The War of Invention
Scientific Developments, 1914–18

Brassey's titles of related interest

Bellamy
Red God of War: Soviet Artillery and Rocket Forces

James
Imperial Rearguard: Wars of Empire 1919–85

Liddle
Home Fires and Foreign Fields

Shaker
War Without Men: Robots on the Future Battlefield

Simpkin
Deep Battle: The Brainchild of Marshal Tukhachevskii

Sokolov & Erickson
Main Front: Soviet Leaders Look Back on World War II

The War of Invention

Scientific Developments, 1914–18

by

GUY HARTCUP

BRASSEY'S DEFENCE PUBLISHERS
(a member of the Pergamon Group)
LONDON · OXFORD · WASHINGTON · NEW YORK
BEIJING · FRANKFURT · SÃO PAULO · SYDNEY · TOKYO · TORONTO

U.K. (Editorial)	Brassey's Defence Publishers, 24 Gray's Inn Road, London WC1X 8HR
(Orders)	Brassey's Defence Publishers, Headington Hill Hall, Oxford OX3 0BW, England
U.S.A. (Editorial)	Pergamon-Brassey's International Defense Publishers, 8000 Westpark Drive, Fourth Floor, McLean, Virginia 22102, U.S.A.
(Orders)	Pergamon Press, Maxwell House, Fairview Park, Elmsford, New York 10523, U.S.A.
PEOPLE'S REPUBLIC OF CHINA	Pergamon Press, Room 4037, Qianmen Hotel, Beijing, People's Republic of China
FEDERAL REPUBLIC OF GERMANY	Pergamon Press, Hammerweg 6, D-6242 Kronberg, Federal Republic of Germany
BRAZIL	Pergamon Editora, Rua Eça de Queiros, 346, CEP 04011, Paraiso, São Paulo, Brazil
AUSTRALIA	Pergamon-Brassey's Defence Publishers, P.O. Box 544, Potts Point, N.S.W. 2011, Australia
JAPAN	Pergamon Press, 8th Floor, Matsuoka Central Building, 1-7-1 Nishishinjuku, Shinjuku-ku, Tokyo 160, Japan
CANADA	Pergamon Press Canada, Suite No. 271, 253 College Street, Toronto, Ontario, Canada M5T 1R5

Copyright ©1988 Brassey's Defence Publishers, Ltd.

First edition 1988

Library of Congress Cataloging in Publication Data
Hartcup, Guy.
The war of invention.
Bibliography: p.
Includes index.
1. World War, 1914–1918 — Technology.
2. World War, 1914–1918 — Science.   I. Title.
D639.S2H37 1988   940.3   87-26805

British Library Cataloguing in Publication Data
Hartcup, Guy.
The war of invention: scientific developments, 1914–18.
1. World War, 1914–1918 — Technology
I. Title
940.4   D639.S2

ISBN 0-08-033591-8

Printed in Great Britain by A. Wheaton & Co. Ltd. Exeter

FOR
RUSSELL

'When the history of the present war is really written one of the most curious chapters will be the marvellous manner in which in almost every field the scientific layman has come to the aid of executive ignorance'.

KARL PEARSON, FRS, *1919*

Preface

In recent years the employment of scientists in World War Two and post-war military applications of science and technology have received considerable attention, especial interest being kindled by the clash of personalities like Lord Cherwell and Sir Henry Tizard and by the arrival of new technologies such as the development of the atomic bomb, radar and the deciphering machines used in cryptanalysis. Yet, apart from a number of valuable studies on naval and military scientific policy, few attempts have been made to assemble and assess the scientific and technological equipment introduced to try to end the tragic, drawn-out struggle that was the First World War — the opponents themselves immobilised on account of the power of modern weapons. It was, indeed, the first major technological war in history.

This book is an attempt to fill the gap and to relate well-known inventions like the tank and the introduction of chemical warfare with less familiar advances involving physical, chemical and medical research which changed the face of warfare. Above all, it was a war in which, to a surprising extent, the man of science (scientist was still an unfamiliar synonym) and the engineer began to assume an importance which would vastly increase over the next forty years. The book is as much about these men — and women — the first 'boffins', as an account of the techniques and equipment that they were responsible for developing.

I have taken advantage of the voluminous documentation on World War One in the Public Record Office at Kew. By comparison the French, German and Austrian archives contain much less material throwing light on the technical side of war, but at least they have yielded some information. Although the United States did not become one of the Allies until 1917, American scientists had responded to the threat of war long before the politicians. However, space has not permitted more than brief references to their activities.

My thanks are due to the following for advice, commenting on first drafts, and other kinds of assistance and encouragement: Dr Peter Alter of the German Historical Institute, Professor Lawrence Badash, the late Mr Patrick Beesly, Dr Alan Beyerchen, Dr Rainer Egger of the Kriegsarchiv, Vienna, Major General David Egerton, Lieutenant Colonel R. Eyeions, Curator of the Royal Army Medical Corps Museum, Mr Harry Wesley, Technical Information Officer of the Materials Quality Assurance Director-ate, Royal Arsenal, Woolwich, Sir Christopher Hartley, son of Sir Harold

Hartley, for permission to examine his father's papers in Churchill College Archive, Cambridge, Dr Lutz Haber, Miss Doreen Hanson, Colonel P. N. B. Jebb of the Ordnance Board, Dr Gabriel Khoury, Brigadier R. J. Lewendon of the Royal Artillery Institution, Professor Russell McCormmach, Herr Jürgen Möllers, the late Mr J. L. Nayler, Dr Michael Pattison, Mr D. P. Segal and Dr Erich Watzke.

Finally, I am grateful to the staffs of the following: The Public Record Office, Kew, the Militärarchiv, Freiburg-am-Breisgau, the Kriegsarchiv, Vienna, Churchill Archives Centre, Churchill College, Cambridge, the archives of the Imperial College of Science and Technology and the Medical Research Council, the libraries of the Imperial War Museum, the Institute of Hygiene and Tropical Medicine, the Institution of Electrical Engineers, the Institution of Mechanical Engineers, the Naval Historical and Old War Office Libraries of the Ministry of Defence, the Royal Aeronautical Society, the Royal Army Medical College, the Royal Society and the Science Museum.

East Sheen   GUY HARTCUP
1987

Contents

List of Illustrations   xi

Introduction   1
Changes in the nature of war from the mid-19th century — Smokeless powder
and ballistite — Importance of chemical industry and munitions — State-
sponsored science.

1 Prelude to Armageddon, 1900–14   6
New forms of high explosive — Fire control for the new warships — Beginning
of continuous wave wireless telegraphy – Aeronautical research.

2 Mobilising and Organising the Scientists   21
Britain. The Royal Society War Committee — Formation of the Board of
Invention Research, Munitions Invention Department and Air Inventions
Committee — French scientific organisation — Formation of Naval Consulting
Board and National Research Council in the United States of America —
Russian and Italian scientific organisation — Central Powers reliance on
industry.

3 'Science moves, but slowly slowly'   38
Scientific liaison between Britain and France — British liaison with Italy and
Russia — Liaison of European Allies and the United States — American need
for operational experience.

4 'The Monstrous Thunder of the Guns'   44
Expansion of chemical research for munitions in Britain — Shell fillings: TNT
and Amatol — Defects in armour-piercing shell — Propellants: RDB, Acetone
— French munition making — German nitrogen fixation — Fuse development
by British and French — Mechanical fuses.

5 Breaking the Deadlock   61
New weapons for trench warfare: grenades and trench mortars — Sound ranging
— Wireless in static warfare — Earth currents — The Fullerphone — Acoustic
instruments in mining operations — Development of the tank by the Allies —
The German response — Movement of supplies: tracked vehicles and aerial
ropeways.

6 'The Ghastly Dew'   94

Beginning of chemical warfare — Discharge of chlorine by cylinder: German
and Allied attempts — Use of projectors, mortars and shell — Phosgene —
Respirators — Mustard gas — Chemical warfare on the Eastern and Italian
Fronts — Gas casualties.

7 Failure and Success at Sea   118

British fire control failure — Stability of gun platforms — Torpedo propulsion
— Direction finding: use in naval intelligence — Wireless communication
between ships — Submarine detection: hydrophones — Offensive measures
against submarines — Development of echo-ranging — Underwater protection
of warships — Paravanes.

8 'Tumult in the Clouds'   145

Aircraft armament: synchronised machine-guns — Machine-gun sights — Bomb
sights — Continuous wave sets for aircraft — Valve development — Introduction of wireless telephony — Rotary engines — Incendiary weapons against
airships — Control of anti-aircraft guns — Sound location of aircraft: early
warning — Inventions for the future: helicopters and pilotless aircraft.

9 The Unseen Enemy   166

British shortages of anaesthetics and drugs — Treatment of wounds: new
antiseptics — Wound and surgical shock — Enteric fevers — Dysentery —
Cause of Typhus — Gas casualties — Trench warfare diseases: nephritis and
trench fever — Malaria and Bilharziasis — Oxygen masks for airmen.

10 Aspects of Wartime Industrial Research   181

British deficiencies in optical glass — New process for annealing — X-ray tubes
— Allied experiments in nitrogen fixation.

Conclusion   189

Respective value of 'inventions' and development of existing techniques —
Relations between scientists and 'users' — Conflict between 'short term' and
'long term' aspects of research — Post-war developments — Effect on World
War Two.

Sources   199

Select Bibliography   216

Index   219

List of Illustrations

PLATES

1. Lord Rayleigh
2. Mervyn O'Gorman, Superintendent Royal Aircraft Factory
3. British Army wireless set, mounted on a horse-drawn limber, 1909
4. Lee de Forest Audion valve, 1911
5. Lee de Forest
6. Sir J. J. Thomson
7. Sir Horace Darwin
8. Colonel (later General) Gustave Ferrié. Head of the French Military Telegraphy Service
9. Ammonium nitrate, packed hot, from the United Alkali Company
10. Women munition workers guiding shells from an overhead crane
11. 24.5 centimetre German mortar
12. Mills Hand Grenade No. 5
13. Stokes mortar
14. Parleur TM2 (French equivalent of the Fullerphone) being operated in a listening post
15. Killen-Strait tractor
16. British tank ('Mother') climbing a one-in-two incline
17. Newton Universal Military Tractor being tested
18. Fritz Haber
19. Sir William Pope
20. British small box respirator
21. French respirator
22. German respirators for man and horse
23. Livens Projector
24. Poulsen Arc Generator
25. Hydrophone Watch, Otranto Barrage 1917
26. Paravane
27. Synchronised Vickers machine-gun for testing
28. Wimperis bomb sight
29. Effect of Threlfall incendiary bullets fired from a Lewis gun on target aircraft
30. Sound Locator
31. Mobile Pathological Laboratory
32. British oxygen mask for pilot being fitted.

FIGURES

1.1 Dreyer fire control table   13
4.1 The 106 fuse   59
5.1 Sound ranging. Arrangement of microphones   70
5.2 Valve amplifier for field telephone   79
8.1 Norman gun-sight for aircraft   149

Introduction

The first contact of the British, French and German armies in August 1914 was made by cavalry patrols armed with rifles and lances. There were, indeed, a few aeroplanes on both sides making reconnaissances or controlling artillery fire. Yet within four years the character of war had utterly changed. Movement across the ground had become impossible without preparation entailing the expenditure of thousands of tons of high explosive shells; poison gas and tanks had been used, though with little appreciation of their best method of employment, to break the deadlock of trench warfare. Blockade, either by German submarine or by the Allied navies, compelled both England and the Central Powers to turn to their chemists and physicists to develop new processes whereby substitutes for raw materials originally brought from overseas and necessary not only for munitions but for medical supplies might be obtained, or for substitutes to compensate for the lack of foodstuffs. The air became an additional sphere of conflict; rival air forces fought for superiority over the battlefield; while more powerful aircraft, both lighter and heavier than air, were developed to launch attacks on industry, or to lower the morale of the civilian population by bombing.

All these changes could not have been achieved without the cooperation of scientists and engineers, and the creation of research establishments and laboratories drawing extensively on the limited resources of scientific manpower. In the autumn of 1915 an English physicist could truthfully write: *It is beyond any doubt that this war is a war of engineers and chemists quite as much as of soldiers*[1]* Yet in 1808, only just over one hundred years earlier, Napoleon, in the middle of the war against England, allowed the great chemist Humphrey Davy to come to Paris and receive an award for his electro-chemical discoveries.

How did these revolutionary changes come about? By the middle of the 19th century, war was being transformed by science and technology. Rifled, breech-loading guns improved the accuracy of artillery and in 1850 the invention of gun cotton marked the birth of explosives more powerful than gunpowder — the high explosives. Such new developments and others in

---

* Superscript numbers refer to notes at end of book.

1

pyrotechnics, for example, all required the attention of chemists. The effect of them would eventually lead to the break-down of what had been an international brotherhood of men of science meeting each other and exchanging ideas. It was a change of attitude that was to have a profound effect upon the history of warfare.

In England the change was first marked by the Crimean War which began in 1854 and demonstrated to the British Army that it could no longer rely on the muzzle-loaded musket and the cast iron smooth bore cannon with which it had fought the Napoleonic Wars. Already the War Office had asked Michael Faraday, who was then professor of chemistry at the Royal Military Academy at Woolwich, to provide advice, but on conclusion of the war in 1856, it appointed the twenty-seven-year-old Frederick Abel as War Department chemist.[2] Abel had not long been professor of chemistry in succession to Faraday, and had also been consulted during the recent war. Belatedly recognising the advance of technology, the War Office, in 1864, asked Abel to form a small research department at Woolwich to investigate chemical and metallurgical problems. By 1871, Abel had built up his staff of assistant chemists to eleven and they covered the whole field of chemical research and inspection. Abel served the War Department until 1888 and made several important contributions to military science. At the same time, the study of ballistics was begun by the Reverend Francis Bashforth, an ex-Cambridge don, who was induced to leave a remote Essex parish to become Professor of Applied Mathematics at Woolwich. In that capacity he investigated the reasons why British artillery had failed to make any impact on the Russian defence at Sevastopol. Although Bashforth returned to Essex in 1872, he was recalled the following year as adviser on ballistics to the War Office and retained that appointment for the next five years. Bashforth's laws on the resistance of projectiles in flight continued to be relevant for another forty years.[3]

By the outbreak of the American Civil War in 1861, breech-loading guns and rifled barrels were in general use. During that war, primitive machine-guns, sea mines and torpedoes were used for the first time, while telegraphy, photography and balloons improved the efficiency of communications and reconnaissance. In the medical field, anaesthetics were used for the first time to alleviate the sufferings of the wounded. Abraham Lincoln was possibly the first national leader to recognise the importance of science when he appointed the National Academy of Sciences in 1863 to provide the Federal Government with scientific advice. Yet the new weapons were not 'war-winning' as they generated logistical problems which were then impossible to solve; hand-to-hand encounters characteristic of traditional warfare persisted, but with heavy loss of life due to the power of modern weapons.

A few years later, the Franco-Prussian War was remarkable for the use of railways as a means of bringing armies rapidly into action, and for improved types of firearms and artillery. Less well known was the original and quite extensive use of civilian scientists by the French Government, particularly during the siege of Paris when *ad hoc* committees were formed for the purpose of making recommendations both on technological aspects of military operations and the nutrition of the civil population.[4] One of these scientists was Marcelin Berthelot who became a leading French chemist and an expert on explosives. In 1887 he was appointed president of the *Commission d'Examen des Inventions de Terre et de Mer* which eventually had five scientific members in addition to naval and military officers. In 1906 the Commission (still headed by Berthelot, then Professor of Organic Chemistry at the Collège de France) was reported by an English military observer to be far ahead of the War Office's Ordnance Committee, which could only boast of two scientists among its members.[5] There was a close rapport between scientists and the armed forces in France; scientists taught in military and naval academies and corresponded with the Academy of Sciences.

By the last decade of the 19th century, further significant changes had taken place in the technology of war, including improved breech-loading guns resulting in higher rates of fire, the magazine rifle, the submarine and the torpedo. The value of a number of these weapons lay in the introduction of smokeless powder for ammunition. In this the French led the way with smokeless ammunition for their Lebel magazine rifle.[6] Of greater significance, however, was the invention of ballistite by the Swedish chemist Alfred Nobel. This was a celluloid-like material composed of glycerine and nitrocellulose which could be cut up into suitable portions for use in the projectiles of small arms, artillery and even for the recently invented machine-gun.[7]

Nobel was more than an inventor. He was a superb commercial organiser and by the end of the century had set up a chain of firms manufacturing explosives in England and Germany with branches in France, America and Australia. While their products were primarily intended for industrial use, such as mining, there was no doubt about their value in war and the leading armament manufacturers became keenly interested. The centre of research for the Nobel ring of explosive firms was the *Centralstelle für Wissenschaftliche Technische Untersuchen* near Potsdam. Founded in 1897, the laboratory was probably the most up-to-date of its kind in the world, carrying out experiments on the properties of nitrocellulose and investigating the strength of gun barrels. The great firm of Krupp, principal supplier of arms to the German services, was represented on the board of trustees and naturally benefited from the research.[8]

While continental powers like Germany and Austria-Hungary introduced ballistite for their armed forces, the British decided to find an alternative. In 1888 Abel, assisted by the physicist James Dewar, produced cordite. This could be cut into strings or cords, the rate of burning depending on the thickness of the cords. Cordite differed from ballistite in that it was made with insoluble rather than soluble nitrocellulose.

Chemical research had indeed become an essential adjunct to the development of weapons; chemists were appointed as members of ordnance committees, and the major armament firms like Krupp, Schneider, Le Creusot and Armstrong-Whitworth had their own experimental establishments. By the end of the century, a small number of scientists were working on explosives, torpedoes and developing wireless technology. What the general staffs of Britain and the continental powers did not anticipate, however, was the possibility of a *long* war, demanding both the expansion of the munitions industry and the necessity of finding alternative forms of raw materials like nitrates after normal supplies had been cut off by naval blockade.

Fortunately for the military, the organic chemical industry had made great advances in the latter part of the 19th century and the plants for producing dyes and fertilisers could be rapidly converted to warlike use. The country that was farthest ahead in exploiting these new processes was Germany. Production had to be complemented by a corps of scientists to assist in their preparation. Again, the Prussian Government had taken steps before other nations to ensure that the research chemists in the universities met the requirements of industry. Anticipating the growth of the chemical industry, the government had from 1864–75 stimulated the creation of a number of technical institutes, or *Technische Hochschule* as they were called, which specialised in applied chemistry, their students eventually forming a cadre which would be employed by industry to carry out research. Further moves to strengthen the links between science and industry were taken in 1911 by the founding of the *Kaiser Wilhelm Gesellschaft zür Förderung der Wissenschaften (KWG)* by private enterprise, the intention being to promote the sciences by the foundation and support of research institutes. One of them was the Kaiser Wilhelm Institute for Physical and Electrochemistry (*KWI*) which would become the centre of research for chemical warfare from 1915 onwards.

Although scientists like W. H. Perkin had pioneered new processes such as indigo dye in organic chemistry, British industrialists failed to exploit them. Unlike Germany, relations between universities and industry in Britain were remote; eminent men of science like Ramsay and Rayleigh, after following an academic career, would retire to conduct further experiments in their private laboratories. Some of the younger scientists, however, appreciated what was happening in Germany and during the turn of the century formed pressure groups, like the British Science Guild, urging the Government to follow the German example and provide a state laboratory to investigate the latest advances in physics, and an institution for the training of scientists and technologists.[9] Their efforts led to the foundation of the National Physical Laboratory (NPL) at Teddington near London modelled on the *Physikalisch-Technische Reichsanstalt* in Berlin. It was administered by the Royal Society and funded partly by the Government and partly by scientific and technical institutions. Its prime purpose was to provide reliable physical standards and methods of testing scientific instruments; secondly, to carry out original research in physics. In 1907, five years after the founding of the NPL, and after further agitation by scientists and a few science-oriented politicians like Richard Haldane, the Imperial College of Science and Technology at South Kensington was created on the lines of the *Königlich Technische Hochschule* at Charlottenburg in Berlin. Completion of the laboratories came just in time for their extensive use during the war. Meanwhile from 1900 onwards, a small organic chemical industry was growing around Manchester and its university; it, too, would be used for wartime scientific applications.

Likewise in France little had been done to cultivate relations between industry and academic science. The state had not created an equivalent of the NPL or the *Physikalisch-Reichsanstalt*. In the sphere of organic chemistry and the industries that were based upon it, France was no further advanced than Britain; ironically it was Berthelot, the authority on explosives, who was opposed to the atomic theory from which the latest chemical developments were derived.[10] France had, however, seen a resurgence in physical research since the Franco-Prussian War. New institutions such as the *École Supérieure de Physique et Chimie* took their place alongside the long standing *École Normale Supérieure* and the *Collège de France*. The emphasis on the study of electricity and metallurgy was to find an important outlet in war technology.[11] Another new centre of research was the *Institut Aérotechnique* of the University of Paris established in 1911 and which reflected the considerable interest of the French in aviation. Scientists, engineers and the military foregathered there to study aerodynamics.[12] Paris had also become a world centre for the manufacture of binoculars though in the production of lenses the French, like the British, were a long way behind the Germans. The French automobile industry led the world and later provided a foundation for the production of tanks and heavy motor vehicles.

1

Prelude to Armageddon, 1900–14

The fourteen years of peace preceding the 'Great War' — known variously as the Edwardian era in England, the triumphant conclusion of the Wilhelmine period in Germany, and the recovery of confidence in France after the Franco-Prussian war and the Dreyfus affair — also witnessed the germination or early development of most of the technology in modern warfare such as submarines, torpedoes, improved propulsion for warships and even radar. We shall be concerned for the moment with four of them: new high explosives like trinitrotoluene (TNT); electrical transmission for controlling heavy guns; wireless; and the new science of aeronautics. All of them demanded the employment of chemists, physicists, and engineers.

However, while the continental powers like France and Germany had civilian scientists serving on ordnance or inventions committees, the British naval and military authorities adopted an attitude of complacency. A scientific advisory committee, originally formed by Abel after the Crimean War, was dissolved in 1891 despite its warning to the War Office that *'unremitting systematic investigation and practical experiment [were] absolutely indispensable'.*[1] How far the technological backwardness of the British Services which, as a chemist working at Woolwich was later to remark, had relied on a classical education and the old school tie to win wars, had gone was revealed in the Boer War. The British found in South Africa that they were not only being outwitted by the enemy, but that their armament and the supply of munitions were undoubtedly sub-standard.[2] Some British scientists had used the Services' neglect of these matters as yet another stick with which to berate the government for its failure to support science and technology.

Explosives

On 6 April 1900, just over a month before the relief of Mafeking, Major F. L. Nathan, who had a chemistry degree as well as being Superintendent of the Royal Gunpowder Factory, suggested to the Director General of Ordnance, Major General Sir Henry Brackenbury, that there ought to be *'a small committee of experts to direct experiments and researches'* in order to

6

keep abreast of foreign powers.[3] Brackenbury, a well known authority on artillery, who had already observed on the outbreak of the war that the British were *'attempting to maintain the largest Empire the world had ever seen with armaments and resources that would be insufficient for a third class military power'*,[4] wasted no time. Within a matter of weeks, he had obtained permission to invite a small number of scientists to suggest how the Army's guns and projectiles could be improved.

The president of the Explosives Committee, as it became known, was Lord Rayleigh, former Cavendish professor of physics and shortly to receive the Nobel prize for his discovery of argon. Supporting him were Sir William Crookes, the celebrated chemist and President of the Royal Society at the outbreak of war; Sir William Roberts-Austen, metallurgist and chemist at the Royal Mint; Sir Andrew Noble, chairman of Armstrong-Whitworth, who had made significant contributions to the advancement of modern ballistics and gunnery; and, finally, the Liberal Party member and savant, Richard Haldane, shortly to be Secretary of State for War and probably the prime mover in suggesting the names for the committee since he knew the leading scientists of the day. After the death of Roberts-Austen, Alfred Ewing, Professor of Mechanical Sciences at Cambridge, joined the committee for a brief period before he was appointed the first Director of Naval Education. In that capacity he began to remedy some of the deficiencies in science and engineering in the Royal Navy; and early in the war he was to become celebrated for founding Room 40, the birthplace of British naval cryptanalysis.[5]

Within a year, the Explosives Committee had been responsible for establishing a small team of chemists under the direction of Oscar Silberrad, a brilliant organic chemist who had studied in Germany, to carry out such experiments as were necessary. The age of this team, according to one of them, *'did not exceed around twenty-five, but they were full of beans and worked till all hours of the night to make a success of the Chemical Research Department'* as they were called.[6] An up-to-date laboratory was built to the design of Silberrad, quite distinct from the Royal Laboratory of the Arsenal, concerned with designing shells and fuses. It worked hand in hand with the Proof and Experimental Establishment, responsible for the proof of guns since the 16th century, which was conveniently situated nearby.

The use of high explosive, as opposed to shrapnel, shell was still quite novel and the Research Department played an important part over the next six years studying continental practices and suggesting new fillings for shell which were both sensitive to detonate and safe to handle. The filling of a high explosive shell consisted, firstly, of the fuse, a mechanism designed to produce a flash at the point at which the shell was to burst. It had to be capable both of being roughly handled before firing and of resisting the great pressure placed upon it when discharged from the bore. Secondly, there was a capsule which provided a spark to ignite an intermediate explosive packed in the *gaine* (or sheath) which in turn detonated the main filling; the latter also had to be insensitive to the shock of discharge but sufficiently sensitive to transmit the initiating flash to the next stage, once the shell had left the bore.

Silberrad's first problem was to improve on the picric acid used as an intermediary in the *gaine*. He investigated a new compound called trinitrophenylnitramine at that time no more than a laboratory curiosity. After test tube experiments and field trials, this compound, renamed tetryl, was adopted for use by both Services and proved to be safer and more effective than previous substances.[7] The Research Department also investigated the possibility of using TNT instead of lyddite as the main charge of the shell. Lyddite, invented by Abel and similar in composition to the picric acid used by continental armies and navies, had not come up to expectation in the South African war, failing to detonate properly, especially in small shell when it '*just fizzled*'. Considerable pressure to adopt TNT was applied to the War Office by several British dye manufacturers producing it as a by-product. In fact, TNT was safer to handle, more chemically inert, and cheaper to manufacture than lyddite. Crookes urged the Ordnance Committee to adopt TNT for the Services, pointing out that it was already being extensively used abroad.[8] However, in 1908 the Ordnance Board, as it had now been renamed, decreed that lyddite should continue to be the main filling for shell, principally because it was more powerful than TNT and there was some doubt about using fulminate of mercury in the capsule to detonate the intermediary charge.[9] It was a decision that the War Office came to regret in the Autumn of 1914.

Experimental work on TNT was nevertheless continued by the Research Department and it was used in a very pure form as an exploder charge for field artillery. Meanwhile, the manufacturers of TNT continued to campaign for the introduction of the new high explosive, in particular the Chilworth Powder Company which had acquired the ex-secretary of the Explosives Committee — Major T. G. Tulloch — who was one of the first to anticipate the use of tracked vehicles for military applications, as well as the need to introduce TNT. As late as April 1913, he persuaded a German scientist to lecture to the staff of HMS *Vernon*, the naval torpedo and mining establishment at Portsmouth, on the merits of TNT as a filling for shell, mines or torpedoes. Tulloch also told naval authorities that 6-inch shell filled with TNT could pierce 12-inch armour plate '*without even igniting the explosive*'.[10]

The propellant required to fire the shell needed to be improved. Hitherto the British had used cordite — a combination of nitroglycerine and nitrocellulose. This had the drawback of causing rapid erosion in gun barrels and was unstable in warm climates and when an unexpected change in temperature occurred.[11] The defects had been responsible for a number of serious accidents on land and at sea. The Research Department found that much greater stability was obtained by reducing the proportion of nitroglycerine to nitrocellulose from fifty to thirty per cent. This would have the effect, according to Rayleigh, of doubling the lives of the bores of guns. In November 1901 Cordite MD, as it was called, was recommended for use by the Services in guns of all calibres. By the end of that year, the Ordnance Committee had approved large scale production of Cordite MD for heavy calibre naval guns and, before long, improvements in their operation were reported. In May 1904, the Commander-in-Chief Mediterranean noted that whereas six-inch guns were capable of firing only eight hundred rounds without serious deterioration with the old type of cordite, they could now fire as many as two thousand rounds without undue damage to the barrels.[12]

Reforms in the War Office, such as the creation of a General Staff and Army Council in 1904, the appointment of Haldane as Secretary of State for War in the Liberal Government of 1906, committed to a large programme of social services, had important repercussions on the direction of research at Woolwich. Scientific work was now put more directly under the control of the Services. These changes became imminent when the Director of Artillery, responsible for implementing decisions taken by the Ordnance Board, expressed the view in the Autumn of 1905 that the Ordnance Board and Explosives Committee should work more closely together; it would also save money. The impending resignation of Rayleigh would make a change easier to execute.[13]

However, the opportunity was taken to make one more improvement by adding a metallurgical section to the Chemical Research Department. Criticisms had recently been made, in particular by Sir Benjamin Baker, the distinguished civil engineer and long-standing member of the Ordnance Committee, that there ought to be facilities for research on metals at Woolwich to improve the quality of artillery as there were '*in all Foreign Establishments*'. Baker complained that the practice as regards research '*has been to begin experimenting, and finally to drop it without coming to any definite conclusions, as there was no one able to devote his time to the work*'.[14]

The Explosives Committee held its last meeting in April 1906 and control of research passed to the Ordnance Research Board, shortly to be amalgamated with the Research Committee — the two bodies eventually becoming known as the Ordnance Board. Although distinguished scientists like Crookes, Noble and other Fellows of the Royal Society continued to act as consultants, they exerted far less influence on the proceedings. In 1907 (a year in which there was a serious explosion at Woolwich damaging the laboratory), a Service officer replaced Silberrad as Superintendent of Research. All research and the trials and proving of guns were now included in a single Research Department. A young Scots chemist named Robert Robertson, recently home from India where he had been advising on safety measures in cordite magazines, became head of chemical research and in that capacity was responsible for the development of explosives until after the war.[15] Robertson was a good organiser but, so it was said, terrified his staff. These numbered no more than a dozen; they carried out a number of important experiments on the stability and detonation of high explosives and propellants, but their recommendation that more attention should be given to the development of TNT for the Services was not accepted by the Ordnance Board.

Fire Control of the New Warships

Just as the Boer War had revealed deficiencies in the British Army's equipment and munitions, the new breed of capital ships like *Dreadnought* and fast battle cruisers created several new problems for long-range naval gunnery. Firstly, the firing of salvoes now needed to be more flexible and concentrated; a system of fire direction was required. Secondly, when warships were operating at high speed and at great distances from the enemy, it was very difficult for fire control officers to estimate the course, speed and bearing of a target.

The problem of fire direction was largely solved by Captain Percy Scott who had made his mark as a gunnery expert and was commanding *Excellent*, the naval artillery experimental establishment. He appreciated how difficult it would be to elevate and train guns on a target, especially when the latter was obscured by smoke or sea spray. In 1905, he proposed that the elevation, train and movement of heavy guns should be determined by a single fire director placed high up on the foremast. This post would contain an observer officer, a layer and a trainer with telescopes providing elevation and azimuth respectively.[16] The layer elevated or depressed his instrument to get the target on the *horizontal* line of his telescope and the trainer moved his instrument to get the target on the *vertical* line of his telescope. The intersection of the two lines provided the aiming point. These movements were transmitted electrically to dials in the gun turret. Here the gunners followed them, as indicated by a needle, elevating and depressing the gun in accordance with the directions from the fire director's post. When the target appeared on the cross wires the gun was fired. One drawback was that in a rough sea the firing ship might roll through angles between two and twenty degrees. Up to two degrees the layer could operate the telescope quickly enough to hold the target, but when the roll increased, the target was only visible for a few seconds making it impossible to obtain an accurate fix.

Scott's proposal did not meet with unanimous approval at first, but after trials on the battleship *Neptune*, it was acknowledged that the ability to fire guns simultaneously and in poor visibility would probably increase the fighting efficiency of the fleet by about fifty per cent. In 1913, the fire director was approved and, by August 1914 eight battleships had been equipped with directors for their main armament.

The problem of fire control proved to be more difficult to solve. There were two main operations: (1) finding the correct rate of change of range and the rate of change of bearing and (2) integrating this information and continuously impressing the results on the gun sights. A further problem was how to counteract the motion of the ship when bringing the guns to bear on the target.[17] The first attempt to provide a correction was made by Lieutenant (later Rear Admiral) J. S. Dumaresq who invented a trigono-metric slide calculator named after him which, used in conjunction with a rangefinder, when set with the firing ship, course and speed of the target and its bearing, could estimate the change of range rate and the deflection. But any variation in setting had to be guessed and, in order to provide greater accuracy, another device called the Vickers clock, with its face divided into ranges instead of hours, was introduced. From the clock, range rates and bearing rates from zero ranges and bearings previously obtained could be used and, by integrating the data, the range and bearing of the moment could be read. However, this instrument was also unreliable because the change of range rate would alter considerably between settings, which had to be done by hand.

What he believed to be a system overcoming these deficiencies was submitted to the Admiralty by Arthur Hungerford Pollen, the forceful managing director of the Linotype Company, who since the Boer War had been obsessed with the idea of devising a method of enabling naval guns to fire with an accuracy equal to that obtained by artillery used by the Army. Pollen's system could obtain from simultaneous mechanical transmissions of range and bearing a plot of the true course and speed of the enemy ship. From this plot by means of a clock (later known as the Argo* clock) the future range and bearing at any particular moment of the enemy ship were obtained by a mechanically integrating process. Pollen also worked out how to combine with the mechanical transmission of range and bearing a gyroscopic control to eliminate errors of aim due to the yaw of the firing ship and slight changes of course. Pollen, who had influential friends like the great scientist Lord Kelvin, won the support of Admiral Fisher, First Sea Lord and his Director of Naval Ordnance, Captain J. R. Jellicoe; both were officers with an open mind of new methods of naval warfare. A number of trials with the Pollen system were carried out by the Navy from 1905 to 1910.

Meanwhile the Navy was trying to improve the Dumaresq-clock system by developing a new manually-operated fire control system. The inventor was Commander F. C. Dreyer who submitted his first idea to the Admiralty in 1906. He had recently served on *Dreadnought* for an experimental cruise and in 1907 was appointed assistant to Captain R. H. S. Bacon, the new Director of Naval Ordnance. Although without academic qualifications, Dreyer had a scientific background as his father was a distinguished astronomer and his brother, serving in the Royal Artillery, also had a talent for invention and, indeed, helped him to improve his instrument. The Dreyer fire control table,

* The Argo Company was formed by Pollen in 1908 to make integrating systems.

as it was called, provided (1) plots of time and range and (2) time and bearing from information provided by the rangefinders which was then converted through the combined Dumaresq-clock into change of range and change of bearing.[18] The plots were recorded by pencils on a moving sheet of paper. But there was one serious drawback to the Dreyer table. This was that accurate readings could not be taken when the firing ship and target were converging or diverging at steep angles and at high speed, or when the firing ship was under helm.

Trials to test the reliability of the two systems were held in the winter of 1907–08 in the cruiser *Ariadne* under the direction of the sixty-seven-year-old Admiral Sir Arthur Wilson, recently Commander-in-Chief of the Channel Fleet, who had seen action in the Crimea and in several colonial campaigns, but who may not have appreciated the significance of recent advances in gunnery.[19] Captain Bacon, his chief adviser, although very technically-minded, did not believe that long-range guns would be effective in the murky weather usually experienced in the North Sea which was the most likely place for a contest with the German fleet. Before the trials a good deal of prejudice had arisen against Pollen who, for his part, became convinced that Wilson never grasped the advantages of his scheme. Moreover, the trials failed to assess the value of the Pollen plotting system as both the firing ship and its target were made to steam at almost equal speeds and on parallel courses. Wilson, in his report to Fisher, claimed that Pollen's instruments were unreliable and recommended that the Dreyer table should be used by the Navy. His decision was confirmed by the Admiralty which considered that the Dreyer table was possibly easier to operate and cheaper than the Pollen apparatus.

After 1908 Pollen was excluded from further fire control experiments though he continued to press his ideas on the Admiralty with great vehemence. In 1911, assisted by Harold Isherwood, he further improved the Argo clock by introducing a slipless drive which enabled an automatic and continuous integrating process to take place instead of having to reset the clock after each correction of bearing. On 4 September of that year, Pollen and Isherwood assigned their invention to the Admiralty as a secret patent and it remained on the secret list until long after Pollen's death in 1937. As a result, Dreyer soon abandoned manual operation and eventually incorporated so many features of Pollen's apparatus that in his Mark V table (introduced late in the war) the Dumaresq-clock combination was almost identical with corresponding parts in the Argo clock. Dreyer tables began slowly to be installed in battleships from 1910 onwards and the Admiralty purchased five Argo clocks which, after some time, were incorporated into the Dreyer Mark II table.

Instead of relying on inventive naval officers or private inventors, the German Admiralty assigned the design of its fire control system to the experienced electrical firm of Siemens & Halske.[20] From 1892 they had

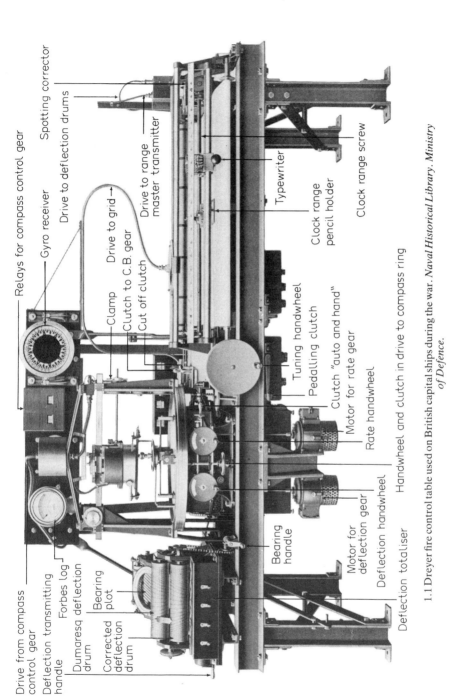

1.1 Dreyer fire control table used on British capital ships during the war. *Naval Historical Library. Ministry of Defence.*

experimented with electrical transmissions for controlling the fire of coastal batteries and then naval guns. This work was directed by August Raps, a physics lecturer from Berlin University, and the firm's engineers installed the first electrical control system for warships in the early 1900s. Known as the direct current '*six roller*' system, it computed figures for elevation and lateral training of the guns. But the apparatus, which required endless tapes to carry the data, was inconveniently large when installed in the ship's command post. In about 1905, the engineers of Siemens & Halske reduced the size of the apparatus by introducing an entirely new system in which electrical transmitters and receivers operated by very small motors provided essential data for firing the gun, being mounted alongside the gun itself. A powerful receiver was also put in for simultaneously adjusting the telescopic sight. All the gunner had to do was to set the target on his sight and fire. At the same time the process of measuring range was improved by employment of a base range finder in which the target was sighted from two points at a prescribed distance from each other. When the measuring device was coupled to an alternating current transmitter, the transmitters of the various instruments were connected in series. The arithmetical mean of the estimated range was then transmitted to the telescopic sight telegraph to indicate finally the required elevation of the guns. Orders were placed in 1913 for equipping the High Seas Fleet with this new apparatus, no expense being spared.

Raps, who by then had become enthusiastic about seeking ways of improving fire control, began to consider the use of gyroscopes but his experiments had to be abandoned on the outbreak of war when ships were no longer available for trials. At about the time that the British and German experiments were being conducted, the French began to introduce into their fleet a fire control system rather similar to Dreyer's.

Continuous Wave Wireless Telegraphy

The possibility of improving communications in war by wireless telegraphy — and eventually by wireless telephony — was quickly appreciated, though it was equally well understood that wireless was also extremely vulnerable to interception. Its use in naval warfare was perceived as being its most valuable application. In 1896, Marconi offered his invention to the British Services not realising that a British naval officer, Captain Henry Jackson, had been following the same line of development and had just succeeded in obtaining intelligible signals along the length of his ship.[20] Marconi formed a company in England and Jackson, who was soon elected a Fellow of the Royal Society for his experiments, was put in charge of equipping the Royal Navy with wireless supplied by Marconi's and instructing staff to use the equipment. A small wireless section was formed at HMS *Vernon*, the torpedo school, where the staff contained a number of officers trained as electrical engineers. A close relationship was formed between *Vernon* and Marconi and one of the latter's engineers was attached to the establishment to supervise experimental work and train operators; he was H. A. Madge, a young Cambridge graduate, who continued to work for the Royal Navy until the outbreak of war.[21] By 1908 spark sets were being operated by the Fleet and experiments in direction finding were in progress. At the same time, the German Fleet was being equipped with wireless by the *Telefunken* Company. This had been formed by Professor Adolph Slaby and Count Arco, who amalgamated with the firm of Siemens & Halske. Wireless was being installed in units of the French Fleet by the physicist and naval officer, Maurice de Broglie.[22]

In the British Army, wireless became the responsibility of the Royal Engineers. During the Boer War, its use was subject to continuous interference due to climatic conditions. Then, in the early 1900s, wagon and pack sets based on the *Telefunken* system were already operating with the cavalry and modest development was taking place at a small signals experimental and training section at Aldershot. Most of the experienced wireless operators, in fact, received their training from the Post Office and were contained in a special Territorial Army battalion.

It soon became apparent that the Army was not keeping abreast of recent developments. In 1911, a special committee was appointed under Sir Henry Norman MP, an enthusiast for new technology such as automobiles and wireless, to suggest how Army wireless communications could be improved.[23] Assisting him were Bertram Hopkinson, Professor of Mechanical Engineering at Cambridge, and Russell Clarke, a barrister and early wireless 'ham' who was to play an important role in the interception of German naval signals during the war. A study was made of the equipment made by foreign wireless manufacturers and evidence was taken from, among others, Colonel George Squier, the American military attaché in London, an electrical engineer with a degree from Johns Hopkins University, who was interested in both wireless and aeronautics. The committee reached the depressing conclusion that the state of wireless in the Army was such that it would be better to abandon it altogether as '*an inefficient wireless service in war would be a constant source of doubt and danger*' — a verdict with which the Chief of the Imperial General Staff concurred.[24] The committee recommended that wireless operators should be better trained, the experimental section enlarged and moved to Woolwich, and that mobile sets should be transported in motor rather than in horse-drawn vehicles.

Much greater interest was shown in wireless by the French Army on account of thirty-five-year-old Gustav-August Ferrié, commandant of the *Radio-télégraphie Militaire*, who was a qualified electrical engineer and responsible for military wireless throughout the war. In 1903, he established an experimental station on the Eiffel Tower offered to him by the builder in order to save it from destruction. From the top of the tower, long distance communication was established with units of the French Army as far away as Morocco.[25]

What particularly occupied scientists engaged on radio research up to 1914 was the need for replacing the spark transmitters by a system for the transmission and reception of continuous waves to improve the quality of sending morse signals and making long distance wireless telephony possible. This could be done either by using the Poulsen arc system invented in Denmark in 1903, or by a thermionic tube or valve, the most promising being the three electrode valve (known as the audion) devised by the American engineer Lee de Forest in 1906 and which was already being used for amplifying normal telephone conversation. Slightly less successful attempts to emulate de Forest was made by the *Telefunken* engineers in Germany, while in France Ferrié actually acquired an audion valve after a visit to Paris by de Forest but neglected to do anything about it. In England, experiments with thermionic valves were being made by a small group of engineers at Marconi's. The intention was to adapt these valves for use by the Fleet but nothing had been installed by the summer of 1914.

By this time the Russians and the Japanese had made use of wireless at the battle of Tsu Shima and the Royal Navy had recognised it as being a *'strategical factor of the highest importance'*, though much remained to be done in reducing the size of the apparatus and over the training of personnel to use it properly.[26] Experiments had also been made in transmitting signals from the ground to aircraft in Britain and on the Continent; signals could be received up to about thirty miles.

Aeronautical Research

Only three years after the first two-man flight by the Wright brothers in 1908, the possibility of using aircraft, aeroplanes or airships in war was being given serious consideration. But fundamental research to ascertain the principles of flight had to take place and following that, the needs of the land and sea forces had to be discovered. France set the pace, a number of scientists taking a keen interest in aviation, in company with the military. Fundamental research began in Paris and in Goettingen. However, the British were the forerunners of state-controlled research in military aeronautics. In 1908, again largely at Haldane's instigation, the government set up a committee under Lord Esher to enquire into the future of what was quaintly termed *'aerial navigation'*.[27] Following up its conclusions that it was important to continue the development of both heavier and lighter-than-air craft, an Advisory Committee for Aeronautics was formed in April 1909 under the presidency of Rayleigh who had been for some time well aware of the potentiality of aviation.[28] Only recently he had asked General Nicholson, Chief of the Imperial General Staff, who was his companion at a dinner, whether flight would not give a new dimension to war. The General thought not. *'Not even for scouting?'* queried Rayleigh. *'Not even for scouting'* answered Nicholson. *'Well, you must remember that Wolseley could see no advantage in the proposal to use smokeless powder'*, responded Rayleigh.[29]

As Rayleigh's committee was to function throughout the war, some account of its members is called for. Most of them either were, or became, Fellows of the Royal Society. The chairman was Richard Glazebrook, the first director of the National Physical Laboratory (NPL), a Cambridge mathematician with experience of the business world, able to get things done, largely because he was trusted, and a man possessing inexhaustible energy. However, it was W. N. Shaw, also a Cambridge mathematician, who became the first director of the Meteorological Office, who was probably more responsible than anyone else for setting up the Committee. He was extremely bright, quick to appreciate new ideas and deliberate in his approach to his work. Horace Darwin, the fifth son of Charles Darwin, was an engineer and designer who became the first chairman of the Cambridge Scientific Instrument Company which also played an important part in the war. H. R. A. Mallock was another engineer who had been an assistant of Rayleigh's and was familiar with military problems, having been a member of the Ordnance Board. Sir Joseph Petavel, Professor of Engineering at Manchester, had a special interest in the measurement of high pressures and in meteorology which led him to design instrument-carrying kites; and his practical bent was only satisfied by actually learning to be a balloonist and to fly an aeroplane. Finally, the engineer F. W. Lanchester was outstanding even in this assembly of talent. Not only did he design the famous Lanchester car, but wrote two seminal books on aerodynamics and aerodonetics in 1907 and 1908 which are still consulted. His mind ranged over a wide variety of subjects and he wrote several remarkable papers on the theory of aerial warfare which foreshadowed operational research some thirty years later. In addition, he enlivened discussions with his sense of humour and was exceptionally quick as a committee member.[30]

Representing the Services was Captain Bacon who, on account of his technical qualifications, prepared reports on the building and steering of airships. In 1910, he was joined by Captain Murray Sueter, RN who was interested in non-rigid airships. Major General Hadden, Director of Artillery, spoke for the Balloon Factory, the birthplace of British military aeronautics at Farnborough, and was soon joined by the new Superintendent Mervyn O'Gorman, a capable engineer and leader of men who attracted to the Factory a highly talented group of young scientists and engineers, most of whom were to distinguish themselves in various aspects of aeronautics. F. J. Selby, another mathematician and secretary to the NPL, performed similar duties for the Advisory Committee. Three other members who joined later and were to make their mark were George Greenhill with a special interest in mechanics and hydromechanics, T. E. Stanton who worked on the effect of wind pressure on engineering structures and the fatigue of materials, and L. Bairstow who also worked on fatigue and was credited with making original suggestions.

Rayleigh himself provided a sense of direction in the new science, his aim being to define the limitations of the primitive flying machines of the day. He only wrote two short notes on the subject but, according to his biographer (his son and the fourth Lord Rayleigh), they were the foundation stone of the Committee's work. Its value was demonstrated by the quality of the flying machines produced during the war. Rayleigh indefatigably presided over ninety-six of the 126 meetings of the Committee from 1909 until 1919, a few months before his death. In his latter years, though, he became a figurehead, control of the proceedings passing to Glazebrook.

Little more than two months after the formation of the Committee, Blèriot made the first flight across the Channel, dramatically proving that England was no longer isolated by a narrow strip of sea from the Continent. The effect on the public of his descent on the cliffs of Dover was similar to the first landing on the moon and must have inspired the members of Rayleigh's committee. Their first annual report, submitted to the Prime Minister, dealt with the work at the NPL on stability, propellers, light alloys and petrol engines. According to one of the first members of the staff, J. L. Nayler, the atmosphere was not unlike that of a research laboratory at a university. Scientists were used to working with their hands as *'mechanics were scarce and money short'. 'The hours of work were laid down but were never rigid . . .; those interested in their problems often worked late at the laboratory or continued until late hours at home as well as at week-ends . . . It was mainly a world of carry on with your own research, which people did because they enjoyed it, and when no ancillary staff were available, each man went into the workshop or office and did it himself'.*[31] Thus aeronautical research was transformed from the uncoordinated and secretive work of a handful of enthusiasts into a highly sophisticated activity, requiring various kinds of novel apparatus and employing some of the best brains of the country.

Foremost among the new equipment was a wind tunnel (already being used by the French, thanks to the patronage of the industrialist, Henri Deutsch de la Meurthe) for testing small model aeroplanes, a fifty-feet high steel wind tower, the purpose of which was to discover the behaviour of flat plates and models in winds, and a large whirling arm (or whirling table as it was called) designed to test model propellers with the aid of a dynamometer. In the theoretical field, discoveries on the nature of streamlining were made by Rayleigh and Lanchester, and pioneer work on the nature of stability was carried out by G. H. Bryan of Bristol University. But the work at the NPL was by no means exclusively academic. After a number of accidents to monoplanes of the Royal Flying Corps, a special committee was set up to investigate the causes, and Bairstow wrote an important paper setting out methods of calculation which could be used to determine stresses in the spars of wings.[32]

The Advisory Committee also set in motion experiments on fabrics for airships and was especially concerned about the permeability of covers enclosing the inflating gas — hydrogen. In February 1911, the Committee visited the first British naval airship then nearing completion in the Vickers yard at Barrow-in-Furness. *Mayfly*, as she was ironically named, broke in half seven months later when being towed out of her floating hangar.

By then the future of military flight almost certainly seemed to lie with aeroplanes. The outcome of the theoretical work at the NPL was embodied in the Reconnaissance Experimental (RE1) aircraft built at the Royal Aircraft Factory, as the Balloon Factory at the insistence of O'Gorman was now designated. In charge of its development was E. T. Busk who had obtained a first class honours degree in the Mechanical Sciences Tripos at Cambridge. He may be fairly described as being one of the first 'boffins', as war scientists were affectionately called in World War Two. Combining designing ability with practical application, his approach was quite different from that of Bairstow who was '*sometimes puzzled as to how Busk was step-by-step modifying his aeroplane to make it wholly stable*'. In November 1913, he flew his machine for several hours in winds up to thirty-eight miles per hour without the assistance of balancing, controlling or steering mechanisms except for landing. The RE1, as Glazebrook reported the following spring, was the first machine to fly for fifteen minutes without the pilot touching the controls; it was the first machine in which the '*balancing of its various parts has been so calculated as the result of experimental work that it shall be inherently stable and because in actual flight it has shown that these calculations have been verified*'.[33] The RE1 was the prototype of the BE2C which, with a speed of 140 miles per hour, was to become the standard two-seater biplane with which the Royal Flying Corps went to war in August 1914. The staff at the Royal Aircraft Factory had also designed and tested an airborne wireless set and had fitted a machine gun in an aeroplane and fired it. The Factory was the first military research establishment applying theoretical propositions to practical applications.

And yet, while in certain respects recognition of what modern war might entail was made by the small staffs at Farnborough and Woolwich, when war actually came in 1914 Britain, more than the other belligerents, had failed to make provision for a *major* war. The lessons of the South African War, such as the failure of explosives and fuses, had still not been properly digested, in spite of the probings of committees of enquiry. In fact, the capacity to wage war had even been reduced because of the Government's programmes for expenditure in other fields; and little pressure had been applied to the armament firms in the private sector to keep abreast of new developments. Prophetic words like those spoken by the Superintendent of the Royal Laboratory at Woolwich in 1906 went unheeded. '*If we ever come*', he said, '*to a really big war, ourselves, the trade, and everybody working as hard as they can go, will never keep pace with what* [the Services] *will want us to supply . . . the productive capacity of the country would be stretched almost to breaking point'.*[34] Similar words might have applied to research and development. As a naval officer was to write in August 1923, when financial cuts were once again threatening the development of weapons and equipment: *'Peace and not war is the time for methodical research; had this country been better prepared in this respect at the outset of the late war, our advantages would have been enormous in the increased capabilities for supplying information for use in the field and afloat which was so urgently needed at the time'.*[35]

2

Mobilising and Organising the Scientists

In each of the belligerent countries the scientific community, normally more international in outlook because of the need to study at foreign universities and exchange ideas at conferences than their fellow citizens, were no less fervent in their support for the war; foreign honours were renounced; manifestos or statements were issued by leading scientists declaring, on the one hand, that German so-called 'culture' had fostered a military caste which now rode rough-shod over Europe and, on the other, identifying with the spirit of the German people and condoning the German Army's invasion of Belgium and France.[1] For the French intellectuals, there was no question but to retaliate immediately against an enemy that after only forty-four years was again occupying a substantial part of their homeland.

While the young scientists, who might have contributed to new techniques of war, enlisted or were called to the colours, the professors and senior engineers began to take a more sanguine view of the possible length of the conflict after the abrupt halt of the German armies on the Marne. British scientists had been warning their fellow countrymen for some years of the great advances being made by the German chemical industry. Now they had to persuade the professional soldiers and sailors of the importance of the new techniques described in the last chapter; they had to learn how to gain access to the 'corridors of power' if new ideas were to be transformed into weapons. In each country, scientists approached the problem in a different way. The French were more politically-minded than the British; in Germany, scientists were more accustomed to dealing with industrialists; in the USA there were closer links between industry and the universities.

The Royal Society is Involved

No time was lost by the French when on 4 August 1914, the day after the German declaration of war, the Academy of Sciences put itself at the disposal of the Government and agreed to act as an agent between the latter and scientific institutions.[2] Two months later, William Ramsay, a senior

British chemist and sharer of the Nobel prize with Rayleigh, who in his youth had been contemptuous of the Armed Forces, proposed that the Royal Society should take similar action.[3] Early in November, a War Committee was set up at Burlington House including Ramsay, Sir Oliver Lodge, Sir Alfred Ewing and Richard Glazebrook from the NPL, while Sir Henry Jackson, then Chief of the Naval War Staff, provided a link with the Admiralty. Its aim was to provide 'assistance to the Government in conducting or suggesting scientific investigations in relation to the war' and sub-committees were formed to cover chemistry, engineering and general physics.[4] A circular letter was sent to each of the Services calling for problems needing solution. While the Admiralty response was more positive than that of the War Office, Ramsay later observed that 'if we have to confine our attention only to the suggestions formally referred to us by the Government Departments, we may as well close our work. What we are there for is not to answer questions, but to make suggestions.'[5] In fact, Ramsay continued, the committees were at that stage more concerned with 'chemical problems connected with industry rather than with physics and engineering; there were a mass of things to attend to, all of them useful'. A prolonged debate between the Government and the Royal Society and other scientists was held during the summer of 1915 on the correct policy for scientific and industrial research.[6] In the autumn, an advisory council was set up of Fellows of the Royal Society headed by Lord Rayleigh to make recommendations for research on vital raw materials deficient because they could no longer be obtained from Germany. Among the items discussed were optical glass, essential for the artillery, which will be discussed in a later chapter. The council was responsible to the Privy Council and before the end of the war was expanded into the Department of Scientific and Industrial Research.

Meanwhile the failure of the German troops to reach Paris led to concern by German scientists about the shortage of raw materials for munitions on account of the imposition of an Allied blockade. Emil Fischer, a Nobel prizewinner for chemistry and a leading promoter of industrial scientific research (and incidentally a pre-war friend of Ramsay's) in company with several leading chemists and industrialists, induced the Prussian War Ministry to set a Kriegsrohstoffabteilung (KRA) or Raw Materials Section.[7] Their prompt action undoubtedly saved Germany from an acute shortage of munitions that autumn.

Within eight months of the outbreak of war, the British scientists' warnings about the failure of industry to keep abreast of the Germans were vindicated. Chemical industry now had the task of developing counter-measures after the German use of chlorine on the Western Front, and the unexpectedly high consumption of shell required a vast expansion of the munitions industry by both the state and private sectors. The use of submarines and mines by the Germans at sea required the development of complex underwater apparatus for detection and location. On 17 June 1915, the Royal Society expanded its advisory activities by constituting its Council as a War Committee with sectional committees dealing with applications of science, emphasis being placed on chemical and trench warfare. Liaison with the Army was maintained through Colonel (later Major General Sir Louis) Jackson at the War Office who had been put in charge of developing new weapons, while a link with the War Cabinet was maintained through its Secretary, Colonel Maurice Hankey, who in both world wars took a close interest in the scientific aspects of warfare.[8] Unfortunately the Royal Society greatly restricted its influence for authoritative advice by refusing to sponsor any recommendations directly affecting government or industry, unlike its German counterpart, the *KWG*. Its activities were henceforward conducted in secret, so diminishing its authority to discriminate between so-called 'inventions' often submitted by cranks and the application of a particular branch of science to solve an operational problem. The Society did, however, produce several important confidential reports, including one on the physiological effects of battle gases, and specific items of research (mainly dealing with the production of drugs in short supply) were carried out at universities and technical colleges at the request of the sectional committees. Further impetus was given to this work when Sir J. J. Thomson, Professor of Physics at the Cavendish Laboratory and discoverer of the electron who was already deeply involved in war research, was elected President at the end of 1915.

The Society was naturally concerned to prevent the indiscriminate call-up of scientific man power to the armed forces. In November 1915, it appeared that men working on projects for the sectional committees might be taken away. As the Society was not their employer, the question arose as to whom these men should appeal for exemption on the grounds that their work was essential to the war effort. After appealing to the Reserved Occupations and War Badges Committees, the Society was able to obtain a number of badges which signified exemption from national service for a select number of physicists, chemists, metallurgists, and biologists (needed for medical research).[9] In January 1918, for example, there were three hundred and twelve analytical and consulting chemists and a number of protozoologists on the reserved occupations list. Being responsible for the administration of the NPL, the Society was able to ensure that it was fully utilised for research into the more fundamental aspects of war research including aeronautics and acoustics in sea and air warfare. By 1917, the permanent staff had been increased to about one hundred and fifty.

British Control of Invention and Research

During June and July 1915, British science was somewhat uneasily hitched to the chariot of war after a public outcry, led by well-known figures such as

H. G. Wells, who had years before anticipated the technical nature of modern war, that '*available resources were not being used to the fullest extent and that the British had not so far produced any counterstroke to the enemy's submarines and no protection against his improved torpedo*'.[10] The flood of inventions from the general public that these criticisms engendered led to scientific advisory boards being set up by the Admiralty, War Office and Ministry of Munitions but without a coordinating panel to ensure that there was no overlapping and that the ideas related to what the fighting men wanted.

In the case of naval science, the new First Lord of the Admiralty, Lord Balfour (who had just succeeded Winston Churchill) was, like Haldane, deeply interested in science. He proposed a board of Service officers, engineers, physicists and chemists who would be less concerned with assessing the value of '*inventions*,' of which only a fraction would be worth investigating, than with '*formulating practical demands for new devices*' with the help of the Admiralty departments concerned. The board would be independent of naval administration, so that in effect '*the Admiralty would not be deprived of any of its present powers but relieved of some of its present labours*'.[11]

Balfour's choice of Lord Fisher, the outgoing First Sea Lord, as President of the Board was an unfortunate one. Although the latter was a keen advocate of new weapons like submarines, aeroplanes and airships, he was too intemperate and idiosyncratic in his method of conducting business to sell scientific advice to the traditionally-minded Admiralty departments. It was hardly surprising that the Board of Invention and Research (BIR), as Balfour's proposal was to be called, acquired the name in some quarters of the 'Board of Intrigue and Revenge'. Under Fisher was a Central Committee headed by J. J. Thomson, Sir Charles Parsons, inventor of the steam turbine and head of his own engineering company, and George Beilby, a notable industrial chemist and director of one of the handful of British chemical firms, Castner-Kellner Alkali; he had some knowledge of the ways of the Admiralty, having served on a Royal Commission on Fuel for the Royal Navy.[12] This committee was supported by a panel of well-known physicists, chemists and engineers including William Bragg, the crystallographer, Bertram Hopkinson, Sir Oliver Lodge and Ernest Rutherford, then on the brink of his great discoveries in atomic physics. The work of the panel was divided into six sections with accompanying sub-committees covering all the technical aspects of naval warfare such as naval construction, marine engineering, explosives, anti-aircraft weapons. The most important was Section II covering submarines, mines, wireless and acoustics.

What was lacking was a working relationship between these eminent men of science and the relevant Admiralty departments. As J. J. Thomson later complained, the BIR was regarded by senior naval officers as an '*excrescence rather than a vital part of Admiralty organisation*',[13] there being no contact with the officers in charge of torpedoes and mining and naval ordnance to *'plan a campaign in applications of science for the Navy'*. On account of this the Navy was to suffer from deficiencies in fire control apparatus and up-to-date wireless for most of the war. Another serious deficiency was the lack of laboratory accommodation to carry out experiments and Thomson's repeated requests for a central research institution were never fulfilled.

Meanwhile the BEF was faced with the problem not only of introducing new weapons like mortars and grenades, which the Germans were using in profusion, but with developing countermeasures against chemical warfare initiated by the Germans in April 1915. Provision of all this novel equipment was the responsibility of the Assistant Director of Fortifications and Works, Colonel Jackson. On 25 June, in order to relieve his burden, Kitchener asked Christopher Addison, the young Parliamentary Secretary of Lloyd George, to *'take up the whole supply connected with trench warfare, of hand grenades, bombs, etc, whether charged by hand or mechanically and whether charged with explosive or any other abomination'*.[14] Addison, a doctor by profession, had an ability to master technical problems. Before the war he had been a member of the recently-formed Medical Research Committee (MRC). He immediately formed a Trench Warfare Department in the Ministry of Munitions responsible for both research and supply of new weapons, putting it in charge of A. (later Sir Alexander) Roger, a forty-year-old accountant and director of an investment trust then working in the War Office. Although quite unfamiliar with scientific matters, Roger proved to be an excellent organiser and mastered enough of the technicalities to give weight to his decisions. A Commercial Advisory and Scientific Advisory Committee was set up to help him. Most of the scientists were already members of the Royal Society War Committee, but on account of the importance of chemical warfare two professors, H. B. Baker and J. F. Thorpe, in charge of the new chemistry laboratory at Imperial College, which was to be a centre of research for new equipment, were enlisted. Sir Boverton Redwood, a fuel expert, and W. B. Hardy, a physiologist, were also included.

The most important new weapons like the Mills bomb and the Stokes mortar were already in the development stage; others like the tank were being developed by other departments, while all were required to fulfil the exacting standards of the War Office. Roger soon found himself *'trying to please the research mind foreign to commercial ways and . . . reconcile* [his] *ideas of running the department on commercial lines with the military and experimental spirit that met* [him] *at every turn'*.[15] By the end of 1915, the exasperated Roger had divorced supply from research, leaving Jackson aided by the Scientific Advisory Committee to concentrate on research which, as will be seen, became increasingly concerned with chemical warfare.

But there were other aspects of land- and air-operations such as explosives, aircraft armament, and anti-aircraft weapons that needed scientists to provide new ideas. Quite early in the war Sir John French, the Commander-in-Chief of the BEF, had appointed one of his staff officers, Major General J. P. Du Cane, to form an Inventions Committee to examine suggestions sent up from the front which, if considered favourable, were then passed on to Jackson in London. However, Lloyd George as Minister of Munitions wanted a body of civilian scientists comparable to the BIR and which would absorb the small section of Army officers under the Director of Artillery (A4) which hitherto had been dealing with inventions submitted to the War Office. After obtaining Kitchener's approval, Lloyd George charged E. W. (later Sir Ernest) Moir, a well-known civil engineer who had recently been responsible for constructing the defence of Dover harbour, with forming a Munitions Invention Department (MID).[16] It was to consist of a panel of twenty scientists and engineers and met for the first time on 20 August 1915 with the aim (like that of the BIR) of sifting new ideas, developing promising ideas, carrying out original research and investigating anti-aircraft weapons (England was now subject to attack from Zeppelins). Some of the members of the MID like J. J. Thomson, F. W. Lanchester, Horace Darwin and Glazebrook were already serving on the BIR or on Jackson's Scientific Advisory Committee, but there were others who had not yet been called upon to contribute to the war effort such as S. Z. de Ferranti, the Manchester electrical engineer. Sir Alexander Kennedy, Professor of Mechanical Engineering at Imperial College, and Wilfrid Stokes, who had just come into prominence as inventor of a trench mortar. Unlike the BIR, the MID succeeded in obtaining experimental grounds for the testing of weapons and equipment at Wandsworth, Wembley, Imber Court near Esher, and elsewhere.[17]

Moir had hardly had time to assess the extent of his duties before he was switched to New York as head of a commission to deal with promising ideas being developed in the United States.[18] He was succeeded by Colonel H. E. F. Goold-Adams who had served on the Ordnance Board and in A4 for the past five years but who did not have the scientific prestige to help him win inter-departmental battles. For as long as the War Office retained responsibility for weapon design, much of the work done by MID was in danger of being duplicated or even ignored by the recently expanded A4 or the Research Department, Woolwich. These anomalies came to a head over the failure of the Ordnance Board to introduce an efficient fuse for high explosive shell, the one currently in use causing not only damage to the guns but sometimes injuring or killing the crews as will be described in greater detail below. Advantage was taken of the absence of Kitchener abroad to wrest control of ordnance matters from the War Office. Addison prepared for his Minister a memorandum illustrating the dangers of divorcing design from production and pointed out the superiority of the French fuse which was safer and cheaper to produce than the British equivalent. This finally clinched the matter and on 25 November 1915 the Ordnance Board, the Research Department at Woolwich, the proving grounds at Shoeburyness and A4 at the War Office all came under control of the Ministry of Munitions.[19]

The Aircraft Crisis

The next crisis concerning scientific participation in the war arose over the failure of British aircraft and their equipment in the spring of 1916 to match the German performance. The Royal Aircraft Factory was the prime target for attack in Parliament and the Press and that May a special committee was formed under the odd choice of Sir Richard Burbidge, the chairman of Harrods, with Sir Frederick Donaldson, an ordnance administrator and Sir Charles Parsons to help him.[20] They were to find out whether the resources placed at the disposal of the Factory by the War Office and the organisation and management could not be improved. Since the beginning of the war the Factory under O'Gorman had become the largest experimental establishment in the country with a staff of some 4,500, including a small core of mathematical physicists 'of the order of senior professors in charge of such an engineering laboratory as Cambridge, Dundee or Manchester'.[21] They were responsible for engine design, armament and other equipment, and for the testing of new aircraft. In the early days of the war O'Gorman had 'dragooned the War Office into concentrating its supplies for the Royal Flying Corps on Factory-designed aircraft and engines',[22] but now the growing British aircraft industry claimed its share of research and development. It was proposed that the Factory should be allowed to concentrate on research and improvements in management were suggested and approved, but the senior staff were sacked including O'Gorman who was relegated to an advisory post under the Director General of Military Aeronautics. He was replaced by Sir Henry Fowler, a railway engineer who had recently been employed as an armaments adviser. One of the members of the Factory, later to become a leading aeronautical engineer, wrote years later, 'Surely no country but Britain would have acted in such an astounding way in the middle of the most shattering war in history'.[23]

Even though the Royal Aircraft Factory was reformed and later renamed the Royal Aircraft Establishment, it could not cope on its own with the insistent demand for better gun sights, bombs, navigational aids, wireless, and other equipment. It therefore concentrated on the testing of aircraft, full-scale experiments on aircraft and research into light alloys and other materials used in construction of aircraft. New ideas for armament and other forms of equipment were investigated under the aegis of the BIR, MID and the NPL. Many of the most promising ideas emerged from the Royal Naval Air Service (RNAS) which had the advantage of being able to call on personnel with experience of naval engineering.[24]

In May 1916 the newly formed Air Board under Lord Curzon concluded that it needed a single scientific body to *'investigate all aeronautical inventions'* drawing on the resources of all the agencies engaged in aeronautical research.[25] Perhaps predictably this proposal was rejected by both the Admiralty and the MID, the former claiming that it should be free to carry out all experiments and research for the Royal Naval Air Service (it was trying to duplicate wind tunnels already in existence at the NPL) while the MID maintained that there was adequate coordination between itself and the BIR.

Just at the point when the air arm had been recognised as being an essential adjunct to land operations, research and development was divided between the RNAS and the RFC at their respective experimental establishments with inevitable overlapping and delays in bringing equipment into service. Only in September 1917, after a year's futile argument, was an Air Inventions Committee formed.[26] Again it was asserted that the main function was to *'sift new inventions'* which its chairman, Horace Darwin, rightly foresaw would mainly consist of ideas *'old or obviously useless'*. Of the twelve members, some like Bairstow, Glazebrook and Petavel were members of the Aeronautical Advisory Committee (which continued to do valuable work on structures and propulsion problems) while others, like Dugald Clerk (an authority on the gas engine, who had recently been directing naval engineering research), Kennedy and a newcomer, A. V. Hill, a physiologist, were members of the BIR or MID. The usual sub-committees were formed to deal with aeronautical engineering, armament and navigational equipment.

From the start there had been no *'clearing house'* for new ideas in the British organisation of war science, nor had there been any attempt, despite several protests by leading scientists, to expand the body of scientific advisers already enlisted. Some leading academic scientists such as William Pope, Professor of Chemistry at Cambridge, and Percy Frankland of Birmingham University had not been called upon to furnish advice on chemical warfare. The attention of the War Cabinet was drawn by Sir Henry Norman, now liaison officer for the MID in Paris, to the lack of coordination compared with the French system.[27] Taking wireless, a subject in which he was particularly interested, he noted how little progress had been made in Army wireless over the period 1915–16 and the existence of a short range wireless set made by a British commercial firm had never been communicated to GHQ in France. The useful Experiments Committee at GHQ had in the meantime been dissolved. Earlier in the war J. A. Fleming, inventor of the two electrode valve, had remarked on the need *'to organise to a far higher degree than we have yet done what may be called the strategy of research, and* [he urged] *that the learned societies should act in some capacity like the general staff of an army towards the subordinate generals and corps commanders'*. Norman now proposed a small scientific committee under a cabinet minister with Captain T. G. Tulloch, the first secretary of Rayleigh's Explosives Committee, as the chief executive. Nothing came of the idea because the Admiralty refused to allow the BIR to coordinate research with the Army and the RFC.

Ironically, it was the inability of the Admiralty to accept the BIR that led in the autumn of 1917 to the setting up of an enquiry on the work of the latter by the new First Lord, Sir Eric Geddes, and resulted in its dissolution and replacement by a Department of Experiment and Research within the Admiralty itself.[28] The Admiralty had by then belatedly recognised the need to call on scientists to help in combating the U-boat threat. The report of the committee headed by Sir Sothern Holland, a senior civil servant who had been organising the supply of munitions, assigned blame for the ineffectiveness of the BIR quite impartially. While the Navy had failed to cooperate with the scientists and the growth of experimental stations run by the Admiralty had led to dispersion and confusion of effort, the Central Committee under Fisher had wasted time discussing purely administrative matters while the advisory panel had not always pushed new research projects. In January 1918, after a period of uncertainty during which the morale of the scientists plummeted, the Admiralty decided to dispense with the sub-committees of the BIR, leaving the Central Committee and the consulting panel. C. H. Merz, an eminent electrical engineer, was appointed head of the Department of Experiment and Research.

Since June 1917 Winston Churchill had taken charge of the Ministry of Munitions and his unique insight into the possibilities of mechanised warfare and the use of new weapons as well as his appreciation of the importance of air supremacy was beneficial to the scientists working in MID. Yet, as in the BIR, there was overlapping of work and a tighter rein was needed to control the processes leading '*from the inception of the idea to the issue of the finished design*'.[29] But proposals for improved coordination of the department by Admiral Bacon, the new Comptroller who early in the war had recognised that of all others it was a '*war of science and mechanism*', failed to obtain the agreement of the Admiralty and his reorganisation never took place.

French Scientific Organisation

The way the French handled their scientific effort had an urgency lacking in that of the British. The Germans had deprived them of nine-tenths of their steel production and much of their chemical output. Paris, the centre of intellectual life, was threatened and general mobilisation had emptied the workshops, arsenals and laboratories. The French were fighting for survival.[30] Soon after the outbreak of war the long-standing *Commission d'examen des Inventions Intéressant les Armées de Terre et de Mer* was replaced by the *Commission Supérieure Chargée d'Étudier et Eventuellement d'Experimenter des Inventions Intéressant la Défence Nationale*. Like the BIR, however, it suffered from a lack of experimental facilities where scientists could give shape to their ideas.[31]

The man who was to give effective direction to the French scientific effort was fifty-two-year-old Paul Painlevé who, apart from being a distinguished mathematician, took a keen interest in aeronautics and had flown with Henri Farman and Wilbur Wright, holding jointly with the former the record for the longest pre-war flight in a biplane. Painlevé, like several French scientists, was interested in politics, and was elected a Deputy for Paris in 1910, after which he was head of a number of naval and aeronautical commissions intended to prepare the country for a future war. In October 1915, Painlevé was appointed Minister of Education and one of his first actions was to ask the President to set up the *Direction des Inventions Intéressant la Défense Nationale* which would provide the counterpart for the industrial mobilisation that had become necessary after the loss of territory to the Germans. The new Board was placed under Emile Borel, another mathematician turned politician from the *École Normale Supérieure*, who assumed the rank of captain for the duration of the war. It was divided into seven sections, ballistics and ordnance, physics, chemistry, applied mechanics, trench warfare, sanitation and hygiene and naval warfare, all housed on two floors of a modern building situated in the heart of the university area. Each section was in charge of two or three scientists or officers specialising in the branch of knowledge with which the section was concerned. Sections were represented in a cabinet presided over by Borel who became permanent technical adviser to the Minister with an office adjoining that of Painlevé. Like its British counterparts, the Board sifted ideas submitted to it and promising ones were examined by the appropriate section. Immediate action was taken if experiments proved to be favourable. They took place in the laboratories of institutions placed at the disposal of the Minister and an experimental workshop for the investigation and development of mechanical appliances was acquired. Limited funds were provided by the Government periodically and the *Comité des Forges* of the Association of Iron and Steel Workers provided both financial support and facilities for experiment.

It was during this period that a considerable chemical warfare organisation was set up with the assistance of professors from the universities and several Parisian laboratories were turned over for analysis of and experiment with toxic substances. Under the stimulus of the soldier-scientist Gustave Ferrié, wireless development was undertaken by a combination of scientists and industrialists. Research was carried out on sound ranging for the artillery, the location of aircraft and submarines by acoustic methods, aerial photography, new forms of explosive, and ground and aircraft armament. As a recent historian of French science has written, this effort '*showed the great resourcefulness of the French scientific community and French industry. Integrated into the mechanisms of the state, the scientific community was totally at ease in collaborating with the Army and with industry before and during the war*'.[32]

In 1917 Painlevé was promoted to War Minister, but before his transfer, he further increased the collaboration of scientists, technologists and the military by locating the *Direction des Inventions* in the Ministry of Armament and Munitions, something which British scientific administrators had longed to achieve. It was put under the overall supervision of J. L. Breton, another scientist with political ambitions. In April 1917 the Board, still under Borel, was renamed the *Sous-Secrétariat à État des Inventions, des Études et des Experiences Techniques* combining all the technical offices and research organs of the Ministry. New sections were formed including aeronautics, technical information and statistics. Also under control of the *Secrétariat* was the centre of physical studies at Toulon responsible for underwater research and sections dealing with artillery and infantry weapons. In September 1917 the *Secrétariat* came directly under the authority of the Minister of War. Compared with a total of 482 scientists and technicians working for the British Ministry of Munitions, the French equivalent was employing a total of 747 in January 1918.

Although the French had nothing quite comparable to the British Aeronautical Advisory Committee and the Royal Aircraft Factory, the Institute Aérotechnique of the University of Paris, which had been dissolved at the outbreak of war, was revived in 1916 after the growth of air warfare and became the headquarters of the *Section Technique de l'Aéronautique Militaire* under Commander Cagnot, and a good deal of fundamental research was carried out using the wind tunnels and chemical laboratory available. At the same time a military laboratory was built by the Technical Section at Issy-les-Moulineaux for the development of aircraft armament and navigational equipment.

The United States Research Council

Not entering the war until 1917, the Americans had time to profit from the early mistakes made by the Allies. In 1914 the amount of scientific research done for the Armed Forces was negligible. Reliance was placed on civilian inventors and industrial firms for new equipment, the small Service laboratories being restricted to the testing and inspection of equipment. Study of aeronautical problems was limited to the Bureau of Standards in Washington, but as the grand total of naval and military aircraft was less than twenty-four, opportunities for extensive research were limited. In the summer of 1915, the Secretary of the Navy Josephus Daniels, discussed with the great inventor Thomas Edison how the equipment of the Navy might be brought up to date for modern sea warfare.[33] The result was the formation of the Naval Consulting Board (NCB) under Edison in October 1915. Members were selected by the presidents of the leading engineering and scientific societies but, in the end, the engineers heavily outnumbered the rest. The Board was divided into sub-committees, each of which handled a special problem in the fields of physics, chemistry, wireless, aeronautics, and a variety of engineering subjects. Among the members were E. A. Sperry, inventor of the gyroscope, L. H. Baekeland, inventor of bakelite, and representatives from a number of electrical and engineering firms. Later, a military branch was added to the NCB called the Inventions Board composed of officers from the Central Staff. But research was not encouraged as Edison was more interested in the standardisation of inventions and their production.

As it did not appear that the National Academy of Sciences, the Federal Government's official scientific advisory body, was going to make any provisions for a possible war, a small group of members of the Academy led by George Ellery Hale, director of the Mount Wilson Observatory at Pasadena, California, took the view that the United States could not remain neutral indefinitely and that they should prepare for war with Germany.[34] Hale, who had original views on the value of scientific application, believed that the country needed a research body to '*promote scientific research in the broadest and most liberal manner, for the increase of knowledge and the advancement of the national security and welfare*'. His ideas crystallised after talks with his friends, the physicist and future Nobel prize-winner, R. A. Millikan from Chicago University, and Arthur Noyes, a leading chemist from the Massachusetts Institute of Technology. But they realised that, without the backing of the President, they could achieve little. President Wilson was still sticking to a neutralist policy and an initial talk with him by the scientists was unpromising. Hale then won the support of Colonel House, the President's confidential adviser, and almost immediately authority was given for the formation of a National Research Council (NRC) in the autumn of 1916 with Hale as chairman and Millikan as vice-chairman. By a stroke of good fortune the Council's headquarters in Washington was in the same building as that of the Council of National Defence recently set up to mobilise and direct the civilian effort in the event of war. Immediately, therefore, the NRC achieved the authority and ability to coordinate its activities that were so lacking in the British organisation. Furthermore, its members not only consisted of scientists, engineers and academic administrators but chiefs of the technical bureaux of the Services and representatives of electrical engineering firms like the General Electric Company and Western Electric which had already begun war research on their own initiative.

The usual committees were formed, covering all the scientific and technical applications for war. Since 1914, American iron, oil and other supplies had been crossing the Atlantic to sustain the Allied effort and it was certain that the U-boat campaign would be intensified once a state of war existed between the States and Germany. Special attention therefore had to be paid to this topic and Millikan became chairman of the Physical Science Division under which fell nearly all the anti-submarine, meteorological and sound ranging activities.[35] Indeed, American entry into the war on 7 April 1917 coincided with the sinking that month of 900,000 tons of Allied shipping by U-boats. What was lacking on that side of the Atlantic was actual experience in this novel form of warfare. Early in May this deficiency was speedily rectified by a scientific delegation of British, French and Italian scientists including Rutherford. More positive direction could not be given to research and a new experimental station was set up at New London on the east coast. The NCB also participated in the attack of underwater problems, though there seems to have been little cooperation between the two organisations: 'inventions' were left to the NCB while the NRC concentrated on research.

Chemical warfare was taken no less seriously after the despatch of the American Expeditionary Force to Europe. A research programme was launched by the Bureau of Mines, specific items being farmed out to the universities.[36] American aeronautical research, which was the responsibility of the Signals Corps, was taken over early in 1918 by Millikan at the request of General Squier. Some months later control of Army aviation was divided between civil and military agencies. Complaints were made by the latter that Millikan's scientists were spending time on 'interesting and fascinating research to the total neglect of immediate problems ahead'.[37] This was a charge that was repeatedly levelled against scientists engaged on war work everywhere and could only be answered by pointing out that research needs time for, as J. J. Thomson expressed it, 'the quarry to be tracked down'.[38] The ambitious plans for aircraft production were never fulfilled and the U.S. Air Service relied on British and French aircraft manufacturers for nearly fifty per cent of its aircraft.

Russia and Italy

Any discussion of the scientific mobilisation of the other Allies such as Russia and Italy is limited to the sparse documentary evidence available. Russia, although, as will be seen, possessing talented scientists and engineers, was heavily dependent upon her Western allies for technological aid (as indeed she would be in World War Two). Scientists were attached to the Army's Ordnance Committee and after the Russian reverses in the spring and summer of 1915 a special Council of Defence was created to try to remedy the deficiencies in munitions and artillery. Scientific committees were formed to meet the chemical and military needs of the nation. Like Germany, Russia was short of raw materials for munitions and had to resort to the production of synthetic substances like the synthesis of ammonia.[39] The need to produce chemical warfare weapons after the German use of chlorine in 1915 required the participation of scientists, of whom Vladimir Ipatieff was one of the most distinguished. However, the Russians were eventually supplied with British and French anti-gas equipment.

In Italy the Department of Invention and Research under Vito Volterra was, as in France, run by the Minister for the Army and Munitions. There was a Central Office where Italian and foreign inventions were pooled, experimented with and reported upon and where original research could be conducted. But according to the British liaison officer attached to the department, research was, in fact, mainly carried out in existing institutions and was largely uncoordinated. More effort went into studying the natural resources of the country for post-war reconstruction and development.[40] Like Russia, Italy had to depend on Britain and France for technological aid.

The Central Powers' Reliance Upon Industry

It is perhaps not surprising that industrial research being so well established in Germany and the recently-created *KWG* providing a bridge between academic science and industry, there appeared to be no need for the state-controlled or semi-independent groups of scientific advisers that had to be rapidly improvised in Britain, France and the United States. But military requirements had to be defined for the civilian experts, and the Prussian Army being such a stiff, hierarchical institution, it was not easy to find a suitable individual. There was, however, Major Max Bauer, according to Ludendorff, when Quartermaster General, *'the cleverest man in the Army'*.[41] Bauer was an artillery specialist on the General Staff of the Prussian Army; he had the advantage of being acquainted with some of the leading industrialists like Carl Duisberg, a brilliant research chemist before becoming managing director of the Bayer dye factory at Leverkusen, Wichard von Moellendorf and Walther Rathenau, an unusual combination of electrical engineer, chemist, financier and amateur philosopher who was the first head of the *KRA*. Bauer also knew senior chemists such as Emil Fischer, Walther Nernst and Fritz Haber.

Haber, then aged forty-six, was already celebrated for his system of nitrogen fixation making it possible to obtain ammonia nitrate which was an essential ingredient for the making of munitions. Since 1911 Haber had been director of the new Kaiser Wilhelm Institute for Physical and Electrochemistry at Dahlem in Berlin. Haber, like Fischer and Nernst, was a staunch patriot but was also a Prussian with *'an uncritical acceptance of the State's wisdom'*.[42] He immediately placed his institute (then almost depleted of staff through call-up) at the disposal of the military authorities and at the same time actively engaged with Fischer and other scientists in planning industrial mobilisation.[43] The Army soon made use of the *KWI* which was asked, in the opening months of the war, to provide a formula for anti-freeze in motor vehicles on the Eastern Front and to solve a problem relating to high explosive in shell. But not long after the decision to launch chemical warfare, the *KWI* became the centre for research on this subject, Haber being placed in sole charge and dealing directly with the General Staff.

In the meantime, development of other types of new weapons for trench warfare was the responsibility of the *Artillerie Prüfungs Kommission*. Quite informally, it called upon a number of prominent scientists from the universities for assistance. They had to don uniform (a habit to which some of them never became accustomed) and had little opportunity of influencing policy on new weapons. Another group of scientists conducted experiments on wireless communications between aircraft and the ground. The Navy (whose officers came from a less narrow background than those of the Army and who were more open to new ideas) relied mainly on the research facilities of *Telefunken* and other electrical engineering companies, but with the growth of submarine warfare and the need to communicate with U-boats over long distances, invited Wilhelm Wien, a Nobel prize-winner for physics, to take part in experimental work. But there was no attempt to mobilise scientific manpower even on the relatively small scale that took place in the Allied nations, so much so that, in August 1916, complaints were made by some scientists, Wien in particular, that the talents of German physicists were not being employed to the best advantage of the state.[44]

That month saw the launching of the Hindenburg Programme which was intended (unsuccessfully in the event) to maximise munitions production. In November, when the Prussian War Office was reorganised, so as to coordinate the war economy, a scientific commission of two hundred expert advisers was formed to improve weapon development. Another step was taken by Fischer and Haber in January 1917 when they founded the Kaiser Wilhelm Foundation for the Science of War Technology, the intention being to bring the '*Army and Navy into close contact with representatives of natural science and technology*'.[45] By then, with increasing shortages of raw materials, it was already too late to make any impact on events. At least it was recognised by the Prussian *Junkers* that scientific applications were changing war while the scientists could reflect that '*our military circles should thank God that industry sprang to their side in 1915 and dragged the wagon out of the mud*'.[46]

The German Army did not begin to concentrate on making the aeroplane into a weapon of war until August 1915. Previously it had depended on development of new aircraft being carried out by the manufacturers like Fokker and Albatross. It now assembled a number of scientists and aeronautical engineers to work at the experimental ground at Doeberitz. Aeronautical research of a more fundamental character was sponsored from March 1914 onwards by the *Deutsche Versuchsanstalt für Luftfahrt* — a body of civilian scientists and engineers.[47] The leading German aerodynamicist was Ludwig Prandtl, the forty-year-old Professor of Applied Physics at Goettingen (later to become celebrated for his work on boundary layer control) who had a small laboratory built for him before the war. A much more extensive research establishment was constructed during the war under the auspices of the *KWG*, a large wind tunnel being one of the features. Here Prandtl carried out important research on wing structure.

Germany was the only belligerent nation to use large rigid airships exten-sively. Although the Zeppelin company had briefly a rival in the Schütte-Lanz Company which built airships with a wooden framework for the Army, the Zeppelins were favoured by the Navy which took control of the works at Friedrichshafen. A number of aerodynamicists and engineers were enrolled in the development section which was responsible for the new high altitude, long-range bombing and reconnaissance aircraft that absorbed so much of the Allied air defences.[48]

As the grip of the Allied blockade tightened on the Central Powers, Fischer, Haber and Nernst turned their attention from military problems to trying to improve the nutritional value of food supplies. In January 1917 they asked the War Ministry to set up a commission to deal with alternative foodstuffs for both humans and animals. Fischer's last experimental work of the war concerned the extraction of glucose from grapes.[49] By the end of 1917 he had lost his fervour for supporting the war after two sons had been killed by enemy action. His colleague, Nernst, though receiving the highest decoration *Pour le Mérite* for his research on applications for trench warfare, shortly after Count Zeppelin had received the same award, was likewise soured by the turn of events; he too had lost two sons on the battlefield and he now returned to Berlin to find solace in his laboratory.[50]

The Austro-Hungarian Empire lacked the drive that produced the great advances in German science and technology. Its head, the aged Emperor Franz Joseph, was resolutely opposed to change — unlike Kaiser Wilhelm II in Berlin. A spirit of conservatism was reflected in the Services. Even the Academy of Sciences in Vienna was antipathetic to original research; an occasional genius like Ernst Mach or Bolzmann were exceptions to the rule. Yet technical changes affecting warfare could not be ignored and the small technical committees that served the Army and Navy before the war continued to function. Membership was largely restricted to staff officers with a sprinkling of civilian experts from the arsenals, ordnance factories, and the electrical engineering and shipbuilding industries. They concen-trated on the improvement of explosives, artillery and optical instruments. In the development of large trench mortars the Austrians were probably ahead of the Germans. Much engineering effort was expended on the development of land mines which were used extensively on the Eastern Front. Physicists were needed to improve wireless communications between aircraft and the ground forces. But no attempt was made to emulate the Germans in chemical warfare. The first occasion on which poison gas was used by the Austrians on a large scale was in October 1917 in an offensive against the Italians on the River Isonzo leading to their defeat at Caporetto, the gas projectors being operated by German scientists and technicians.

Like the Germans, the Austrians were forced to seek new processes for munition-making and in 1916 the *Technische Hochschule* in Vienna was turned over to research into methods for the extraction of toluene from

PLATE 1. Lord Rayleigh. Pre-war President of the Explosives Committee and President of the Advisory Committee for Aeronautics throughout the war. *Science Museum Library*.

PLATE 2. Mervyn O'Gorman. First Superintendent of the Royal Aircraft Factory. He insisted that the War Office should rely on Factory-designed aircraft and engines. *Royal Aeronautical Society*.

PLATE 3. 'Carpet' aerial wireless telegraph station. Installation waggon and 4 horse power petrol engine at Aldershot, August 1909. *Private collection*.

PLATE 4. The triode Audion valve invented by Lee de Forest. *Science Museum Library*.

PLATE 5. Lee de Forest, inventor of the triode valve which revolutionised wireless. *Science Museum Library*.

PLATE 6. Sir J. J. Thomson, Chairman of the Central Committee of the Admiralty Board of Invention and Research and President of the Royal Society from 1916 to the end of the war. *The Royal Society*.

PLATE 7. Sir Horace Darwin. First chairman of the Cambridge Scientific Instrument Company, member of the Advisory Committee for Aeronautics and chairman of the Air Inventions Committee. He was also instrumental in promoting scientific liaison with the Americans. *The Royal Society.*

PLATE 8. General Gustave Ferrié. Head of the French Military Wireless Telegraphy Service and pioneer of continuous wave wireless communication. *Science Museum Library*.

PLATE 9. Ammonium nitrate from the United Alkali Company packed 'hot'. This method of pouring liquid Amatol into shells superseded the 'cold' method of filling shells with a dry mixture. *Public Record Office.*

PLATE 10. Women munition workers guiding shells from overhead crane. *Public Record Office.*

PLATE 11. A 24.5 cm German trench mortar captured by the French. *Public Record Office.*

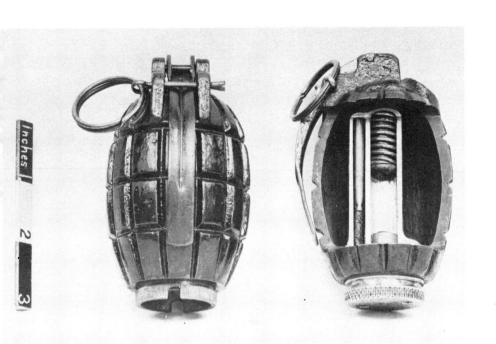

PLATE 12. Mills hand grenade No. 5. *Public Record Office*.

PLATE 13. A 3-inch Stokes mortar with shell ready for loading, adapted for use by the French Army. *Public Record Office.*

PLATE 14. British troops using a *Parleur TM2* earth telegraphy set. It did not have to rely on surface wires which could be cut by shell fire. *Imperial War Museum*.

PLATE 15. First attempt at wire-cutting with Killen-Strait tractor fitted with torpedo wire-cutter, Wormwood Scrubs, 30 June 1915. The demonstration was watched by Lloyd George, Minister for Munitions, and Winston Churchill, recently First Lord of the Admiralty. *Public Record Office.*

PLATE 16. 'Mother'. Prototype for the first tank, February 1916. The tail wheels enabled the machine to turn on a wide radius and acted as counter weights to the tank's point of balance. *Imperial War Museum.*

PLATE 17. Universal Military Tractor. Designed by Colonel Henry Newton to carry supplies up to the front line, but it arrived too late to go into service. *Public Record Office.*

benzene.[51] In other parts of the Empire attempts were made to extract alcohol from various organic substances. In the same year, Austria-Hungary began to suffer from the Allied blockade and a scientific commission on the war economy was formed to make suggestions on obtaining raw materials, the improvement of industrial output, transport, health, and other aspects of the national war effort.

Aeronautical research at the aviation arsenal at Fischamend outside Vienna was handicapped by the reluctance of the aircraft manufacturers to exchange information with the military. One of the scientists working at this establishment was the Hungarian Theodor von Karman who later became a leading aeronautical engineer in the United States.[52] He had been prevented by the authorities from going to work for the Germans but, instead of employing his talents on the improvement of military aircraft, he was allowed to preoccupy himself with the design of a helicopter.

3

'Science moves, but slowly slowly'

Exchange of ideas and information on subjects of mutual interest are essential ingredients of the scientific process and no more so than in the development of military applications. The liaison that was slowly established between Allied scientists in World War One would be repeated and extended in World War Two with such outstanding examples as the arrival in Britain after the fall of France of the group of French scientists who had been working on nuclear fission and, shortly after this, the despatch of the British mission to the still neutral USA carrying with it the latest radar equipment and other devices which could be further developed and manufactured beyond the range of enemy air attack. In the early stages of World War One, however, scientists found it hard enough to discover what was needed at the Front, let alone find out what their Allied colleagues were doing.

At first information was acquired, as it had been in peacetime, by the exchange of military and naval attachés who occasionally had some form of technical education. Through this means useful information about foreign equipment could be obtained. Information was also gathered by individual scientists obtaining permission to visit colleagues abroad, as happened from time to time between British and French scientists. But as the war lengthened into 1915, the manufacture of explosives, fuses, poison gases, the development of aircraft armament, and the sensitive equipment required for detecting submarines had become too complex for non-specialists to master. Hence the emergence of the scientific or technical liaison officer and the scientific mission.

Anglo-French Scientific Liaison

After Painlevé had formed his *Direction des Inventions* at the end of 1915, he met Lloyd George, in charge of the Ministry of Munitions, and both agreed that regular exchanges of information should take place. But no action was taken until April 1916 when Sir Henry Norman, who had chaired the War Office Committee on Army wireless before the war, was attached to Painlevé's department in Paris.[1] In return, Captain de Jarny was despatched to the MID, later being replaced by the Marquis de Chasse-Laubat after de Jarny left for Washington on special duties.[2]

Norman quickly appreciated how little exchange of information about new techniques existed between the Front and London as well as between London and Paris. In company with members of the *Direction des Inventions* he organised weekly meetings attended also by Russian and Belgian officers in addition to himself and occasionally a naval ex-gunnery officer, Commander Cyprian Bridge, who had won the Ryder Memorial Prize for French, representing the BIR. As Norman was knowledgeable about wireless he was able to hasten the provision of new wireless equipment to some extent. More serious, however, was the absence of a permanent British liaison officer on chemical warfare in Paris until May 1917, two years after the first German gas attack. The officer chosen was Victor Lefebure who had studied under Ramsay at London University and had recently been a lecturer at Wye Agricultural College before joining one of the Special Companies formed to launch gas attacks. He spoke French and Italian well. After setting up an office in the university quarter of Paris, which had become the hub of French chemical warfare research, he visited laboratories and factories and attended Allied committee meetings. His experience was that the French were more forthcoming than the British in imparting information.[3] Due to Lefebure and other British officers in France, exchange of information on the processes of manufacturing mustard gas was expedited in the critical months after its first use by the Germans in the summer of 1917. That September the French formed the *Secretariat Interallié* on chemical warfare, attended by British and Italian as well as by American officers from the American forces recently arrived in France.

Liaison between French and British chemists on new developments in explosives tended to be spasmodic. From time to time small parties of British experts visited French munitions factories.[4] But there was no permanent British scientific representative stationed in Paris until the appointment early in 1918 of Sir Charles Ellis, an industrial chemist, to coordinate the supply of munitions and to find out what new processes were being developed by the French.[5] By then both British and French had begun to work seriously on the production of ammonia nitrate by the fixation of nitrogen from the air and the latter were anxious to learn about recent advances in England.

Collaboration between the French and British on technical aspects of naval warfare proved to be even more difficult to establish than between the respective military authorities.[6] This was apparently due to the Admiralty's fear of imparting confidential information which might get into the wrong hands. During a visit to Paris in July by William Pope, Professor of Chemistry at Cambridge, who was a firm believer in scientific intervention in the war, strong representations were made by the French for a permanent representative of BIR to be located in Paris. Not long after, this request was backed up by a long and frank memorandum by Commander Bridge to his superior in BIR pointing out that the French had a number of important inventions to offer, not the least of which was the underwater detection apparatus being developed by Paul Langevin, and which would be invaluable to British experiments in anti-submarine warfare. Bridge continued: *'Practically all the most important inventions of recent years which have any great bearing on war have been originated and first developed in France, the machine-gun, the aeroplane, the automobile, the submarine, smokeless powder, etc. The French are more imaginative and consequently more inventive than we are, and study of scientific matters has probably received more encouragement in France than it has here'.*[7] And he concluded with the pertinent observation that, with science developing so rapidly, what was confidential today would become common knowledge tomorrow. While Bridge was perhaps being over-generous to French inventiveness, there was little doubt that the British were failing to take advantage of what was being done on the other side of the Channel.

At last, in October 1916, Balfour, the First Lord, was persuaded to authorise the mutual exchange of scientific liaison officers between the British and French scientific establishments. Maurice, Duc de Broglie, the pioneer of naval wireless and elder brother of Louis de Broglie who later became famous for research on the electron, was appointed Liaison Officer in London in December 1916. Maurice de Broglie was now working on wireless and submarine communication at Toulon. Bridge joined the *Direction des Inventions* in January 1917,[8] though as soon as the Americans came into the war, he accompanied the Anglo-French scientific mission to the States in May.

Anglo-French exchange of information on aeronautical matters only began in 1916 when Lord Curzon of the Air Board appointed Viscount Tiverton as Liaison Officer to the *Section Technique* under Cagnot. Tiverton was a lawyer like his father, Lord Halsbury, who had been Lord Chancellor for ten years, and was serving in the RNAS. He was given a free hand, meeting French technical officers in Paris once a fortnight and exchanging information on items of mutual interest. A good deal of this information concerned aircraft armament.

British Liaison with Italy and Russia

Italy declared war on Austria-Hungary in 1915 and on Germany a year later. Although the Italians had made important contributions to electrical and motor engineering and aeronautics, neither the British nor the French had much to gain from their military scientific applications. Representatives from the Italian Board of Inventions arrived in London and Paris in August 1916, but it was only after the defeat of the Italians at Caporetto in October 1917 that the Allies appreciated that something would have to be done to bring the Italians up to date in the latest techniques in making explosives and anti-gas precautions. In February 1918, therefore, a special mission was sent from London to Italy to report on Italian deficiencies and provide advice to their technical departments.[9] The scientific side was headed by Professor Percy Frankland who had already served on a special mission to the Western Front when the Germans began to use poison gas and who was then a member of the British Chemical Warfare Committee. He and his colleagues visited universities and factories and offered advice; in recognition of his services, Frankland was decorated by the King of Italy.

Shortly afterwards, Captain C. W. Rawes, an artillery officer, was permanently stationed in Rome as Technical Liaison Officer and contributed a number of reports on the progress of Italian scientific research. To their credit, however, the Italians produced an alloy called biametal, a shell fuse, and a design for an artificial limb.[10]

Russia likewise required technical assistance, especially in chemical warfare. The British sent Daniel Gardner, to Petrograd in March 1916 to advise on the use of gas shell. A substantial French mission spent some weeks in Russia imparting information about explosives[11] and arranging for the supply of French anti-gas equipment, though the latter did not equal the British respirators eventually sent to the Russians.

And with the United States

As described earlier, American radio engineers were well in advance of their European rivals. The military significance of this new form of communication was most of all appreciated by the French, though they had failed to take advantage of the audion valve which they had in their possession. The way in which they were given a second chance to acquire the valve after the outbreak of war provides an unusual example of 'unofficial liaison'.[12] It came about through a deserter from the French Army named Paul Pichon who had settled in Germany, trained as an electrical engineer, eventually being employed by *Telefunken*. In due course Pichon became a commercial traveller for his firm, exchanging information with foreign competitors. Gustave Ferrié was one of those interviewed by Pichon in an attempt to discover what progress had been made by the French. On 3 August 1914 Pichon was in London returning to Germany after a visit to the United States. Feelings of patriotism, to which was added sensible advice from Marconi's, induced him to give himself up to the French authorities. He was immediately arrested but allowed to be interviewed by Ferrié to whom he handed over the latest audion valve designed by de Forest. Pichon was quickly instated in the *Radio-télégraphie Militaire* and after a brief period of development by French scientists, a version of the American valve known as the TM tube was put into mass production. By the end of the war over 100,000 valves had been supplied to the French Services; some of them were sent to the British for experimental purposes. Ferrié, when reminded about the first valve presented by de Forest, which had lain for some years in a storeroom awaiting a report, is said to have exclaimed '*How could I have forgotten it!*'

America's entry into the war in 1917 provided further opportunities to take advantage of recent progress in radio communications. It has already been noted how an Anglo-French scientific mission crossed the Atlantic with all haste to the States. Its members soon discovered that the American Services were far more generously endowed with experimental facilities, especially in regard to underwater experiments for detecting submarines. Nevertheless, the British and French had the edge on the Americans on account of their operational experience and were instrumental in realigning various aspects of research. It was not long before the Americans, who learned quickly, were making important contributions to the anti-submarine war.

But operational experience was the first requirement. Before the United States became one of the belligerents, Hale, who, it will be remembered, was the astronomer responsible for coordinating military and naval scientific research, made a brief visit to England to find out how scientists were employed. A few months later, Darwin and other scientists in the MID wrote to George Squier, now a General in charge of the Signal Corps, suggesting that liaison between British and American scientists should be improved.

The way in which liaison could be achieved was outlined by Darwin in a memorandum of 8 July 1917 and eventually circulated to the American Ambassador in London. It indicated how the Americans could avoid the mistakes made by the British in the early stages of the war, such as allowing valuable scientific workers to be swallowed up by the Services. Darwin made a frank comparison with the way the French had employed their scientists. They had, he wrote, '*recognised the importance of selecting for service with heavy or anti-aircraft guns, or with the engineers and other similar corps, men who by their previous experience were qualified to deal with scientific and engineering problems. The matter, which is only a particular instance of the intolerant contempt for knowledge and technical skill which affected this country before the war, has to some extent been put right now; and such subjects as sound-ranging, aeroplane or field wireless, submarine or Zeppelin attack, aircraft equipment, anti-aircraft gunnery, explosives, metals, gas poisoning and anti-gas precautions, medical and surgical questions, etc, are now being dealt with and investigated very largely by men from the scientific and engineering departments of the universities of this country.*'[13]

Darwin went on to propose that the Americans should lose no time in taking advantage of operational experience in the UK, especially in anti-aircraft gunnery and wireless. This could be done by the NRC selecting about a dozen young scientists, commissioning them, and attaching them to MID which would also enable them to make visits to the front. While this proposal was not acted on quite as Darwin had intended, the NRC did form sound-ranging and chemical warfare sections, manned by scientists in uniform, which were soon in action in France.

Meanwhile, Millikan had drawn up a plan designed to facilitate full cooperation between the Allied scientific groups and to avoid unnecessary duplication of effort.[14] This was to be called the Research Information Service, financed by the President's emergency fund. Offices were set up in Washington, London, Paris and Rome, Hale himself directing operations from Washington in company with the naval and military intelligence services. Among the well-known scientists sent to Europe were Henry A. Bumstead, a physicist from Yale who had spent a year at the Cavendish under J. J. Thomson, and was now posted to London, and William F. Durand, an aeronautical engineer from Stanford University and a fluent French speaker, who went to Paris. Senior American officers in Europe welcomed the arrival of the scientists and, by the spring of 1918, information was flowing back to the NRC headquarters in Washington.

The British, for their part, established an ordnance mission in Washington in February 1918 composed entirely of artillery officers.[15] Its aims were, firstly, to help the Americans in the development of their artillery programme, drawing on British experience both in regard to manufacture and use in the field; and the spare parts needed for their maintenance. It also investigated American artillery inventions, such as a pilotless aircraft for target practice and new types of fuse, including a mechanical fuse then under investigation in England.

It is unlikely that there was any comparable liaison between Germany and Austria-Hungary, but certainly exchanges of information took place between Berlin and Vienna on technical matters, mainly on aspects of armament.

4

'The Monstrous Thunder of the Guns'

Never before in the history of warfare had so many guns been assembled or so many rounds fired as on the battlefields of the Western Front. The number of guns increased as the impasse continued. In March 1915, at the battle of Neuve Chapelle, 306 British guns were disposed along a 2,000 yards front, and in June 1917, at the battle of Messines, 2,571 guns were deployed along a nine and a half mile front — about one gun every seven yards. While expenditure of ammunition was often very light, when required it could be astronomical. During the battle of the Somme, for example, each battery of one British field artillery brigade fired 30,000 rounds in five weeks — a total of 120,000 rounds for the whole brigade. In March 1918 a single battery fired 1,700 rounds in one day. In a heavy engagement, a single gun might fire about 200 rounds in a twenty-four hour period.[1]

Expansion of Chemical Research in Britain for Munitions

It was at the battle of Neuve Chapelle that the British realised that their pre-war calculations for consumption of shell were hopelessly out of date and that large quantities of lyddite *and* TNT were necessary. The Germans were believed to be expending on occasion as much as 480 tons in fifty-three hours; while the French had just estimated that they would require sixty tons of high explosive a day — nearly 2,200 tons a year. The British, and to some extent the French, now paid the penalty for neglecting the possibilities offered by an organic chemical industry, in particular the production of synthetic dyestuffs. Apart from lyddite and tetryl, the explosive used for detonating shell, very little high explosive was manufactured in Britain.[2] As soon as the war began, a committee of leading industrial chemists was formed under Haldane to suggest alternative sources of supply of vital chemical products now no longer obtainable from Germany. A sub-committee on dyestuffs was chaired by Lord Moulton, a law lord entering his seventies but who had been a senior wrangler and Cambridge Apostle, expert on patent law, and had distinguished himself sufficiently in research on electricity to be elected a Fellow of the Royal Society. He had also been a Liberal member of Parliament and was chairman of the recently-formed Medical Research Committee.[3]

Haldane made Moulton responsible for the supply of explosives.[4] It proved to be a good choice for, apart from Rathenau in Germany, no other individual on either side had such heavy responsibilities for supplying munitions. As soon as the Ministry of Munitions was formed, Moulton's committee moved from the War Office and was enlarged into a Department of Explosives Supply served by a scientific advisory panel under R. C. Farmer, who had been Robertson's chief assistant at Woolwich for the past twelve years. Moulton worked in close conjunction with the Ordnance Committee and the Research Department at Woolwich which had acquired so much importance that Lloyd George declared that the *destruction of Woolwich would be a worse piece of news to us than the loss of two army corps*.[5] During the course of the war, Robertson's staff of eleven was increased to 107 chemists and physicists and half a dozen women *probationary assistant analysts*. He himself regularly attended meetings of the Ordnance Committee and with his extensive knowledge of explosives could quickly assess the difficulties that had to be overcome with the minimum of investigation.[6] His staff continued to work in the one storey Victorian building within the Arsenal, but new laboratories had to be erected for research and several out-stations were set up in other parts of the country near munitions factories.

Shell Fillings: TNT and Amatol

Instead of merely being an advisory body for the Ordnance Board, the Research Department now embarked on original experiments to discover alternative ways of producing nitric acid, toluene, glycerine, and the like and to introduce new forms of high explosive.[7] Indeed, almost half of its work was fundamental in character, such as the study of the decomposition of explosives in order to make them safer, or finding out the temperature at which combustion took place in various types of explosive.

But by 1916 the production of high explosive had become so extensive that additional laboratories were needed for analysing chemical substances like toluene and tetryl and for carrying out large scale practical experiments. One of them was the Explosives Research Laboratory set up by the Ministry of Munitions on the wharf at Chiswick.[8] It was placed under the charge of J. T. Hewitt, a Fellow of the Royal Society, who had studied chemistry in Germany and had recently been acting as chemical warfare adviser at the Dardanelles. Before another year had passed, the nation-wide manufacture of explosives had burgeoned so rapidly that still more chemists were needed to inspect their products. The heads of five chemistry departments at the universities of Birmingham, Edinburgh, Liverpool, Leeds and Manchester were asked to make regular inspections of manufacturing processes in government factories and commercial firms in their vicinity. In January 1918 the Deputy Inspector of High Explosives reported that *The work of the*

universities is so well carried out that it would be invidious to draw compari-
sons between them'.[9] There was also considerable academic research of a
fundamental nature carried out; it was supervised and coordinated by
Farmer, Hewitt and other members of Moulton's scientific staff.

On account of the complex processes demanded in shell filling, described
below, a special section of some seventy-five chemists had to be formed in
the Gun Ammunition Filling Department of the Ministry of Munitions. It
was headed by Martin Lowry, an able chemist, aged forty-two, who was in
charge of the chemistry department at Guy's Hospital, the first teacher of
chemistry in a medical school to be appointed a professor of London
University. He was also a Fellow of the Royal Society and after the war,
became Professor of Chemistry at Cambridge.[10] Lowry, as will be seen,
made notable contributions to the safety of shell filling. This work was
largely independent of Woolwich and, perhaps inevitably, friction
developed between the two groups of chemists. The long-established Woolwich staff tended to look askance at the improvements in processes or
machinery design made by the new organisation and the young Controller
Gun Ammunition Filling, Brigadier General Lionel Milman,* who had
complete control over the national filling factories, and after the war became
a manager of Imperial Chemical Industries, wryly stated at an enquiry that
he had no *locus standi* at Woolwich.[11]

How then did the chemists at the Research Department and elsewhere
improve high explosive production? The first urgent problem was to discover
a method for rapidly producing TNT. There was little experience of making
this compound, which usually took place in three phases involving the
treatment of toluene with strong nitric and fuming sulphuric acid known as
oleum. Moulton asked one of his committee members, W. R. Hodgkinson,
for many years Professor of Chemistry at the Ordnance College, Woolwich,
to discover whether it would be possible to make TNT without oleum, which
was extremely scarce as it had been imported from Germany. Hodgkinson
had been urging for a long time that the Services should use TNT. He found
that the British chemical industry was incapable of making TNT to the high
standard demanded by the Services.[12]

At least the Research Department had carried out experiments with TNT
before the war and might be able to produce small quantities of the
compound to serve as a stop-gap until the new munitions factories were in
action. Hodgkinson went to his laboratory in the College and carried out a
series of experiments in the hope that he could merge the second and third
nitrations into one operation by using highly concentrated sulphuric acid
with toluene and nitric acid. He stirred this mixture at a low temperature
which, when slowly raised produced between one and two pounds of TNT.
By 18 October 1914, he was confident of making enough TNT without oleum

---

* A captain at the beginning of the war.

to ask Robertson to work out a process for making three tons of TNT a week as an emergency measure.

Robertson and his colleagues now set about making a pilot plant. The main aim was to eliminate impurities in the compound so as to make it safe to handle. During the winter of 1914–15, they carried out, according to Robertson, '*a programme which was settled in committee the night before and these experiments embodied all the variants we could think of. From that work emanated our process with its distinctive features, the acid mixture, the running-off when hot, the process of detoluation, the counter-current process for the purpose of conserving the strength of the sulphuric acid, the cyclic process, which means that one starts with the mono and through the di to the tri, the sulphuric acid going into the counter-current and the temperature time rise. Having got out the process at the laboratory, we applied it on a semi-industrial scale and I can well recollect going up to the Arsenal one Sunday to acquire what we could from the scrap heaps. We got old coal skips, which were covered with lead, and we picked up wheels here and there. From that we erected the small experimental plant . . . in order to put our laboratory experiments to the proof. In that plant we conducted the process in all its special features exactly as it had been done in the laboratory. The first run was on 17 January 1915; it gave us good TNT and showed that the laboratory process was a sound one*'.[13] By June, Woolwich was producing the three tons of TNT a week originally called for.

This process was eventually adopted by the munitions factories built at great speed around Britain under the direction of K. B. Quinan, an outstanding chemical engineer loaned to the British by the Cape Explosives Works in South Africa.[14] The first factories to start production were Oldbury and Queensferry. Oldbury was used as a training centre in the processes of nitration for young chemists who had received preliminary training at Woolwich. Commercial firms also sent representatives to Oldbury in order to improve their techniques. It is worth noting that one of the firms making munition material was the Government-financed company called British Dyes, recently formed to fill the gap made by the absence of German synthetic products. By the end of the war thirty factories were producing 1,000 tons of TNT per week. It was filled in shell fired by field, medium and heavy artillery and the Navy used it in guns of 9.2 inch calibre and above. It was not put into naval armour-piercing shell on account of the difficulty of devising s suitable fuse, but mines and torpedo warheads were filled with it. Lyddite continued to be used for all other calibres of naval gun.

In April 1915, Farmer and the Explosives Supply Department appreciated that the large supplies of toluene needed to make TNT (every three tons of TNT required two tons of toluene) would soon become scarce. Toluene was derived from coal tar, large stocks of which were produced by the gas industry, at that time providing the main source of lighting in towns. Dr Carpenter, chief engineer of the South Metropolitan Gas Company, after lengthy and difficult experiments, was responsible for synthesising phenol from benzene and thus providing adequate supplies of toluene to meet the emergency.[15]

In the meantime Lord Moulton suggested that as ample supplies of ammonia existed in Britain, the addition of nitric acid to make ammonium nitrate, which could then be combined with TNT, would make an effective high explosive. E. R. Deacon, a member of the Research Department, made a comparison of ammonium nitrate and TNT with the French high explosive called *schneiderite* — a combination of ammonium nitrate and dinitronaphthalene — and found that the former process had a higher degree of combustion.[16] Forty per cent of ammonium nitrate was mixed with sixty per cent of TNT, the compound being called Amatol. It was first tested on 8 March 1915. Although the War Office at first doubted whether it was sufficiently powerful, Kitchener authorised it to be used straight away. Amatol was actually easier to handle than pure TNT because it did not become moist so quickly; more important, less raw materials were required to make it as one ton of Amatol only required 1.5 tons of imported materials, whereas the same amount of pure TNT absorbed 7.5 tons.[17]

The next stage was to ensure that there was a plentiful supply of ammonium nitrate for making Amatol. The firm of Brunner, Mond, used to making ammonia soda, was asked to work out an economical process for making ammonium nitrate.[18] Their chief chemist, F. A. Freeth, then serving in the BEF, was brought home to resume his experiments on combinations of ammonium nitrate. After trying out a number of methods, Freeth, assisted by one of his colleagues, H. E. Cocksedge, discovered that ammonium nitrate could be crystallised with a solution of sodium nitrate and ammonium sulphate. This process was used successfully in a trial plant at Sandbach, Cheshire and manufacture on a large scale began at Swindon in September 1917. Most of the British ammonium nitrate was made by Brunner, Mond. Freeth later recalled being told by Lord Moulton that the 'safety of England' had depended on his work.[19]

Meanwhile the Woolwich Research Department had discovered that eighty per cent of ammonium nitrate and twenty per cent of TNT (80/20 Amatol) was just as effective as 40/60 Amatol, saving an even greater amount of TNT — a fact of some importance should supplies of nitrate be cut off by German U-boats. The new compound was fired in shell in April 1915 and gave good results.[20] At first shells were filled with this new compound by what was known as the 'dry' or 'cold' method, Amatol in the form of a powder or cake being poured into the shell. This filling method was used throughout 1916 and provided most of the shell fired during the battle of the Somme. An effective way of speeding up output was introduced by Lord Chetwynd, managing director of the national shell filling factory at Chilwell, Nottinghamshire. Although possessing neither chemical nor engineering knowledge,* he invented a hydraulic press with a revolving table

* But he had been an enterprising and inventive manager of Vickers Steel Works.

on to which the powdered explosive was fed into the shell. It could be easily operated by two or three girls. Chetwynd received an award for his machine after the war.[21]

However, the gunners found the 'dry' shell filling method to be too unreliable and caused a large number of 'duds'. The Research Department therefore proposed that 80/20 Amatol should be heated and poured into the shell in a liquid form. But the transitional temperatures for heating the compound had to be accurately determined and special tables and graphs were worked out by Lowry for the purpose. In December 1916 80/20 Amatol was approved for firing by the BEF and was subsequently adopted by the Americans when they came into the war in 1917. Amatol had now become the main filling for shell and bombs, pure TNT being retained for certain types of naval shell. In mid-1917 about 400 tons of Amatol were being produced weekly. At an Amatol conference held that April, both Lord Moulton and General Milman paid tribute to the research which had made Amatol such an efficient explosive, though Moulton recalled that when 80/20 Amatol was first suggested he and Colonel Craig, in charge of the Research Department, *were its only supporters. Great credit was due to Woolwich and they were all aware of the services of Lowry with Amatol*.[22] At the conclusion of the war Moulton was surely justified in remarking that *'Amatol was the greatest single thing of importance in the supply of that wealth of munitions that enabled our armies to expend shell on an unlimited scale'*.[23]

Defects in Armour Piercing Shell

The filling of shell for the attack of ships whether armoured or unarmoured was governed by the need to penetrate, and then detonate in the ship's vitals, neither before nor after. Such a combination of penetrability and correct fusing has never been easy to achieve. In the early 1900s trials were conducted at Portsmouth, but difficulties arose over the construction of the shell which at that time was in one piece with a hole in the base for the fuse and for filling. But after a serious explosion in 1902 it was decided to protect the burster by putting it into an inner shell to guard against the outer shell cracking or breaking up and generating heat. This proposal was evidently assessed and approved by Woolwich and manufacture taken on by Messrs Hadfield at Sheffield.[24] Up to 1914, armour-piercing shell trials were carried out with guns ranging from six-inch to twelve-inch, but in the light of war-time experience they had clearly not been tested stringently enough, especially on account of the much thicker armour plating with which battleships were then being built. Nor, as far as it can be ascertained, was the armour plate subjected to the scientific analysis that was devoted to the development of other types of high explosive, especially after the lessons learned from the Russo-Japanese war.

In 1914, armour-piercing shell (APC) was available for the heavy (13.5

and 15 inch) guns of the Fleet.[25] Although the inability of APC to affect the vitals of enemy warships was apparent in the Coronel and Falklands actions, the crucial test came at Jutland.[26] Here engagements took place mostly at long range, so that the shells struck their targets at a steep angle. Although capable of penetrating thick armour when making a strike at or near the vertical plane, the sensitivity of the fuses made these long range shells burst on impact and so at the wrong angle to the plate. Hence the force of the explosion was often wasted. In addition, the lyddite filling was oversensitive and the shell produced a low order of explosion before the fuse had functioned and the armour had been properly penetrated. Captain Dreyer, who became Director of Naval Ordnance in March 1917, considered that with better APC shells the British should have sunk at least six German capital ships in that engagement. The Germans, for their part, had always used TNT as a filling and used armour-piercing shell far more liberally than the British. Closely connected with all these difficulties was the inadequacy of the fire control apparatus then in service, as will be discussed elsewhere.

After Jutland, the Admiralty set up a shell committee '*to determine most suitable nature or natures of projectiles and their filling and fusing for use in the Navy from turret guns, 12-inch and above*'.[27] Robertson's staff at Woolwich had to devise a less sensitive filling for an armour-piercing shell.[28] A lengthy period of experiment and trial ensued until in June 1917 a new 15-inch armour-piercing shell (called Green Boy) filled with a TNT compound called '*Shellite*' was introduced.[29] It was capable of penetrating 10–12 inch armour plating and bursting well inside the ship. But Green Boy did not become available until mid-1918 and, moreover, naval ordnance officers continued to prefer the old filling of lyddite which exploded when the shell broke up.[30] Luckily, the British Fleet never had to put '*Shellite*' to the test in a major action and further research uninterrupted by other pressing problems was continued by the Research Department after the war.

Woolwich did, however, devise a valuable explosive for naval operations and that was the star shell which, in certain conditions, illuminated a target better than searchlights, as the star shells did not give the enemy a point of aim to fire at. Robertson claimed that the British star shell was superior to that used by the Germans.[31]

Propellants

So much for high explosive. The shortage of raw materials also affected the manufacture of propellants. As we have seen, the British services used cordite, which was a combination of nitro cellulose, nitroglycerine and a percentage of mineral jelly, the solvent for gelatinising this mixture being acetone. Acetic acid, or acetone, was usually obtained from the United States of America or Austria and was made by the destructive distillation of hard woods in iron retorts. After August 1914, the United States became the main source of supply, British production of acetone being negligible, especially when the demand for cordite rapidly increased, and when acetone became an important ingredient for dope to cover the fabric of aircraft.

Apart from trying to increase the supply of acetone from America, an unsuccessful attempt was made to obtain the acid from vinegar. The only alternative therefore was to find an effective substitute. As the Research Department at Woolwich was already familiar with the composition of cordite, it was instructed to discover a suitable raw material from which, at the outset, some 400 tons of solvent a week could be produced. A new form of cordite had to have the same heat energy and ballistics as Cordite MD so as to avoid altering the calculation of range data, and it had to be capable of being manufactured by the machinery already installed in the munitions factories.[32]

Three possible processes were evolved.[33] The first, and most successful, depended on the use of alcohol and was originally suggested by William H. Perkin, the first Wayneflete Professor of Chemistry at Oxford, who was the eldest son of the famous Sir William Perkin, discoverer of aniline dye. Here was a good example of the use made of the most skilled research chemists of the country who gave their services voluntarily and usually without payment. Further details were worked out by Nevil V. Sidgwick, another fine Oxford research chemist, and a mass production process was devised by Messrs Joseph Crosfield of Warrington. The new variety of cordite was introduced in the latter part of 1916 and was called Cordite Research Department B, or Cordite RDB, ether alcohol being the solvent. This change required the use of a nitrocellulose which had a lower degree of nitration than gun cotton and the modification of the proportions of the other ingredients.

As ether alcohol was not as powerful a solvent as acetone, even for the modified form of nitrocellulose, careful research into the nature of the cellulose and its manufacture was required in order to make it conform to a strict system of chemical control. It was necessary, in the first place, to eliminate the woody matter in the cellulose and, secondly, to regulate the amount of viscosity, or 'stickiness' in order to simplify the mixing of nitroglycerine and mineral jelly, and thus to produce uniform cords of the explosive. It became possible to identify woody matter in the cellulose by selective dying while viscosity was measured by the rate of fall of a steel sphere through a solution of cellulose.

The supply of alcohol was drawn entirely from British distilleries and a large plant for converting it into ether was erected at Gretna in Scotland under the supervision of the American engineer, Quinan. Nearly 1,000 tons of alcohol, or the equivalent of about 200,000 gallons of proof spirit, were required for the production of the target of 1,500 tons of Cordite RDB a week, and it was this requirement which led to the restricted sale and increased cost of whisky.

The second process involved the use of calcium carbide and originated from experiments made at McGill University in Canada. An industrial process was designed by the Canadian Electro-Products Company. Both processes were responsible for providing acetone, but as the requirement for aeronautical purposes grew, the three stage process had to be reduced to two in order to provide the necessary quantities.

The third process concerned the production of acetone by bacterial fermentation from maize and other substances containing starch. It is of particular historical interest because the chemist who proposed it was Chaim Weizmann, better known as a pioneer of the Zionist movement, eventually becoming the first President of Israel. Weizmann was a Russian Jew who, after studying science in Germany and Switzerland emigrated to England in 1904 and settled in Manchester which not only boasted a flourishing school of organic chemistry under Professor William Perkin, before he went to Oxford, but was a cultural centre where liberal views were held in high regard. Weizmann believed that here both his scientific and political ambitions would be recognised. Perkin provided research facilities for Weizmann at the University and, two years later, he began to work on the production of synthetic rubber which was then in great demand and very expensive.[34] He spent a number of vacations working at the Pasteur Institute in Paris under Auguste Fernbach, the bacteriologist, to learn about the latest developments in fermentation chemistry, in particular those making use of alcohol.[35]

Although Perkin was not altogether impressed with Weizmann's research ability, and Weizmann himself was disappointed at not being elected a Professor of Chemistry, he was nevertheless awarded a readership in biochemistry at Manchester University for his research. He supplemented his income by working as a research chemist at the nearby Clayton Aniline Dye works.

Shortly after the outbreak of war Weizmann, then aged forty and a naturalised British subject, offered to provide the War Office with details of his process which he had now adopted for the production of acetone, making use of bacteria to ferment grain or other substances containing starch.[36] The process was not altogether unknown, as it had already been used at a factory in Norfolk, potatoes being the raw material, but very little acetone had been produced. The War Office did not reply. Evidently Weizmann then got in touch with the Nobel Explosive Company at Ardeer in Scotland. In February 1915, he was visited by William Rintoul, head of the company's research department, who had earlier been one of the founder members of the Woolwich Research Department. Rintoul was favourably impressed with Weizmann's experimental work and arrangements were made for him to work at the Nobel factory. But a serious explosion at the works put this out of the question.

Instead, Rintoul reported his opinion of the value of Weizmann's work to Frederick Nathan who, after leaving Waltham Abbey had become manager of one of the Nobel explosives plants in Scotland and was now adviser to the

Admiralty on cordite supply. He soon decided that a full scale trial of extracting acetone from fermented grain should be put into operation. Weizmann, in the meantime, had won the support of the First Lord, Winston Churchill, promising him that if he could produce a ton of acetone he would be able to multiply that amount by any factor required. The trial was laid on at the gin distillery of J. W. Nicholson at Bromley-le-Bow at the end of July 1915.[37] A brew of a thousand pounds of maize was made and a seven and a half per cent yield of acetone solvent was obtained — roughly the amount that Weizmann had hoped for.

Favourably impressed, the Admiralty engaged the services of Weizmann, giving him the title of Chemical Adviser on Acetone Supplies and providing him with a laboratory at the Lister Institute in Chelsea. There he began to develop the possibilities of another substance — butyl alcohol — which then had limited military and industrial applications as a possible solvent for cordite.[38] In the event of this process being successful, plans for a larger laboratory at Wandsworth were drawn up.

Meanwhile, Lord Moulton had become interested in Weizmann's proposal and engaged him to work simultaneously for the Ministry of Munitions. As he was now fully occupied, Manchester University agreed in August 1915 to release Weizmann from his academic duties. For the next year he devoted himself to the development of solvents for cordite, although this by no means curtailed his activities in promoting the Zionist cause.[39]

In 1916, Nathan became the Director of Propellant Supplies under Lord Moulton and therefore was responsible for the mass-production of acetone. The principal customer was the Admiralty, which erected an acetone plant at the Royal Naval Cordite Factory at Holton Heath near Poole, capable of producing some 25,000 gallons annually. By 1917 acetone was being produced on an annual scale of 90,000 gallons, mainly from damaged rice as maize was then in demand for foods stuffs.[40] A distillery at Greenock in Scotland was also adapted for the Weizmann process.

Weizmann by this time had collected a small staff of assistants to help with research and installation of plant. One of them had been recruited from Switzerland which, according to Weizmann, had even better chemists than Germany. (Moulton had objected to him travelling abroad to recruit staff and exchange ideas with other scientists and their relationship was evidently an uneasy one. Furthermore, Weizmann was never invited to serve on the panels of either the BIR or MID.) Another assistant was a woman graduate of Cambridge, Ida Smedley MacLean, who had won a Beit research fellowship to Manchester. Early experimental work and development did not always run smoothly. Special precautions had therefore to be taken in the preparation of the culture and in sterilising the mash; fermentation was then likely to succeed although failure sometimes occurred.

On 17 August 1916 Weizmann was able to tell Nathan that '*the manufacture of acetone by process is now on a proper footing*' and that his services in this direction were no longer required, though he wanted to continue to engage on long term research to discover a process for the conversion of butyl alcohol into methyl-ethyl-ketone as an alternative solvent for making cordite. His preference was to continue serving in the Admiralty, though the Ministry of Munitions would continue to enjoy the benefit of his researches. On 26 October 1916, the Admiralty prolonged his appointment, which was to be extended until the closure of his laboratory in May 1918. By that time, Weizmann was already deeply involved in political activities in Palestine.

The butyl-alcohol process gave promising results in the experimental stage and a pilot plant was erected in Toronto early in 1917 but the manufacturing capability had not got under way before the end of the war. In the meantime, production of acetone by fermentation had also been transferred to Canada because of the difficulties of importing grain. After the United States had entered the war, a large plant was built in Indiana. By then the need was less for explosives than for large scale aircraft construction. On account of the scarcity of grain, due to the German submarine blockade, experiments were made with extracting acetone from horse chestnuts which contained a high proportion of starch, but difficulties were encountered in large scale production.

The Weizmann process for making acetone fulfilled an important wartime need, especially for the Royal Navy. Although it was much less an important innovation than Cordite RDB, it acquired additional value through its application as a finishing material for aircraft surfaces. Its dependence on matter containing starch required large scale production to be moved across the Atlantic when supplies of grain were threatened by unrestricted U-boat warfare.

Though outside the terms of reference of this book, it ought to be mentioned that there is no evidence that the Balfour Declaration of November 1927 owed anything to Weizmann's scientific work on behalf of the Allies. That must be ascribed almost entirely to political activity. At the same time, Weizmann's contribution was recognised as a positive one to the winning of the war. A patent safeguarding his process was granted in 1916, applicable to France, Italy, Russia and the British Empire, but had to remain on the secret list for the duration of the war.[42] In 1926, Fernbach, Weizmann's mentor in the fermentation process, brought an unsuccessful action against him for infringement of his process.

French Munition Making

Like the British, the French chemical industry was not geared for the possibility of producing materials for munitions, nor were French chemists available to supervise the production of organic materials. Nevertheless, since the French had been pioneers of smokeless propellants and high explosive, they were not slow in organising research particularly in the dye industry centred on Lyon.[43] In some ways they were more advanced than the British, for example, in the production of picric acid used in French shell throughout the war. This was due to their development of synthetic phenol about fifteen years before the war.

In general, French munition production tended to be rather more rapid than the British as they seemed to have lower safety standards, though their accident rate was apparently no higher. One result of a British visit to French munitions factories in October 1915 was a recommendation that the Government should relax some of the restrictions then in force in British factories. French munitions workers were usually mainly wounded or convalescent Servicemen subject to military discipline. This made the task of supervision much easier than in the British factories, where large numbers of women were employed.[44]

German Nitrogen Fixation

It was Germany, on account of her advanced chemical industry, that exploited the latest chemical applications for making explosives above all the other belligerent nations. As already briefly indicated, significant advances were made by German chemists shortly before the war in the process of extracting nitrogen from the air in order to obtain ammonia and nitric acid. Intended primarily for agricultural fertiliser, badly needed by German farmers, these products could equally well be adapted for the production of explosives if the supply of nitrates from Chile was cut off by naval blockade.

The scientific breakthrough in nitrogen fixation, as it was called, was made by Walther Nernst but more significantly by Fritz Haber and, oddly enough, by an English chemist named Robert le Rossignol, once a student of Ramsay, who became an assistant to Haber.[45] Investigation began in 1904, when Haber was asked by some Austrian industrialists to investigate the possibility of obtaining ammonia through catalysis of various substances. As the experiments involved making chemical reactions at extremely high temperatures and atmospheric pressures, the results were not successful at first. Nernst, who was an expert on thermodynamics, then began to apply himself to the same problem and found that, by increasing atmospheric pressures still higher, he could obtain ammonia more easily though his yield was slightly lower than that of Haber's.[46] Stimulated by his lack of success, Haber, with Rossignol's help, built a metal apparatus capable of withstanding very high temperatures and produced a catalyst of a combination of nitrogen and hydrogen at 550° Centigrade.

It was now the turn of the industrial chemists to take over. On 2 July 1909, Carl Bosch and Alwin Mittasch from the *Badische Anilin und Soda Fabrik* (*BASF*), which had been interested in the possibilities of nitrogen fixation for some years, came to see the Haber–Rossignol experiment. They reported favourably to their masters and *BASF* asked Bosch to design a high pressure reaction vessel able to operate at high temperatures and Mittasch to discover the best substance for making a catalyst. Early in 1913, Mittasch, after carrying out numerous experiments, reported that an iron compound was the most suitable.[47] *BASF* acted quickly. By the end of that year, a nitrogen fixing plant was opened at Oppau near Ludwigshafen capable of producing 36,000 tons of sulphate of ammonia corresponding to 7,200 tons of nitrogen per year. There were, of course, many setbacks and even loss of life, because of the need to heat hydrogen to 550°C or 600°C at high pressure which, with the exception of platinum, also caused most metals to wear out.

But as the consumption of shell increased, it became urgently necessary to augment the production of nitrogen. During 1915, therefore, the capacity of the plant at Oppau was increased so as to be able to produce annually 60,000 tons of ammonia or 50,000 tons of nitrogen. Oppau was working at full capacity by the end of that year. It was due to the exploitation of nitrogen fixation that Germany was able to continue to wage war from 1916 onwards.

In the meantime, the *KRA* had the foresight to establish a nitrogen administrator. As the Haber–Bosch process was then still uncertain, an alternative system known as the cyanamide process, which had a relatively simple technology, was given priority. (An electrical process requiring large quantities of hydro-electric power had earlier been abandoned.) But in 1915, after the success of the Haber–Bosch process had been confirmed, the Prussian Government decided to transfer financial support from the cyanamide plants to the Haber–Bosch process at Oppau.[48] In January 1916, *BASF* was instructed to build a second, larger plant at Leuna near Merseburg, out of range of Allied air attack; the terms of the Government's loan were signed on 10 April 1916 — at the height of the battle of Verdun, where the German guns were consuming vast quantities of shell. Leuna came into operation on 27 April 1917. By the end of the war, Oppau and Leuna were annually producing 50,000 and 130,000 tons of nitrogen respectively.

It was ironical that nitrogen fixation should have been used at first for warlike rather than for peaceful purposes. Haber and Bosch both received Nobel prizes for their experimental work on the synthesis of ammonia, Haber in 1919 and Bosch in 1931. As for le Rossignol, he was interned at Ruhleben when war broke out, though he was soon released to improve tungsten lamps.[49] He returned to England at the end of the war. But for the handful of chemists mentioned above, Germany would have been as handicapped as the Allies. Wartime development would have been unlikely to have produced results in time, as the British, who started work on nitrogen fixing in 1916, were to discover. As it happened, Germany, according to an historian of the chemical industry had '*purpose, steadfastness in direction, competent technicians and chemists with a questioning as well as a receptive mind, and, above all, luck*'.[50]

Fuse Development

So far, we have discussed the technical improvements and new compounds for shell-filling. Much scientific study was also required to ensure instantaneous and effective detonation when the shell struck the target. As already noted, responsibility for the design of fuses in Britain lay with the Royal Laboratory at Woolwich. In shell filled with lyddite as the high explosive, detonation was achieved by the ignition of a powder fuse.[51] But this was found to be quite unsuitable for the destruction of emplacements and barbed wire. A series of graze fuses had to be introduced to ensure immediate detonation on hitting the target. Unfortunately, these quick-acting fuses caused a large number of premature explosions in the bore. An average of one in 16,000 to one in 32,000 rounds burst or otherwise damaged gun barrels, killing or injuring the gun crews.

In spite of numerous modifications by the Royal Laboratory, a really reliable fuse was not forthcoming. The 44 fuse, for example, issued to the artillery during the winter of 1915, either failed to burst the shell or detonated after the shell had buried itself in the ground. The shell manufacturers, moreover, complained that the fuse was too complicated for mass production. Modifications failed to bring about any substantial improvement.

Predictably, in 1915 the French had devised a more effective fuse called the *Fusée instantée allongée*. It operated by a brass tape which unwound during the flight of the shell to the target; the inner end of the tape was secured by means of a spigot pin through an eye in the tape; the spigot pin passed through a steel collar made in two halves of great annular thickness and into the stem of a hammer. This hammer was very light and had a needle with a blunt point which produced a tamping effect on the cap of fulminate of mercury causing it to divert to force downwards into the tetryl (the intermediary explosive) and detonate the main explosive of the shell. Unfortunately, the brass tape had a tendency not to unwind fully, so preventing the shell from detonating.

The details of how the British discovered the French fuse are illuminating.[52] During lunch after an Ordnance Committee meeting at Woolwich in the autumn of 1915, a member (probably Colonel J. T. Dreyer, brother of the fire control designer, and also an inventor) handed one of these fuses in a semi-dismantled condition to the chemist, Godfrey Rotter, who had been a member of the TNT research team. He had studied chemistry and physics at University College, North Wales before joining the Research Department. Rotter soon appreciated that the fuse could be improved, even though he had no drawings to show either how the fuse was assembled or how it worked. He was asked to improve the performance of the fuse and at once set to work under the direction of the Assistant Superintendent of Research, Lieutenant Colonel L. C. Adams.[53] Eventually, he made two important modifications; one was to insert a stud in the tape, thus allowing the latter to unwind more readily, and the second was to increase the weight of the hammer, relying on it to cause the detonation rather than the sharp end of the needle. Later, several other improvements to facilitate manufacture were introduced, including a simplified means of inserting the fuse into the shell and the provision of a secure safety cap for it once it was ready to fire. The new fuse was designated by the number 106 and fulfilled the stringent requirements of the British Army for safety, simplicity in manufacture, and instantaneous detonation.

It was first used at the Battle of Arras in April 1917 and, according to Haig, Commander-in-Chief of the BEF, *'enabled wire entanglements to be easily and quickly destroyed and so modified our method of attacking organised positions. By bursting the shell the instant it touched the ground and before it had become buried, the destructive effect of the explosion was greatly increased. It became possible to cut wire with a far less expenditure of time and ammunition and the factor of surprise was given a larger part in operations'.*[54] Within a few months, demand for the new fuse had become so great that instructions had to be issued for even more careful attention to be paid to the manufacture and inspection of fuses, if troops were not to lose confidence in the new store. In the field, experience showed that the shortest range at which it was safe to fire was 1,550 yards when the fuse acted correctly and the best effect obtained against personnel and wire entanglements. The ability of the 106 fuse to explode on impact also made it necessary for advancing infrantry not to advance too closely behind a barrage.

Some 20–30 million of the new fuses were made and were used by various calibres of field gun. The 106 fuse was also supplied to the United States Ordnance Department. Rotter obtained an award from the Royal Commission on Awards to Inventors; he continued to work for the Research Department and in World War Two he won the George Medal for bravery.

As soon as aerial activity increased, it became necessary to devote attention to the development of special fuses for anti-aircraft munitions. Fire control devices, as will be discussed in a later chapter, were very primitive and all that could be hoped for was the introduction of mechanical fuses which would explode a shell at a point where the maximum number of lethal fragments would pass through the targets. Development of mechanical, or clockwork, fuses began at Krupp's some years before the war and patents were taken out by that firm in England and on the Continent. But a reliable mechanism for operating it in a shell had still to be found. At the beginning of the war, the Germans, exploiting their knowledge, pressed ahead with research and development and, by mid-1917, were shooting down Allied observation balloons over the Western Front, employing what appeared to be a satisfactory clockwork fuse. Eventually, a number of these fuses, known as *Dopp Z 16*, were recovered intact by the French and several handed over to the British.

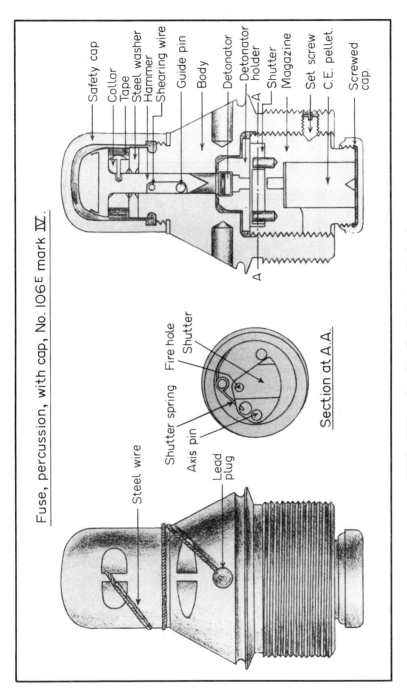

Fuse, percussion, with cap, No. 106ᴱ mark Ⅳ.

Section at A.A.

Safety cap
Collar
Tape
Steel washer
Hammer
Shearing wire
Guide pin
Body
Detonator
Detonator holder
Shutter
Magazine
Set screw
C.E. pellet.
Screwed cap.

Steel wire
Shutter spring
Axis pin
Fire hole
Shutter
Lead plug

4.1 The 106 Fuse. *Royal Artillery Institution, Woolwich.*

In September 1917, the Ordnance Committee decided that clock-fuses, based as far as possible on the German model, should be developed for use primarily in heavy guns, ranging from six-inch to twelve-inch, of both Services and, when an adequate supply permitted, for heavy anti-aircraft guns.[55] As the work was extremely specialised and painstaking, for a German clock had virtually to be reconstructed and tested, Cecil Mason, a director of the Cambridge Scientific Instrument Company, was made responsible for advising both on the design and on methods of production; (no doubt at the instigation of Horace Darwin). Mason was attached for this purpose to the Ministry of Munitions, while he carried out initial experiments at the Cavendish Laboratory, Cambridge.[56] Apart from reconstructing a German clock, he devised special apparatus for testing the fuse at rest under times closely approximating to those likely to be experienced under operational conditions. They were followed by dropping tests and recovery and firing trials on the ranges, the latter taking place in April 1918.[57]

Manufacture of the mechanism and its casing also presented problems as the watchmaking industry in Britain was virtually non-existent on account of the strong competition from American and Swiss companies. Attempts to produce American-made fuses proved to be unsuccessful and it was therefore decided to employ two British companies, one, Messrs Rotherham of Coventry, already an established watchmaking firm, and, second, Messrs Kent of Luton, which was to start from scratch using machinery imported from Switzerland, though making its own jigs and assembly plant. All this highly specialised work had to begin before firing trials were completed, gathering momentum in a surprisingly short time in spite of a number of setbacks, such as the call-up of many technicians early in 1918, a munition strike at Coventry following the influenza epidemic, on top of which the annual August holidays began.

By mid-October 1918, firing trials were deemed sufficiently satisfactory for the Army Council to declare that '*the output of mechanical fuses should be increased as rapidly as possible and to as great an extent as possible*',[58] though the war ended before operational experience could be obtained.

5

Breaking the Deadlock

New Weapons for Trench Warfare

The Germans, on the whole, responded more quickly than the British and the French to the need for specialist weapons in trench warfare — with one important exception, the tank. On 25 December 1914 Sir John French, Commander-in-Chief of the BEF, asked Kitchener for *'an inventive expert . . . to devise means of counteracting the development of German trench warfare. They adopt some new device every day'*.[1] As we have seen, the officer chosen was Colonel Jackson who, in fact, proved to be both inventive and a good organiser. He now became responsible for a multitude of different kinds of weapon ranging from explosives, grenades, mortar bombs, portable shields for the infantry, to pumps to extract water from the trenches; even tanks came briefly into his purview. This chapter will trace the invention and development of weapons and equipment for trench warfare with the exception of chemical warfare which demands a chapter on its own.

Grenades

Kitchener had originally specified that the Trench Warfare Department should be responsible for both research and supply, but, as related earlier, Alexander Roger had to separate the two functions. While this decision proved to be unfortunate in the case of chemical weapons where chemists were required to test the end products before operational use, it became essential for other weapons. Roger claimed that he was the first actually to despatch a complete round to the front; (on one occasion a consignment of grenades was sent to France while their detonators went to Mesopotamia).[2] Another of Roger's innovations was the Outside Engineers Board. This was a team of engineers under Captain Leeming called *'hustlers'* who were responsible for finding suitable factories which could take on an unfamiliar product at very short notice and then ensure that when completed it would be sent to the appropriate theatre of war without delay. During the experimental period of grenades, for example, fuses were made both by

large firms like Brock's, the firework-makers, and Bryant & May, the
match-makers, and by small firework manufacturers in Birmingham and
Huddersfield.[3]

Requests for grenades, or bombs, by the BEF for close-quarter fighting
had become increasingly urgent from the autumn of 1914 onwards. Although
grenades had been used regularly in warfare since the 17th century and
earlier, they had quite recently been revived for modern warfare and were
used in the Russo-Japanese war and were a standard issue in the German
Army. The British had no regular establishment for grenades, but when the
BEF went to France it was equipped with a small number of percussion type
grenades.

The short distances of around 400 yards between the opposing armies led
to the adoption of the grenade as an essential weapon, and it was soon
appreciated that large quantities would be required; as many as 250,000
grenades daily was one exaggerated estimate. Under Jackson's supervision,
various types of grenade were improvised and called 'jam pots' or 'hair
brushes' according to their shape.[4] Their fuses protruded from their sides
and were usually lit by an ordinary match and hurled a distance of about
twenty-five yards in the direction of the enemy. As this procedure had to be
carried out in No-Man's-Land, often in the dark or in the rain, it is not
difficult to appreciate that it was an extremely hazardous operation from the
point of view of the thrower.

A bomb was therefore needed that was safe to handle and self-igniting.
Early in 1915 a Belgian company — the Compagnie Belge des Munitions
Militaires — had developed a new type of grenade containing a striker,
detonating cap and fuse. The striker was brought into play by a lever
attached to the grenade. The lever retained the striker against the force of
the spring which, when released, operated the detonating cap. The explosive
was ammonal — a composition of hydrogen, nitrogen and carbon and the
fuse took five seconds to burn after being activated. The bomb was invented
by Captain Leon Roland, who was taken prisoner of war early in the
campaign.[5] One of his colleagues, Albert Dewandre, met a fifty-nine-year-
old English marine engineer, William Mills, who had set up the first
aluminium foundry in England and had an inventive mind, although he had
never handled explosives before. Mills, with his engineering experience,
quickly appreciated that the bomb could be improved, but he and Dewandre
first submitted the proposal to the Inventions Branch of the Directorate of
Artillery on 23 January 1915. The weapon was considered worthy of
development by the Royal Laboratory, Woolwich which had already produced two percussion type grenades modelled on the German Army's issue.

From then until August 1915, Mills, in close collaboration with the Royal
Laboratory, worked day and night to perfect the weapon. He was helped by
Professor William Morgan, in charge of automobile engineering at Bristol
University. There were three essential improvements which had to be made;

one related to the firing system, especially the detonating cap, while the remaining two concerned the improvement of the lever attached to the grenade which had a delaying system of a jaw and notches which were supposed to prevent premature release when held in the hand. Another aspect which called for improvement was the insertion of adequate vent holes in the sides of the grenade allowing the explosive gases to escape and which otherwise could cause premature detonation.

Unfortunately, the distribution of the Mills Mark II grenade to the troops led to an alarmingly high rate of accidents — around ten a month — many of them fatal. The principal cause was the faulty design of the jaws, allowing premature release of the lever — it often sprang upwards to nearly 90° from the side of the grenade, causing the grenade to explode in the hand of the thrower. A lock manufacturer, F. J Gibbons, who had already devised a machine for the rapid assembly of Mills bombs, invented an improved form of lever early in 1916. This was more effectively slotted and dispensed with the original circular head of the striker, which was liable to become rusty.[6] The grenade thrower now exercised greater control over his bomb, instilling in him a greater degree of confidence.

The improved form of grenade was issued under the designation No 36 and No 23 Mark III; they were, in fact, more or less identical in design. The number of accidents — originally around one in three thousand, was reduced to one in twenty thousand. Thus the Mills grenade, despite being mechanically unsound in its earlier versions, proved to be an outstandingly effective weapon. Well over seventy-five million were manufactured in the United Kingdom and issued to the infantry on all the battle fronts. A discharger cup was devised to give the grenade additional range by firing it from a normal rifle. During the period of trench warfare on the Western Front, the grenade virtually superseded the rifle and ranked in importance after artillery ammunition in the order of priority of supply. In the opinion of senior officers it was more effective than the German stick grenade and the French Army had nothing comparable. Mills, the adapter of the Belgian grenade, set up his own factory in Birmingham which manufactured his bomb, enabling him to amass a considerable fortune. After the war he was knighted and a few years later was awarded the sum of £27,750 by the Royal Commission on Awards for Inventors.[7] Similar sums were also awarded to Gibbons and several others for their valuable work in saving lives by the improvement of safety devices.

Mortars

Static warfare also demanded high angle weapons with short, non-rifled barrels to destroy permanent fortifications or dug-in positions. The long siege of Port Arthur by the Japanese during 1904–05 had shown that steel and concrete emplacements could withstand the battering of conventional artillery; it was not until heavy coastal defence guns were deployed that the Russian defenders were forced to surrender. This lesson was digested by the German and Austrian general staffs who approved designs for huge mortars and short barrelled howitzers able to pulverise the sunken gun positions of modern fortifications. The forts encircling Liège and Namur were prime examples of the military engineer's art in Europe and the Germans knew that unless they were speedily overcome, the momentum of their proposed drive through Belgium and into France would be seriously delayed. Two types of artillery were designed; one by Skoda, the Austrian munitions firm, and the other by Krupp at Essen, both being evolved in the closest secrecy. Skoda's contribution was a 12-inch mortar drawn by a tracked motor vehicle able to travel up to twenty miles a day.[8] At the firing site the barrel was bolted to the separate steel base plate, the operation taking about forty minutes; after firing, the whole contraption could be rapidly dismantled and put on the road. The mortars could fire at an angle of 60°, swivelling over a wide arc, and had a maximum range of seven miles throwing armour-piercing shells fitted with delayed action fuses. The German siege weapon was a heavy howitzer 16.5 inches in diameter, bigger than any British naval gun, firing a shell weighing 1,800 pounds.[9] But it was extremely difficult to move and had to be transported in sections by rail. Shortly before the war began, a more mobile motorised or steam-propelled version was evolved and tested.

Both these weapons went into action for the first time to overcome the defences of Liège and Namur in August 1914. Most of the destruction was caused by the Skoda mortars firing at a range of 3,000 yards; their shells penetrated the steel cupolas housing the guns, killing the crews with high explosive or poisoning them with the fumes. Meanwhile the German howitzers, looking like 'overfed slugs',[10] were brought into action after delays in transportation and crushed other centres of resistance. Liège fell four days after the arrival of the siege artillery, while Namur held out for only three days.

The Austrians had designed even larger mortars ranging from 14 to 16-inch in calibre and, throughout the war, were engaged in improving or readapting the 12-inch mortar for bomb or mine projection.[11] After 1914 there was a more urgent requirement for a light trench howitzer, mobile and easy to conceal, throwing shells over distances of 300–400 yards. The kind of targets they were required to hit were enemy parties working in No-Man's-Land, communication trenches (particularly at a time when reliefs were taking place), snipers and machine guns. Both the German and the Austrian armies had equipped their infantry with mortars of light and medium calibre, but neither the British nor the French had them.

As with grenades, improvisation became the order of the day for the Allies and various forms of apparatus for hurling bombs into enemy trenches were devised, even extending to catapults launched with string or elastic. By early 1915, the British Army had evolved two heavy mortars — the 4-inch and the 3.7-inch, and a light mortar — the 2-inch. What was now required was a portable mortar and a safe and efficient fuse for the shell. During a visit to the Western Front, H. A. Gwynn, the editor of *The Morning Post*, learned about the Army's need and, on returning home, got in touch with Wilfred Stokes, general manager of a light engineering firm called Ransome & Rapier.[12]

Stokes immediately got down to the drawing board. In a few weeks he had produced a design. It was a simple tube, four inches in diameter, mounted on adjustable legs and resting on a metal base plate weighing 70 pounds. It would be able to fire a shell made of cast iron (steel was in short supply because of the demand for high explosive shell); it was cylindrical in shape with eight chambers filled with explosive built round a central core and it weighed 20 pounds. The explosive would be ignited in rotation by varying lengths of time fuse, the outer walls of each chamber flying away and leaving the core intact. The propellant charge of black powder contained in a cartridge would be held in a recess at the base of the shell. The fuse would be set off by the ignition of a percussion cap upon striking a spike in the base of the tube. The shell would be fired on the release of a pin, allowing the shell to slide down the barrel on to the striker. Stokes estimated that a projectile could be thrown over a distance of 350 yards at a rate of thirty shells a minute. The great merit of the gun* was that it could be mass-produced by non-specialist firms not yet engaged in the manufacture of munitions and it was cheap, portable and both deadly and demoralising for the enemy, because of the successive explosions of the multiple chambers.[13]

The initial trials of the mortar at Shoeburyness were not outstandingly successful — the shells either fell short or were thrown wide of the target. The gun was therefore turned down by the Director of Artillery. In the meantime, GHQ France continued to press for an alternative to the 3.7-inch mortar which was causing casualties because of its tendency to misfire. Several proposals for a so-called '*pneumatic*' gun operated by liquid carbonic acid were put forward by the Royal Society War Committee but none of them proved to be practicable.

Undeterred, Stokes withdrew to his cottage at Ripley in Surrey to improve the design of the shell. He changed the cylindrical shape to a streamlined one with a nose which would be more accurate in flight; and, after experimenting with various forms of propellant, selected ballistite (invented, it will be recalled, many years earlier by Nobel). He also realised that better results would be obtained by firing the shell with the cartridge attached to it in a container. He cut vents in the container allowing gases generated to escape.

Further trials took place in March and April 1915, but the shell obstinately refused to land on its nose. A few minor modifications were needed to rectify this. After a successful trial on 14 April, approval for manufacture was

* The terms gun/mortar were, confusingly, interchangeable during the war.

requested from Major General F. R. (later Sir Francis) Bingham, Deputy Director of Artillery, subsequently a member of the council of the Ministry of Munitions. Bingham, who knew about the improved design, was either unaware or had forgotten about the demands from GHQ for a new mortar, now turned down the Stokes gun on the grounds that there were already sufficient types being used at the front.[14]

Meanwhile an urgent demand for a new mortar had been brought from the Dardanelles by a young staff officer who had been wounded there, Captain F. A. Sutton, formerly a civil engineer. Two days after landing from a hospital ship in London he met Stokes and was greatly impressed by his design. Casting discretion aside and oblivious of rank, Sutton pushed his way into the offices of Lord Moulton, Lloyd George and Churchill.[15] On 30 June his efforts were rewarded by the arrangement of a demonstration at short notice for the benefit of Lloyd George and Churchill who were due that day to inspect a forerunner of the tank. Both were impressed with the performance of the mortar, and Lloyd George agreed to recommend production of 1,000 weapons and 100,000 shells once the design had been perfected.* Stokes, anticipating that the gun might again fail to come up to standard, enlisted the support of Lieutenant General M. F. Rimington, commanding the Indian Cavalry Corps, who had an attentive ear for new ideas. He arranged for General Haig and other senior officers to see the mortar demonstrated by Stokes while on an unauthorised visit to the front. Predictably, the tests were disappointing because of the imperfect fuse. But Lieutenant R. H. G. Rimington, the General's son, after discussing the problem with Captain Allen West, an engineer officer, who had originally interested the Rimingtons, suggested that the Mills bomb fuse might be adopted — an idea that was readily accepted by Stokes, as was the suggestion that the mortar could be adapted to fire gas bombs.[16] Back in England, the weapon underwent further trials before the Ordnance Committee during August. Their verdict was that while it was certainly a better performer than the 3.7-inch mortar, the detonating system left much to be desired. On 12 August, Lloyd George, although the weapon had still not been approved, ordered the immediate production of 1,000 mortars with a supply of 2–300 rounds per gun per week. He was prepared to cover his losses in the event of failure with a contingency fund. Yet another month elapsed before official acceptance. Instead of concentrating on perfecting the fuse, Stokes took it upon himself to convene some thirty to forty firms, including his own, to manufacture the weapon. His initiative, not surprisingly, was unacceptable to the Trench Warfare Department, which, instead, placed orders piecemeal. In any case, mass production was premature as the weapon was subject to almost daily modifications by the inventor. The situation was also aggravated by urgent demands for smoke bombs required in the battle of Loos.

* According to Addison, only twenty mortars were originally ordered.

At last, on 4 September 1915, although the final specifications were still not to hand, the Master General of Ordnance gave the go-ahead to manufacture the Stokes mortar,[17] formal assent being given by the Ordnance Board on 15 September.[18] That December, General du Cane, who had recently left the GHQ Inventions Committee to become Director General of Munitions Design, insisted that the mortar should not be used operationally until one thousand rounds had been fired by six guns. The original requirement of 800 mortars was completed by mid-January 1916, and, after rapid-firing trials in the presence of senior Allied officers, went into service at the end of March, though at the outset the mortars were only used to fire smoke bombs. Various structural weaknesses still had to be overcome — the legs supporting the gun tended to buckle after prolonged firing and had to be strengthened, while the traversing gear required stronger rivets. At least Haig, now Commander-in-Chief, BEF could write on 28 March 1916 that '*all reports agree as to the efficiency of the 3-inch Stokes mortar*' and declared his intention of substituting it for the other types of light and medium mortar.[19]

By the end of 1916 trench mortars had become such an important adjunct to trench warfare weaponry that a Trench Mortar Committee was formed to deal with questions of supply and improvements to the weapon and ammunition.[20] Stokes mortars were manned by infantry who had received special training at the Trench Mortar School behind the front in France. In 1916, the BEF, then consisting of 55 divisions, possessed a total of 1,320 mortars of all calibres, each division with an establishment of 24 light and medium mortars. The Stokes mortar gave a good performance on other fronts as well; even in guerilla warfare it proved to be useful as T. E. Lawrence anticipated when he equipped his band of Arabs for attacks on the Hejaz railway with a Lewis gun and a Stokes mortar, one manned by an Australian and the other by an Englishman. The mortar decimated the defenders of a derailed train on one occasion. Mortars retained their value in World War Two attaining a range of just under 3,000 yards with a ten pound bomb and continue to become increasingly sophisticated, and may even be used as an anti-tank weapon in the future.

From 1916–18 mortars undoubtedly increased the available fire power in the trenches. At the same time, they were not always popular among front line troops as their destructive capability tended to upset the equilibrium of '*live and let live*' that existed in certain sectors of the front line.

Development of the Stokes mortar suffered in the first place from being over-hastily designed, and its progress was marred by the shift of responsiblity for new weapons from the War Office to the Trench Warfare Department. It was quite correct for the War Office to be adamant on the need for securing proper safety measures before the gun was issued to the troops, especially as so many fatalities had been incurred when operating earlier models. Development might have been accelerated had a single authority for trench mortars been set up at an earlier stage, but at the beginning of 1915 it was still difficult to anticipate the growth of specialist weapons and the intensive accompanying development that would be required.

Flame

Another close support weapon used first by the Germans[21] on the Western Front was the *Flammenwerfer*, or flame-thrower; it was a rudimentary apparatus made up of lengths of steel tubing bolted together and attached to a base plate. Jets of oil, ignited by automatic lighters, were propelled towards the target by streams of compressed air. The French were the first to experience this new weapon in June 1915 and the British about a month later. Flame-throwers were, of course, cited as being yet another example of German *'frightfulness'* but, in fact, the weapon had antecedents in the history of siege warfare.[22]

The Allies responded with similar weapons of their own, but neither they nor the Germans achieved much success with them. The projectors were usually fired from a fixed position in a trench or underground gallery; in the latter case the tubes were pushed up through the earth just before the signal to fire was given. Semi-portable types were operated from trenches or from the surface. But although the smoke, flames and intense heat were momentarily terrifying for those in the target area, for the operators the apparatus was dangerous, cumbersome, difficult to erect and, after firing, its location was only too obvious to the enemy. The first British flame-thrower was devised by Captain Vincent, an engineer officer, but it was dependent on very heavy oil canisters and was dangerous to operate because the compressed air still had oxygen in it. An improved version was invented by a young officer named F. H. Livens who, as we shall see, soon became celebrated for his contribution to chemical warfare. Livens's projector had a range of about seventy yards and he used deoxygenated compressed air as an inert propellant. He also introduced a semi-portable projector which had a range of twenty to thirty yards. Both the Vincent and the Livens projectors were used in small numbers during the battle of the Somme.[23]

The French continued to employ flame-throwers but without conspicuous success, as did the Germans, especially in support of counter-attacks in the latter stages of the war. But the short range of the projectors was a severe handicap to the teams operating them and they quickly became exposed to machine-gun fire.

Sound Ranging

So far we have discussed the impact of technology on short-range weapons. As indicated earlier, the inability of the infantry to penetrate defence in depth and by-pass the ubiquitous machine-gun led to a great expansion of artillery. Attention was therefore turned on both sides to discovering means whereby enemy gun positions might be identified and then destroyed by counter-battery fire. (It should be remembered that at that stage of the war aerial reconnaissance and aerial photography were still in a rudimentary state.) The French and the Germans lost no time in investigating the possibility of locating enemy batteries by sound. The method was quite simple.[24] Sound generated by firing a gun takes a time T1 to reach station M1, T2 to reach station M2 and so on. The range to the gun from each station is VT where V is the velocity of sound. The difference in time of arrival of the sound at the two stations is $T_1 - T_2$, equal to $t_{1,2,3}$, the recorded difference of arrival as shown on the recorder. If the positions of the stations are plotted on a large scale map, and arcs are struck from the plotted positions of the stations at radii VT_1 and VT_2, for all appropriate values of VT_1, and with T_2 equal to $T_1 - t_{1,2}$, the intersection of these arcs produces an arc of a hyperbola on which the gun's position must lie. If the process is repeated for stations M2 and M3, two hyperbolae are obtained and the gun lies on their intersection. It should be possible to get an intersection from M3 and M4 and so on, improving the accuracy (see Fig. 5.1). In practice, celluloid arcs were fixed to the board with graduations corresponding to the appropriate time differences t, the position of the gun being found by stretching strings between the front and back celluloids.

It was Charles Nordmann, an astronomer from the Paris Observatory, now an artilleryman on the Western Front, who, in the autumn of 1914, appreciated that a gun's position could be discovered by measuring the time interval between the arrival of the report at a series of points along a measured base line.[25] His commanding officer was sufficiently perceptive to allow him to carry out a few rudimentary experiments. Nordmann set in position three observers equipped with well-regulated stop watches who noted the time when they heard a detonation. These crude experiments were promising enough for him to return to Paris to develop his idea.

Nordmann discovered Lucien Bull, a French physicist of Irish extraction, working at the Marey Institute on electro-cardiography and recording heartbeats. After discussing the idea, Bull proposed developing his Einthoven string galvanometer which he used for physiological experiments.[26] By inserting three strings into the magnetic field of the instrument, it might be possible to record signals from three microphones, each placed a kilometre apart along a measured base line. In mid-November 1914 Bull and Nordmann found they were able to locate the position of a gun fired from a distance of twenty-seven miles with sufficient accuracy to convince the military authorities to order the construction of three sound recording sets for use at the front.

Bull at once began to construct a portable set for operations. It comprised a small six string Einthoven galvanometer in which the currents were recorded by the displacement of fine wires in a powerful magnetic field. The wires were strongly illuminated and their shadows were thrown into

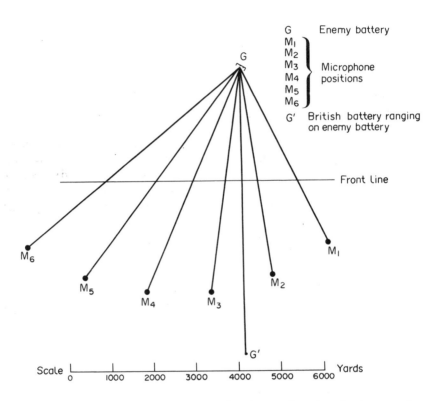

5.1 Method used by the British for obtaining locations by sound ranging, showing general disposition of the recording apparatus. *Public Record Office*.

juxtaposition across a slit by six small totally reflecting prisms. A 35 millimetre cine film ran behind the slit and a toothed time wheel, governed by a tuning fork, interrupted the light one hundred times a second, thus ruling time markings across the film. The apparatus was switched on and off by one or more forward observers in front of the base line who heard the sound before it reached the microphones. When the apparatus ceased running, the operator at headquarters cut off the portion of film which had run, developed and fixed it, and passed it to the reader who measured the time intervals and deduced the position of the gun.

The prototype was ready by mid-December 1914 and the first operational sets were in the hands of artillery units early in February 1915. Meanwhile, other methods of sound ranging were being investigated by French scientists. One was a simpler method than Bull's in which currents from microphones actuated pens whose movements were recorded on smoked paper at the headquarters to which the microphones were connected. This system was used for some time by the French Army signal service. A third set, also using photography like Bull, was developed by the well-known physicists, Aimé Cotton and Pierre Weiss, who directed the magnetic laboratory in Strasbourg.

By the summer of 1915, the existence of sound ranging had been discovered by a few officers in the BEF but had received scant encouragement from the Inventions Committee at GHQ. Eventually a Royal Engineer colonel named H. St J. L. Winterbotham became so persistent in demanding a sound ranging organisation for the British Army that the Experiments Committee authorised the purchase of a set from the French. Lawrence Bragg, then a junior subaltern in a Territorial Army horse artillery battery in England, was asked to collect it from Paris and begin experiments at the Front. Bragg, although only twenty-five, was already well-known as a promising physicist, a reputation confirmed later that year when, in company with his father Professor W. H. Bragg, he was awarded the Nobel Prize for Physics for analysis of crystal structures using X-rays. (W. H. Bragg had already begun to do important work on the detection of submarines, as will be described in a later chapter). Lawrence Bragg, who had been bored with the hunting fraternity to which most of his fellow officers belonged, relished the prospect of doing valuable scientific work.

He and a chosen assistant physicist, H. Robinson (later Vice-Chancellor of London University), arrived in France in October 1915. After a period of instruction from the French in a quiet sector of the front in the Vosges, they settled down at a village called La Clytte, south of Ypres, later moving to Kemmel Hill — an active sector. At first it was as Bragg wrote, 'rather heavy sailing', as neither of them had any operational experience and their only official contact was Colonel E. M. Jack, head of maps at GHQ St Omer. However, before long, the lorry containing the set was collected from Paris, two small Singer cars were acquired and a section of six Other Ranks assembled to operate the apparatus, drive the vehicles and lay telephone line.

Nearly a year passed before any worthwhile results were achieved. The main difficulty was the inability of the microphones to pick up the right kind of noises. They were over-sensitive to high frequency sounds like rifle fire, traffic, or barking dogs, but unable to identify the muffled low boom of a gun report. They were especially sensitive to high velocity shell passing nearby, recording a loud 'crack' but losing the faint boom which was the true gun report. Various ingenious solutions to eliminate disturbance were proposed by the French but none of them were satisfactory. A selective microphone responding to the right kind of noise was essential. Other scientists worked independently on the problem including A. N. Whitehead, the great mathematician and philosopher, in company with his son, who was later killed in action. The proposal was considered by the Ordnance Board and experiments authorised but nothing superior to the Bull apparatus came up.[27]

Experience taught Bragg and his colleagues that, although a gun report made little impression on the ear, it was associated with noticeable changes of pressure in the atmosphere. Merely by sitting in their farm house billet in La Clytte, they were able to classify the firing of different calibres of artillery. The deafening shell wave of a six-inch gun firing over them left their postures undisturbed whereas a faint gun report had a markedly lifting effect. A phenomenon which led them nearer to a solution was that when they were working in the hut which served as a laboratory, a jet of bitterly cold air came through the rents in the tarred paper walls immediately after a gun report.

Eventually a practical solution was provided by a young physicist from Imperial College, W. S. Tucker, then only a corporal. He had been making experiments on the cooling of very fine hot platinum wires, known as Wollaston wires, by air currents. Bragg takes up the story:

> 'Somehow we arrived at the brilliant idea of using the jet of air coming through an aperture in the wall of an enclosure to cool a Wollaston wire, heated by an electrical current, and so alter its resistance. What we hoped was that high frequency sounds, with their very rapid oscillations, would not drag away the film of warm air round the wire, but that the slow but large air movement due to low frequency sounds would do so. We got some fine wire from England, placed it across the hole we drilled in an ammunition box, and made it one arm of a Wheatstone bridge which we balanced with our galvanometer in the usual circuit. I remember vividly the night we rigged it up. A German field battery obligingly fired towards us, and when the film was developed there was a small, sharp "*break*" for the shell wave, followed by a quite characteristic and definite large break made by the gun report which could be read with accuracy. It was a wonderful moment, the answer to prayer. It converted sound ranging from a very doubtful proposition to a powerful practical method'.[28]

The passage of air into or out of the container cooled the wire. Hence the displacement of the galvanometer string was always in the one direction, as if the lower sections of a *sine* wave had been reversed upwards. The characteristic frequency of a field gun report was about 25 cycles, that of a large piece about 10, though this was only a rough guide to calibre. The great advantage of sound ranging was that it recorded shell bursts as well, so that it was possible to determine the kind of gun or howitzer from the time of flight or by recovering fuses from the shell holes. A typical report gave the calibre, number of guns, and target on which the battery had registered.

It was also possible by using the microphone to identify the calibres of guns by the pressure variations. The ammunition box containing the instrument had the advantage of being heavily damped and did not impose its own characteristics. But after the success of this experiment, when instruments were made in England, it was found that they were much inferior to the crude prototype, as they imposed their own character on sounds.

The Tucker microphone came into service in June 1916. It was quite a problem to produce quantities of such sensitive instruments but was resolved by assigning the task to the Research Department of the General Post Office. The staff manufactured 13,540 microphones which were delivered to the sound ranging sections up to December 1918. The officers of the sections (usually numbering four with twenty-four Other Ranks) included several well known physicists and applied mathematicians including C. G. Darwin (a grandson of Charles Darwin), E. N. da C. Andrade and J. M. Nuttall.[29] Thirty seven sections were formed in France from 1916 onwards and were attached for administrative purposes to the Artillery Field Survey Companies. One section went to Italy and four were formed in Egypt and Salonika. Each section had a mechanic with a tool kit, a watchmaker's lathe, and a chest of assorted bits and pieces of wood and metal, enabling each section to try out its own scheme.

In such a novel field of scientific work, exchange of ideas and experience were essential. Every second month Bragg used to hold meetings of representatives from each section at some central point. Before the meeting, new proposals were sent to 'W' Section, the original group, which had now become a centre for training and experiments. Bragg then drew up an agenda for circulation, thus preserving the sense of urgency and eliminating delays which would have been bound to have occurred had the experimental work been done at home. (Later in the war Tucker, now a commissioned officer, formed an experimental section on Salisbury Plain and did good work but by then the problems were well-defined.) The meetings usually ended, Bragg observed, '*with a binge of heroic magnitude*'. But it should be noted that these officers were the first scientists in uniform (though somewhat similar bodies were operating at the same time on similar problems in the French and German armies); they were the first actually to carry out scientific work on the battlefield, setting a precedent for further-reaching and significant activities in World War Two.

Among the topics discussed at these meetings was the need to prevent pressure fluctuations due to wind turbulence from impeding the reception of the microphones. Protection by walls only increased turbulence and it was found that the best results were obtained by placing the instrument near a thick hedge or by draping it with sheets of camouflage netting. Gusts of wind were then converted into a steady flow — a process similar to stretching a piece of gauze across the mouth of a running tap.

Two other inventions improved the effectiveness of sound ranging.[30] The first made it possible to distinguish whether 'breaks' in the film were caused by enemy or friendly batteries, whether ground or anti-aircraft. By putting the microphones at exactly equal intervals in a straight line, the six '*breaks*' on the film fell on a smooth curve. After a while, it was easy to spot a series of '*breaks*' which belonged together even when interrupted by other noises. This was very useful in the overpowering din of battle. Later on, the straight line was abandoned for the arc of a circle with its centre roughly in the most interesting area behind the enemy front. Plotting boards were printed for a few standard sets of radii and distances between microphones, and it was always possible to shuffle a standard layout so that the six microphones fell into convenient places. The surveyors fixed three places correct to a metre. This simple procedure gave the sound ranging sections a certain degree of mobility. In the Battle of Cambrai, in November 1917, one section went into action fifty-six hours after zero hour in an area recently evacuated by the enemy, demonstrating that it could operate at least as fast as a heavy artillery battery.

The second innovation occurred about this time when the first wind and calibration sections were formed. While valuable information was provided by the Army meteorological sections, it was not detailed enough to make accurate corrections because the information derived from such data varied considerably with height and local contours. At the same time upper winds and temperatures varied little along the entire front. A so-called wind section was formed and recorded reports from a known position. A pound or two of explosive was set off at intervals of a few hours and the sound was recorded by a series of microphones in two or three areas at about the same range as the enemy guns. The position of the explosion being known, it was possible to measure the extent to which the wind and the temperature had affected the readings and so circulate to the sound ranging sections the required corrections.

By the end of the war, instrumentation had become sophisticated enough to develop and fix film as it came out of the camera. By using strong solutions, developing and fixing was done in a matter of seconds; but the apparatus was not really reliable, often breaking down and precious records were lost. On the other hand, when an important target was located, it made up for all the trouble incurred.

The Bragg sound ranging system, based on the Bull apparatus, was also used successfully in Palestine, good results being obtained at the Third Battle of Gaza.[31] It was also introduced to the American Army when it went into action in France. Five sections under Colonel Augustus Trowbridge, a physics professor from Princeton, were formed and equipped with the Tucker microphone.[32] According to Bragg, they *'did very well and got lots of useful results'*[33] though they evidently had some difficulty in recruiting the right kind of scientifically-trained officer. A flash ranging section was also formed under Theodore Lyman from Harvard. Both sections performed satisfactorily in the fighting around Chateau Thierry in June 1918.

Whether sound ranging was as valuable as Bragg later recalled is open to question. At the time of his death, one of his brother officers claimed that by 1917 *'seventy-five per cent of all enemy batteries that opened fire were located and that in the great German offensive in the spring of 1918 the outstanding counter-battery intelligence and armour enabled the British Army to withstand the attack and, once the tide had turned, to crush all the enemy's resistance in one hundred glorious days'.*[34] Bragg's wartime correspondence is, however, less eulogistic. Writing early in 1917 he noted that it was *'practically impossible to get any results during the Vimy engagement which was practically a fixed battle and entirely impossible during the moving battle of the Somme. The difficulties arose from interference and the cutting of the telephone line by shells and on the Somme in the difficulty of wiring and surveying fresh positions each time the line advanced. It was agreed that sound ranging would benefit greatly if it could be in closer touch with flash spotting, and the Flying Corps, and Artillery Intelligence'.*[35] Bragg implied that the value of sound ranging was limited in mobile operations, first, because of the time it took to survey accurately new positions for the microphones and, secondly, because of the lack of precise knowledge of wind effects on the sound waves from the muzzle of the gun to the microphones. Another handicap was that the essential line communications were apt to be cut by artillery fire. A wireless link was never evolved because of the primitive state of contemporary wireless sets.

The German sound ranging organisation included a number of scientists, one of them being the future nuclear physicist and Nobel prize-winner, Max Born, then a young lecturer in mathematics at Berlin University.[36] He was responsible for developing a much more simple system depending on the binaural effect. An observer had two horns at the end of a rod, each connected to an ear, and by estimating the direction of the sound with reference to direction posts he deduced its bearing. Intersections from three or more stations gave a location. After the war Born and Bragg exchanged notes on their experiences at the front. Bragg did not think very highly of the German method, believing that the German Army committed itself to the system too soon and was unable to change it when ranges increased and greater accuracy was essential. Born admitted that the British instruments were superior to the ones he was using but stressed their liability to interference. The front line troops, however, had a great respect for the British system and in June 1917 a German order was captured forbidding guns to fire when the sector was quiet, and especially when the wind was in the east, because of the *'excellent sound ranging of the English'*.[37]

Aerial spotting and even more, aerial photography, though dependent on air superiority, had already overtaken sound ranging by the end of the war. Even in the middle of World War Two experiments were being made with the binaural method for locating mortar positions but radar technology was rapidly superseding acoustic appliances for military purposes. Even so, sound ranging equipment was used in the Korean War during a static period of the fighting.

The Use of Wireless in Static Warfare

The use of wireless by the British Army was handicapped both by a lack of policy and by the failure to provide adequate research facilities. The reason for the former was probably due to the slow development of the *'hard'* or vacuum valve and the limited wireless manufacturing resources which compelled priority for continuous wave sets being given to the Navy and the Air Force. Yet never before had Army commanders been so out of touch with the forward troops. One of the most appalling examples in the early part of the war was the inability of General Sir Ian Hamilton, Commander-in-Chief of the Dardanelles expedition, to communicate with his senior commanders and the assault troops from his headquarters ship after they had landed at Gallipoli on 25 April 1915. At least on the Western Front good use was made of the Round/Marconi valve by the posts set up behind the Front for the purpose of intercepting and locating German wireless stations and they became a valuable component of the intelligence service.

As the experimental section at Aldershot was soon absorbed in the BEF, impromptu research had to be carried out in France, and it was here that the first continuous wave sets for the Army were assembled (sometimes with the help of knowledgeable prisoners of war).[38] These sets were immediately monopolised by the gunners for communication with forward observation posts. In the autumn of 1916, the Signals Experiment Establishment was formed at Woolwich and it began to assemble and test spark transmitters for the Front. On account of the lack of skilled operators it was essential that they should be simple to operate.

In the meantime, experiments were made by both sides with what was called *'earth telegraphy'* or *'earth currents'*. Communication between two points was established through electric impulses transmitted by a buzzer powered by a battery, the signals being received through a three-valve amplifier* after crossing a gap 300–600 yards between wires laid in the earth from transmitter and receiver. This system could be used either for tapping enemy telephone communications or for sending signals without having to use land lines.[39] Interception sections were used in the Russo-Japanese War, though Sir Oliver Lodge had suggested that the British Army should use

* See Fig. 5.2 on page 79.

them in the Boer War but to no avail.[40] In Germany the eminent physicist Arnold Sommerfeld, assisted by an electrical engineer named Arendt, discovered they could detect signals through the ground as far distant as 3,000 yards according to the nature of the soil. A listening service was set up in the German Army with a headquarters at Namur responsible for certain sectors of the Western Front.[41] Much valuable information could be derived from listening to casual conversation over field telephone lines and the Germans became so adept at gathering intelligence that sometimes a new battalion entering the front line would be greeted from the other side of No-Man's-Land by its regimental march. Similar experiments were conducted by the Russians and the French.

The French and Germans also found that earth telegraphy was a reasonably secure method of sending signals. General Ferrié was responsible for developing the French instrument called *Parleur TM2*. A similar German equipment was developed by Richard Courant, a twenty-six-year-old lecturer in mathematics at Goettingen, who later became celebrated for his work in quantum physics. After serving as an Infantry officer at the Front, he was transferred to Berlin to do wireless research. The purpose of this work was to provide communication between the guns and their observation posts. He then returned to the Western Front with a small detachment of technicians and took part in operations round Verdun. Courant was later gassed and invalided home.[42]

The British, on the other hand, did not have much success with their experiments with '*earth telegraphy*' which took place at Houghton Regis in Bedfordshire where the chalk soil was similar to that around Arras and Amiens, under the direction of F. G. Baily, Professor of Electrical Engineering at Heriot Watt College in Edinburgh.[43] Experiments with *Parleur TM2* were made at the NPL but the soil at Teddington was unsuitable for the purpose. Meanwhile Sir Henry Norman in Paris had been badgering the War Office and MID to take more interest in the scheme. Communications for the artillery were vital and many systems had been tried '*including telephone lines, rockets, pigeons, whistles, optical signals, wireless and cyclists, but none of them solved the problem*'.[44] Just before the battle of the Somme, Norman wrote to MID: '*The Army needs these sets with the utmost urgency. We have lost thousands of men and our chief offensives have largely failed for want of them. Yet I am sure that GHQ and Woolwich will go on experimenting rather than accept what the French have perfected*'.[45]

In the end, the War Office conceded that the French instrument, although not perfect, was better than anything that could be produced in England and ordered 500 buzzers, half of which had been supplied to the BEF by the end of October 1916. At the end of that year GHQ reported that *Parleur TM2* had been of '*practical use in the late advance after all wires had been cut*',[46] but it was still necessary to eliminate electrical interference from outside and for that fairly high frequencies were required. Work was begun on developing an alternator but at the beginning of 1917 the French had not yet succeeded in improving their system.

The Fullerphone

Since the summer of 1915 the British had found that phone-tapping had become so serious that the Director General of Signals, General Sir John Fowler, had asked the War Office for help. A solution was eventually offered by Major A. C. Fuller, a Royal Engineer officer who had made a detailed study of wireless.[47] In 1910, during a posting to Bermuda, where he was adjutant to the local defence signals unit of the Western Telegraph Company, Fuller kept himself up to date by studying American telegraph and wireless journals, and even constructed his own wireless station. On the strength of this, he was posted on the outbreak of war to the 1st Wireless Telephone Company at Aldershot. Fuller, on his own initiative, began to work on a device which would guarantee speech security over a telephone line. His aim was to devise a combined system capable of transmitting and receiving morse signals but which was incapable of being tapped by the enemy. By setting up an impedance coil and two condensers, he was able to control the rise and fall of current moving up and down the line; the current being 'chopped' by a rapidly revolving commutator to prevent it from surging back through the impedance coil into the line, the current momentarily being stored in the condenser. In the first place, the invention made possible transmission of very weak morse signals which could not be picked up by the enemy and, secondly, once the line had been cleared of alternating current, it could be used for normal telephone speech, though this, of course, was not secure. The combination of telephony and telegraphy was not new, one system having been devised by van Rysselburgh about 1902, but the military possibilities of sending secret signals over the telephone had never fully been worked out, although anticipated by A. C. Brown, an associate of Graham Bell, the inventor of the telephone.

Fuller submitted his proposal to his commanding officer around November 1915 and it was deemed sufficiently promising to be sent out to France for operational testing. It won favourable reports and, on 4 January 1916, was approved for manufacture and distribution to the BEF by General Fowler. Production of the instrument never entirely satisfied demand, as it had to be made by hand, but ten thousand sets were supplied to the British Army and about five thousand to the American Army. The Fullerphone continued to be used by British forces until the adoption of effective short wave radio.

By the end of 1917 the Germans had devised a similar system to that of the British which they called the *Unabhorchbare* (non-tappable) *Telegraph(Utel)* but, like the British, encountered problems with production, in their case mainly because of the lack of raw materials.

Valve amplifier for field telephone

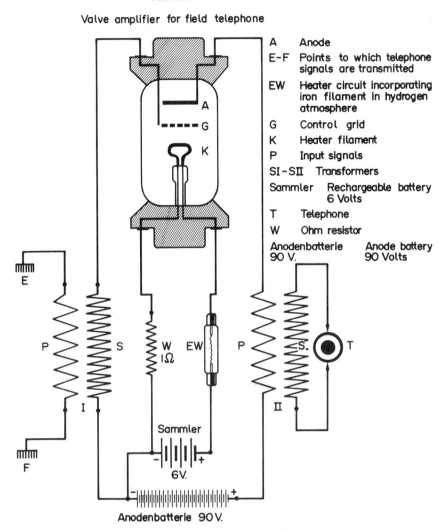

A	Anode
E-F	Points to which telephone signals are transmitted
EW	Heater circuit incorporating iron filament in hydrogen atmosphere
G	Control grid
K	Heater filament
P	Input signals
SI-SII	Transformers
Sammler	Rechargeable battery 6 Volts
T	Telephone
W	Ohm resistor
Anodenbatterie 90 V.	Anode battery 90 Volts

5.2 Valve amplifier for field telephony.

Acoustic Instruments in Mining Operations

The construction of tunnels, in which mines were placed and exploded for the purpose of causing a breach in the enemy line, also provided an opportunity for the use of acoustic apparatus to detect underground excavation. This very old form of siege warfare had been revived by the Japanese during the siege of Port Arthur in 1904–05 where the Russians beat off repeated attacks for seven months and were only overcome when the Japanese tunnelled beneath two forts and exploded mines.

Mining operations were begun by the Germans on the Western Front in December 1914, causing quite a considerable effect on the morale of the Allies. Mine warfare now began in earnest, tunnelling companies being formed by the British and French during the early months of 1915. As soon as this new development in trench warfare got under way, it became imperative to obtain reliable information about underground excavations being carried out by the enemy. As ever, the French Military Telegraphy Service was the first to come forward with listening equipment. In England requests were made to the Royal Society War Committee, but there is no evidence that anything superior to the French appliances was ever devised.[49]

The French appliances were classified under two categories, both being based on the general principle of the seismograph.[50] In the first category they were usually stethoscopes or mine listeners which enabled an observer to listen to sounds on the spot. They had the advantage of being portable and very sensitive to sound but demanded special training for operation. The second kind were microphones set up some distance from the front. The apparatus consisted of two parts, one being placed on the ground and able to respond to vibrations and movement; the other part was mounted above the ground and mechanically separated from the first part. Both parts formed a small airtight compartment containing a small volume of air. An observer could record variations in the air pressure, enabling the subterranean sounds to be identified. The microphones were not as accurate as the stethoscopes. The main disadvantage to this system was that it depended on a number of telephone lines according to whether the purpose was merely to listen to or to locate the position where the sound had originated. On the other hand, there was less interruption to listening such as shelling or gas attacks. No specialist training was required and a single listener could keep a wide area under surveillance. Above all, it was possible to determine the origin of sounds very quickly.

Tunnelling operations on the Allied side culminated in the attack on Messines Ridge in June 1917 when a million pounds of ammonal were fired. But such operations on the whole were inconclusive, being described by one distinguished civil engineer in uniform as '*a gigantic public works operation with the most inferior and inadequate tools and tackle and carrying with it tremendous disadvantages*'.[51] The use of poison gas, aircraft and, above all, tanks made mining redundant after mid-1917. It is the invention and wartime evolution of the tank — the most significant and revolutionary equipment to be used in the war — that must now be described.

The Tank Developed by the Allies

The use of 'battle wagons' for the purpose of assault or for carrying troops into action may be traced back to the beginnings of warfare, like the horse-drawn chariots of Ur protected by hides in 3,000 BC, to the more advanced iron-built chariots of the Assyrians, down to the revolutionary proposal of Leonardo da Vinci for a three-man armoured shell on wheels, through which fire could be directed on the enemy. Mobile forms of equipment like these depended on the muscle power of horses or human beings and it was the invention of steam power and later of the internal combustion engine in the 19th century that made possible consideration of the armoured fighting vehicle as we know it today. Another factor was the improvement in steel plating that made protection against small arms fire possible.

The first step taken towards adopting the petrol driven motor vehicle for military purposes was to cover it with armour plating and the first armoured cars and motor cycles began to appear early in the 20th century, actually operating on the battlefield for the first time in 1912 during the Italo-Turkish War in Libya.[52] Various forms of wheeled armoured vehicle came into service in the French and German armies. But as they were confined to roads or to flat terrain like the desert, their value was strictly limited. One way of remedying this problem was to substitute wheels by caterpillar or endless track systems which had just begun to be applied to agricultural machines, enabling them to traverse hitherto impassable country. The first tracked vehicle to appear on the market was a converted steam tractor built by the American Holt Manufacturing Company for use in the delta lands of Louisiana. Similar types of tractor began to be developed in England by Hornsby-Ackroyd and the Pedrail Company.

Although the advantages of using steam engines to haul heavy guns or supply wagons were quickly appreciated, only a few seemed to grasp the effect that an armoured fighting vehicle, fitted with tracks and able to cross trenches and rough ground and attack enemy positions, might have on the future of warfare. One of these visionaries was the writer, H. G. Wells, in a short story called 'The Ironclads' published in 1903. It was left to two engineers to work out practical details. One was a thirty-two-year-old engineer officer in the Austro-Hungarian Army named Gunther Burstyn who conceived the idea of a 'land torpedo boat' equipped with a cannon. Although he never overcame the problem of designing a track able to carry his vehicle at a reasonable speed across country, he did provide for a sprung suspension which could give a fairly stable platform from which the crew could operate.[53] In October 1911, Burstyn submitted his design to the Military Technical Committee in Vienna, only to be told that it lacked sufficient merit to warrant expenditure from the Army budget. As Burstyn did not have the means to carry on his experiments, his project lapsed and was not even revived when the war came. The following year an Australian civil engineer, L. A. de Mole, also came forward with a proposal for a tracked armoured vehicle with sprung suspension, though in his case he concentrated on developing an efficient steering system. Like Burstyn's his design was doomed to oblivion in a British War Office pigeon hole.

Others, who were not mechanical engineers but who recognised the importance of converting the tractor into an instrument of war, included T. G. Tulloch, already mentioned as being an advocate of TNT. Around 1911 he made some drawings for a steam-driven armoured vehicle based on the Hornsby-Ackroyd design after discovering the importance ascribed to the machine-gun by the German Army.[54] In the summer of 1914 Hugh Marriott, a well-known mining engineer, saw a Holt caterpillar tractor operating at an industrial exhibition in Antwerp. He visualised the machine as a means for extracting soda deposits from dried up lakes in East Africa, but also appreciated its military potential and passed on his observations to a forward-looking engineer officer, Lieutenant Colonel Ernest Swinton, a fluent writer on military tactics who had been commissioned to write the British official history of the Russo-Japanese War and had begun to realise the power of modern weapons that could compel armies to dig themselves in and cause a stalemate. Swinton had recently been Assistant Secretary to the Committee of Imperial Defence, but was sent to France as official war correspondent or 'eye witness' to the BEF. One day it occurred to him that the Holt tractor could easily be converted into a trench-crossing machine and be employed to break the impasse on the Western Front.[55]

While on leave in England in October 1914, Swinton talked to Colonel Maurice Hankey, Secretary of the CID and, as already noted, extremely receptive to novel ideas on warfare. They agreed that Swinton should stir up interest at GHQ, Hankey engage the attention of the War Office and appropriate Cabinet ministers, while Tulloch would seek out likely engineers for design and development. After some weeks, realising that he was not making much progress, Hankey wrote a memorandum, on Boxing Day 1914, for the Committee of Imperial Defence summarising his views on ways of breaking the stalemate on the Western Front.[56] In a few vivid sentences he sketched what mechanised warfare might be like — armoured machines on caterpillars brought up into position at night, then advancing into the enemy's positions, smashing obstructions on the way and sweeping trenches with machine-gun fire. Infantry would advance behind in short rushes using the machines as *points d'appui*. Once the positions had been consolidated the assault would continue against the second line. Above all, surprise would be vital and Hankey suggested that smoke screens might be used to cover the assembly of the force.

Ideas similar to those of Swinton and Hankey occurred to Colonel J. E. Estienne, a French artillery officer serving on the Western Front, some months later.[57] A Holt tractor which he had seen towing guns in the British sector suggested to him the possibility of armoured machines able to cross rough ground and smash through enemy positions. After two unsuccessful attempts to interest his superiors, Estienne decided on 1 December 1915 to write to General Joffre, the Commander-in-Chief, briefly outlining his idea and suggesting that a test model might be made leading to the creation of a force of land ships which would break through a twenty-four mile front followed up by the rest of the Army. On 12 December Estienne was summoned to GHQ for an audience with Joffre. He explained in some detail what his proposed vehicle might consist of and what it might do; it would be manned by a crew of four, be propelled by an eighty horse power engine, armed with two machine-guns and a cannon and if required, tow an armoured trailer carrying twenty fully-equipped infantrymen. As for tactics, the first wave of machines would advance on their objectives after a brief artillery bombardment, behind would follow a second wave supported by infantry, who would consolidate on the trenches just taken and then provide covering fire for a further advance by the leading machines.

Joffre was sufficiently impressed by this exposition to allow Estienne to leave his unit and collaborate with Eugène Brillié, an engineer from Schneider, the armament firm, who was already experimenting with tracks fitted to armoured cars. This combination led to the building and testing of a prototype followed, in due course, by the first French *Chars d' Assaut* built by Schneider under the direction of Estienne.

But the British were the first to give reality to the vision of mechanised war.[58] Their success was due to a rare combination of political drive and effective team work by a very small group of engineers and single-minded Service officers. The political initiative came from Winston Churchill whose imagination had been kindled by Hankey's memorandum. The air defence of Britain was one of his responsibilities as First Lord and early in the war he had established air bases on the Belgian coast from which attacks might be made on enemy airship hangars. Protecting the British airfields were armoured car squadrons manned by the Royal Naval Air Service which were also used to harass the flanks of the enemy ground forces. Impatient at being restricted to the roads, Commander Murray Sueter RN, already noted for his interest in airships, and other officers, began to experiment with caterpillar tracks fitted to their vehicles.[59] Churchill warmly approved their initiative. Similarly, he encouraged experiments being made by Admiral Bacon, who had retired to become managing director of the Coventry Amament Works, to discover whether a tractor towing the 15-inch howitzer he had designed could cross trenches using a portable bridge.

On 5 January 1915, inspired by Hankey's memorandum, Churchill wrote to Asquith, the Prime Minister, suggesting that No-Man's-Land might be crossed with large steam tractors fitted with caterpillar tracks, able to carry men and machine-guns, their advance being covered by smoke screens. He urged that a small committee be set up to consider whether the plan was technically feasible. This was approved and the Director of Naval Construction was made chairman.[60] He had already been called upon to advise on the experiments of Sueter and Bacon, with which, incidentally, the Army had not been impressed. His name was Eustace Tennyson d'Eyncourt, a versatile marine engineer appointed by Churchill at the age of forty-four to be responsible for the design of warships for the Royal Navy. He was also to supervise the development of rigid airships — a field in which the British had a long way to go before catching up with the Germans. D'Eyncourt's committee was called the Admiralty Landships Committee and met for the first time on 22 February 1915. Members included Colonel R. E. Crampton, a mechanical engineer, and Major T. G. Hetherington, a cavalryman with a fertile imagination who had been working with Murray Sueter on armoured car tracks. Their aim was to build a large machine weighing about twenty-five tons. The main problem was how to keep the driving portion of the tracks in contact with the ground. Either the machine should be fitted with immense wheels, as proposed by Admiral Bacon, or it should have some kind of endless track much stronger and lengthier than any existing pattern. They decided to build a sort of mobile armoured fort, or troop-carrier, holding fifty to seventy men with suitable armament and running on endless tracks. For this purpose two Giant Bullock tractors were purchased from the United States; they were delivered to the experimental ground at Burton-on-Trent and a number of experiments made with them. On the strength of these trials a set of creeping grip Bullock tracks was ordered from the States.

Meanwhile, the Army had been independently exploring the possibility of using caterpillar tracks and had tried out a Holt 120 horse-power tractor. Although acquiring a good deal of information, they were disappointed with the performance of the machine in crossing trenches. Seeing that so little progress was being made by the Army, Swinton, still attached to GHQ in France, wrote a paper called 'The Necessity for Machine Gun Destroyers' which ably summarised his ideas on cross-country armoured machines. After examination by the Experiments Committee, the paper was sent to the War Office for comment on 22 June 1915.[61] Swinton then learned for the first time of the progress being made by the Admiralty Landships Committee. At last jolted into action, the War Office specified conditions for the proposed landships, namely that they should be capable of crossing backwards or forwards an earth parapet five feet thick and five feet high, having an exterior slope of one in one, an interior slope vertical, and of bridging directly all gaps up to five feet in width without dipping into them, and climbing up to a depth of five feet all gaps about five feet in width with vertical earth sides. These conditions with others regarding weight, armament and crew, were communicated to the Landships Committee on 1 July 1915.

Two weeks earlier a joint military-naval committee had been formed under Sir George Scott-Moncrieff, the Director of Fortifications and Works to provide fresh impetus to the development of landships which had become bogged down over recent months because of difficulties in finding a suitable track capable of being articulated for steering when the vehicle needed to change direction. D'Eyncourt and the other technical committee members remained in charge of development.

On 30 July a big step forward was taken when it was decided to scrap earlier designs like the big wheel, the Giant Bullock tractor and the half-track, and the whole project was handed over to William Tritton of Messrs Foster & Co of Lincoln which made the Foster–Daimler tractor. Tritton, then forty years old, had joined the firm in 1905 and in six years had advanced to Managing Director. In that capacity he had revived the firm's fortunes which had previously been in the doldrums.[62] As a chief assistant he was given Walter Wilson, a brilliant forty-one-year-old engineer from Cambridge. He was already well known in the motor car industry for designing an engine embodying epicyclic gears and had earlier designed an engine for a powered glider built by the aeronaut Percy Pilcher. He had recently been in charge of tractor experiments at Burton-on-Trent.

Tritton was instructed to build a machine with an endless track which would incorporate the long Bullock tracks already mentioned as being ordered from the USA. Tail wheels were to be provided to enable the machine to turn over a wide radius and to act as counter weights to the machine's point of balance. Power was provided by a six cylinder 105 hp Daimler engine. The machine was to be completed in three weeks. In fact design was started on 2 August and the machine moved itself on the Bullock tracks on 8 September.[63] A model had already been inspected by the Moncrieff committee several weeks earlier, but they found the design did not match the War Office requirements, mainly because the central superimposed gun turret caused the centre of gravity to be too high. The Bullock tracks were continually giving trouble and were replaced by new ones designed by Tritton and Wilson, the machine running satisfactorily on them by 22 November. The machine was christened 'Little Willie'.

As 'Little Willie' could not properly perform the functions laid down, Tritton and Wilson immediately set to work to make an improved design for a machine with a quasi-rhomboidal shape with the tracks running round the periphery. It not only fulfilled all the conditions demanded by the War Office, but dispensed with the superimposed gun turret, the guns now being placed in sponsons between the tracks, each sponson containing either a six pounder naval gun or two machine-guns according to whether it was intended to attack machine-gun posts or infantry positions. It was named 'Big Willie' or 'Mother'. On 29 September 1915, a conference of naval, military and Ministry of Munitions officials, the latter being responsible for supervising development and eventually production, inspected designs and photographs of 'Little Willie', later going to Wembley Park to inspect a full scale model of 'Mother'. Comparative trials of the two machines early in January 1916 clearly demonstrated the superiority of 'Mother' as a fighting machine. It was the design that became familiar to the world as the tank, though for the time being this was a cover name suggested by D'Eyncourt as it was seemingly innocuous compared to the self-revealing designation of landship. Approval of 'Mother' as prototype for the tank was finally sealed when it showed its paces at Hatfield Park on 2 February 1916 in the presence of Kitchener (who apparently remarked that it was '*a pretty toy*') and other general staff officers, Winston Churchill and members of the Cabinet.[64] Several weeks later the tank was demonstrated before King George V.

Approval of the machine, to be known as the Mark I, was merely the prelude to a difficult period during which the first tanks were built, sent into action, and modifications introduced as a result of their performance in the field. At first the War Office, understandably hesitant, only ordered fifty machines, but on 12 February 1916 it agreed to Lloyd George increasing this total to 100 Mark I's.

Initial output might well have been less had not an outsider been put in charge of supply by Lloyd George. He was Albert Stern, a banker who before the war had moved in the 'smart set' as a much sought after bachelor (even Lloyd George's secretary might have succumbed, had she not already been inextricably attached to the former). After several attempts to enlist, Stern was commissioned into an armoured squadron under Murray Sueter where he was initiated into the early experiments in mechanical warfare. He became Secretary of the Landships Committee, not only proving himself to be an excellent organiser, combing industry for essential parts for the prototype tanks, but personally taking a hand in the experiments.

Meanwhile Swinton, with whom Stern saw eye to eye, had taken charge of the Machine Gun Corps Heavy Branch, as the first tank unit was called, again for reasons of security, and trained in a secluded area of Norfolk. Swinton here began to develop the technicalities of mechanised warfare, such as wireless communication between tanks and cooperation with aircraft. Both he and Stern and other tank enthusiasts appreciated that training, formulating tactics, and eliminating mechanical faults would necessarily take time, as would production of a large enough number of machines capable of inflicting a surprise attack on the enemy — the essence of the whole scheme.

Information that Haig intended to use the sixty available tanks in August 1916 in an attempt to offset the failure of the Somme offensive was therefore received with dismay, but protests by Lloyd George, recently appointed Secretary of State for War after Kitchener's death at sea, and Edwin Montagu, his successor at the Ministry of Munitions, were in vain.[65] On 15 September 1916, tanks went into action for the first time at Flers Courcellette. Only thirty-six machines were fit for action, of which eighteen either supported the infantry or consolidated newly-won ground. Five were ditched in shell craters. Although their appearance in some instances caused dismay among the enemy, their tactical employment was absolutely contrary to what Swinton and others had envisaged, in addition to which the possibility for a massive surprise stroke was lost.[66]

In the following months, while Mark I and III tanks continued to be used in '*dribs and drabs*' on the Western Front, efforts were made at home to improve their performance, which left much to be desired. The original Daimler engine was quite inadequate to deal with dust, mud and barbed wire and the lubrication system could not function properly when the machine had to climb out of a steep sided trench. Driving the tank was extremely complicated. Two men, in addition to the driver, were required to operate the gears, and the tank commander had to apply the brakes as well as attend to his other responsibilities. The exhausts emitted clouds of blue smoke when the engines were started from cold, at once revealing the assembly area of the tanks.

D'Eyncourt therefore decided that Wilson, with his experience of epicyclic gears, should design a new transmission system capable of being operated by one man and that Harry Ricardo, a young engineer who had been a student of Bertram Hopkinson at Cambridge, should design a new engine.[67] Ricardo had already been engaged in designing a flying boat engine for anti-submarine warfare and had attracted D'Eyncourt's attention when called upon to suggest a method of lifting tanks onto flat rail cars. Now that the element of surprise was lost, Tritton was asked to design a hull proof against anti-tank weapons.

Wilson, without much trouble, was able to adapt his epicyclic gears so that the torque could be shifted from one track to another. As high quality steel was in short supply, Ricardo had to depend on aluminium for pistons and induction pipes. He designed a 150 hp engine with six separate cylinders in line. The ignition system, hitherto a weak point, was made more efficient by the provision of two magnetos. In order to improve oil control and to eliminate exhaust smoke, he employed a cross-head piston, circulating air on its way to the carburettors around the cross head guides and under the piston crown. The only snag was that the interior of the hull became intolerably hot for the crew because of the length of exhaust pipe running inside it. Ricardo cured this by fixing a metal cowling round the exhaust manifold through which air was circulated by a belt-driven fan and discharged through the top of the tank, partially alleviating the discomfort. Other improvements included the installation of an anti-stalling governor, as machines were liable to come to an abrupt halt on the battlefield exposing themselves to enemy fire. As it was impossible to crawl underneath the machine, the crankshaft was put in the baseplate of the engine making it accessible from above. Ricardo's and Wilson's engine was tested in an experimental Mark V tank in June 1917.

By then the General Staff had at last begun to appreciate what an asset tanks could be, especially in exploiting a breakthrough in the enemy's front line.[68] Formal recognition of the tank was achieved in July 1917 when the Tank Corps was created and on 28 September guiding lines for future policy were laid down at an important meeting presided over by the Deputy Chief of Imperial Staff and attended by Major General Sir John Capper, who had succeeded Swinton as Director General of the Tank Corps and was now chairman of the Tank Committee set up to improve liaison between the Army and the Ministry of Munitions, and Brigadier General H. J. Elles commanding the tanks in the field.[69] Capper's appointment led to disagreement with Stern, now Director General of the Mechanical Warfare Supply Department in the War Office. The latter's policy was to standardise the latest model — the Mark IV — which was essentially the same as earlier marks but was provided with better protection against small arms fire and shell splinters. However, Capper's committee wanted to increase the number of Mark Vs, using the improved engine of Ricardo and transmission system developed by Wilson (now Director of Engineering), both of which could be incorporated into already-completed Mark IVs. The Tank Committee also believed that more attention should be paid to building supply tanks to bring forward oil, petrol and ammunition for the fighting tanks, and that priority should be given to a new fast medium tank able to cover long distances and exploit success and which would become available in the summer of 1918. Stern believed, however, that such sophistication and diversity would merely delay the arrival of one new efficient fighting machine from reaching the impatient tank commanders in France. Having had to battle against disbelief in this new weapon for so long, he now found himself being criticised by the War Office, on the one hand, for not delivering the latest machines in large numbers to satisfy the BEF, and, on the other hand, by Wilson for failing to concentrate on the Mark V incorporating the technical improvements of himself and Ricardo.

Criticism of the Ministry of Munitions, and of Stern in particular, came to a head on 8 October 1917 at a meeting held by Capper to decide how to implement General Staff policy.[70] After a heated discussion it was agreed to cancel 188 out of the 1,400 Mark IVs currently on order, while 212 of these machines were to be converted to supply tanks, having their armament removed. A number of the remaining Mark IVs were to be converted to Mark Vs, of which a total of 800 was to be delivered by the end of May 1918. This was a reversal of Stern's policy and Churchill, who had earlier chosen Stern as the man to accelerate tank production, now as Minister of Munitions had the responsibility for removing him. He cleverly appeased the War Office by transferring Stern to a no less important appointment, that of Commissioner of Mechanical Warfare, Allied and Overseas. In that capacity he would be responsible for supervising the production of tanks to be built for the Americans in a brand new factory in France. In place of Stern, Churchill appointed the fifty-five-year-old Admiral A. G. H. W. Moore, formerly a torpedo officer and commander of a battle cruiser squadron, but who had spent the war in the Admiralty where he had had nothing to do with tanks.[71] Although this might appear to have been an odd choice, Moore, in fact, improved the organisation of the Supply Department and the Mark V, held up by Stern, began to roll off the production line early in 1918. The new tanks were built by the Metropolitan Carriage and Wagon Company under the close supervision of Wilson.

Similar difficulties in deciding on suitable designs had been experienced by Estienne and other tank enthusiasts in France. After dispelling the inevitable clouds of scepticism, Estienne had persuaded his superiors to order 400 heavy tanks from Schneiders in February 1916; they were to be equipped with a powerful gun which was to prove characteristic of all French heavy tanks (in this case the famous 75 millimetre field gun was modified for the purpose).[72] The French Ministry of Munitions also ordered an alternative heavy tank from the firm of St Chamond. Its Panhard engine was more sophisticated than the British, driving a dynamo which in turn furnished electric power to two driving motors, one for each track. Known as the Crochat-Collardeau Drive, it offered better control over track speeds and made the tank more manoeuvrable. Orders were given for 400 Schneider and 400 St Chamond tanks.

In the meantime, Estienne, after visiting England to inspect tank development, concluded that the British should concentrate on heavy and the French on light two-man tanks. This proposal was accepted by the French General Staff and an order placed with Renault for 1,000 two-man tanks. These machines, equipped with a machine-gun, weighing six tons, able to travel at six mph, had an angled tail skid built at the rear enabling them to cross trenches almost as wide as themselves. Their role, as proposed by Estienne, was to operate in swarms like mobile armoured infantry, infiltrating front line defences or enfilading flanks.

The first Schneider tanks to go into action were in support of infantry on 16 April 1917 on the Chemin des Dames near Soissons. As with the British, the operation was spoilt by mechanical failure and deficiencies in design, such as too narrow tracks and the tendency of the forward overhang of the tank to pick up mud and debris. Although French tank doctrine continued to approve of heavy tanks in the role of mobile artillery, in the latter part of the war the operation of small, mobile machines, as approved by Estienne, proved to be successful.

The concept of the tank as a means of breaking the deadlock of trench warfare was vindicated on 20 November 1917 at Cambrai when 378 Mark IVs, supported by ninety-eight other tracked vehicles, made a significant penetration of the Hindenburg Line, only to see the ground lost through poor direction of the battle at Corps and Army level. By the summer of 1918, the idea of mechanised warfare had taken root, as illustrated by a note by the new Chief of the Imperial General Staff, Sir Henry Wilson, written on 20 July.

Instead of being satisfied with local objectives a mile or so ahead of the front line, the main attack was to be directed at the 'brain and stomach' of the enemy by striking at headquarters and communications well beyond field and medium artillery range.[73] This could only be achieved by a force of rapid medium tanks (already referred to) capable of travelling long distances and either crossing trench systems under their own power or relying on bridges being laid by heavy tanks. This force was *practically armoured independent cavalry*, though a concession was made to the traditionalists by including horsed cavalry to assist in the exploitation. The momentum of the advance would be sustained by *large numbers of cross-country vehicles* carrying ammunition, supplies and equipment. Aircraft would provide support throughout the operation.

This was, in fact, the essence of 'Plan 1919', the brainchild of Lieutenant Colonel J. F. C. Fuller, a staff officer at Tank Corps headquarters in France but who, in August 1918, was to become a member of the new Tank Board whose objective was to spread production and improve existing types and develop new tanks. Fuller was to advise on tactical requirements and uses of tanks. So convinced of their future as a war-winning factor did he become in the inter-war years that he won a reputation for being the champion of armoured warfare.[74]

But the war ended before the introduction of these enterprising schemes. Tank technology had in any case been stretched to its limit. More powerful engines were needed and improved track systems — a weak point. Important advances were made, however. In July 1917 the American Packard Company had designed and built the Liberty engine, intended for aircraft.[75] This 300 horse-power engine had the advantage of being light and reliable. Furthermore, it could be mass-produced; as it was supplied to the United States Flying Corps in France, spares and repair facilities were available. British tank officers in France recommended that the Liberty engine should be fitted into the new British heavy tank (the Mark VIII) and the Medium D. The latter, with a range of 150–200 miles and a speed of twenty miles per hour had been proposed in order to meet the ideas of Sir Henry Wilson and Fuller. But members of the tank design team in England were sceptical about its predicted performance; aircraft engines, they maintained, were not suitable for ground vehicles as they had no governor, relied mainly on air cooling and the setting of their valves was only suitable for aircraft. Better value would be obtained, they asserted, from the 300 horse-power engine then being designed by Ricardo.

Unfortunately the adoption of the Liberty engine for tank propulsion never took place because of the failure of the American aircraft programme,* while British losses caused by the German Spring Offensive of 1918 demanded increased production of Mark Vs as replacements, thus postponing the production of the Mark VIII. Only a few of the new Ricardo engines became available therefore and were never put to the test in the field.[76]

---

* But it was a Liberty engine that was used in what was to be the prototype British cruiser tank in 1937.

The German Response

Meanwhile, what of the Germans, usually well to the fore in the field of technological development? The tank idea hardly got off the ground with them until too late. Although they were by no means slow to improve old weapons and devise new ones, it seems likely that the realisation that they would be hard pressed to find the raw materials and manpower to support such specialised artefacts acted as something of a brake. Furthermore, unlike Haig, Hindenburg was more than a little sceptical about the whole business. Proposals for tracked vehicles had been submitted to the authorities early in the war but had been received with as little enthusiasm as by the Allied staffs. By 1916, rumours of large machines built by the Allies for use on the Western Front had begun to circulate, despite the tight security which enshrouded British and French tank development.[77] The appearance of British tanks on the Somme demanded a response. By May 1917, a large machine, designated the *A7V*, based on the Holt tractor chassis, was demonstrated before, and approved by, the German General Staff.[78] Although sprung suspension was employed in the design, the machine was cumbersome and no more than twenty were actually built. Later in the war, some attention was given to developing a light tank embodying the chassis of a large car or lorry to which was fitted a rudimentary track system. On the whole, the Germans were more content in rehabilitating captured British machines. There was at least one case of a battle between British and German tanks, generally regarded as a draw.

In sum, the engineering skill that went into the development of the tank was not matched by the appreciation of its tactical possibilities as foreseen by Swinton, Hankey and Estienne. The all important factor of surprise was sacrificed to Allied piecemeal committal of tanks to the battlefield before they, or the crews, were ready for action, while later operational experience was not readily absorbed by the designers at home due to a failure to liaise. Ironically, it would be the Germans, slow to develop the tank in trench warfare, who twenty years later, would exploit armoured forces so daringly as to drive the British out of France and compel the French Army to surrender.

Movement of Supplies: Tracked Vehicles and Aerial Ropeways

Tracked vehicles were also developed by the British for purposes other than fighting. As time went on and no substantial advance was made in Flanders, the area between the roadhead and the front line became a virtually impassable terrain at times. The desolation has been vividly immortalised both in words and in paint by writers and artists, one of them describing the scene in November 1917 as being worse than the Somme, '*a desert of mangled earth, with innumerable deep pits pierced by shell explosions and filled with water and in its low ground, where the becks have slopped over in gullies, between the slopes, a bog land and lake land, in which men sink to their armpits'.*[79] The supply of essential supplies by men and beasts across such a wilderness became so arduous that offensive operations were impeded.

At first, light railways seemed to provide some sort of alternative but they were too vulnerable to shell fire. The possibility of using tracked vehicles was discussed as early as November 1916, but in the very wet winter of 1917/18 the problem became more insistent, especially with the prospect of substantial advances becoming likely with the introduction of the tank.

One of the members of the Trench Warfare Department, Lieutenant Colonel Henry Newton, a resourceful engineer officer who had pioneered a system of Army workshops behind the front in Flanders, and had devised both grenades and fuses for trench warfare, designed a tracked cross-country vehicle able to carry rifle ammunition, bombs and a three-day supply of rations. Although his original plan was to substitute endless wire ropes passing over grooved tracked wheels for caterpillars, steering proved difficult and he was forced to have recourse to caterpillar tracks, even though they were in urgent demand for tanks.[80] The body and propulsion system was based on that of a large touring car powered by a twenty horse-power engine and capable of a speed of five miles per hour when loaded. Tests were made with the standard Ford touring car carrying a ton load and pulling an 18-pounder field gun and limber. These vehicles were to be made partly in England and partly in the United States. On 20 August 1918 General Seely, Deputy Minister of Munitions informed the War Cabinet that the matter was *'one of quite exceptional urgency'*[81] and his plea was reinforced by one from Haig requesting early provision of some one thousand vehicles able to carry loads across country. But the collapse of the German Army that autumn intervened and probably less than a hundred vehicles were produced by the Armistice.

A more static solution to the problem of supplying war materials over rough ground exposed to enemy fire between the second and first line trenches was the light aerial ropeway. This was based on the Telpher line of 1884 and its military applications for trench warfare were perceived by H. G. Wells during the war and put into practice by Captain Leeming, the energetic officer in charge of the Outside Engineers' Board referred to earlier.[82] An endless hemp rope, gripped by trolleys and suspended from metal cross-trees fixed to the top of ten foot high wooden poles, was the basis of the proposal. Motive power at each pole was provided by two men turning a windlass. Each container carried a load of two hundredweight propelled over a distance of up to a mile. On the return journey the containers could be used to evacuate wounded or to return salvage material. All the posts could be lowered simultaneously in daytime to provide concealment. After a number of experiments during the autumn of 1917, the system went into operation on the Western Front being used by Canadian railway troops to feed batteries with ammunition. In the last months of the war it was tested by the British Fifth Army, small petrol engines replacing manual operation.

6

'The Ghastly Dew'

The Birth of Chemical Warfare

At 17.30 hours on the evening of 22 April 1915 the German Army released from cylinders about 150 tons of chlorine in support of an attack against the Ypres salient. It was the first operation of its kind in modern warfare. An eyewitness later wrote: *'The valleys down which the gas descended were as yellow as the Egyptian desert while the tops of the ridges remained in their spring green'*.[1] Complete surprise was obtained against two French divisions, many of the troops fleeing in panic. Although a large number of men were temporarily incapacitated, the number of fatal casualties was remarkably small. But the German troops, most of whom did not carry any protective equipment, failed to take advantage of the confusion caused by the gas and their advance was soon halted by the combined action of French and Canadian troops. Further attacks with chlorine were made a few days later against the British sector but without decisive results.[2]

In fact, the possibility of filling projectiles with toxic gas had been considered long before the war and formulae published in the scientific journals noting the physiological effects of mustard gas and several arsenical compounds. That there was a strong feeling of repugnance against the use of chemical agents in war (although examples of the use of smoke, incendiary arrows, and Greek fire abound in the history of warfare) was demonstrated by the Hague Convention of 1899 when the contracting powers agreed to 'renounce the use of projectiles, the sole object of which is the diffusion of asphyxiating or harmful gases'.[3] Great Britain and the United States were major powers not to sign, but in 1907 the former agreed to sign the declaration.

Early Allied and German Usage of Gas

Nevertheless tentative experiments with tear gas and more toxic compounds were made in the pre-war years by the British, French and Germans. In England, Ramsay conducted experiments with acrolein — a mild tear gas — before the Boer War and some years later suggested to the War Office that it might be used against an enemy. Tests were later carried out at Woolwich with tear gas and with a derivative from chlorine but no convincing results were obtained. During the Russo-Japanese War, Ramsay was secretly approached by one of his old pupils in Tokyo about the practicability of using toxic gas in the field but the end of the war prevented any experiments being made. The French made similar experiments, the police being particularly interested in the use of tear gas for riot control. In Germany, the Army apparently experimented with various gases and may even have tested phosgene, a highly toxic gas, but no reliable evidence is available.[4]

The unexpected stalemate on the Western Front in the autumn of 1914 led both sides to consider introducing chemical agents in shells or bombs. Ramsay suggested that aerial bombs might be filled with prussic acid, but the War Office rejected the proposal as contravening the Hague Convention. It was not long before Jackson, as we have seen responsible for new devices in trench warfare, contacted Ramsay who instructed Baker and Thorpe to carry out experiments in the new chemical laboratories of Imperial College. They advised that ethyl iodoacetate (named SK after South Kensington) was suitable for filling in bombs and grenades, but no decision was taken to start production before the German surprise attack.[5] The French had gone further and actually accumulated stocks of grenades filled with tear gas to be used to drive the enemy out of trenches and underground shelters. But although the Germans justified their use of gas by claiming that the French had used gas in March 1915 there is no evidence that they had done so.[6]

Meanwhile the Germans, after the failure to drive beyond the Marne, were induced by Haber and Nernst to embark on more ambitious experiments.[7] Although sceptical about the value of such an unpredictable weapon, the German General Staff was prepared to give it a try, especially as high explosive had not had the desired effect on well-entrenched troops, while the serious shortage of raw materials for munitions might perhaps be offset by mixing gas with explosive in shell. Colonel Max Bauer, as we have seen responsible for munition supply, instructed Haber, Nernst and Duisberg to make tests. Their first proposal was to fill shell with a combination of high explosive and dianisidine chlorosulphate — a tear gas. It was made by Duisberg's firm and some three thousand shells were believed to have been fired at Neuve Chapelle but seem to have had no unusual effect on Allied troops. Another tear gas called xylyl bromide was suggested by the chemist, Hans Tappen, whose brother, Gerhard, was Chief of Operations at GHQ. This was filled in shell and used at Bolimov on the Eastern Front early in February 1915. But the gas blew back on the Germans and the scientists had not appreciated that its volatility would be reduced in the extreme cold. Further trials with gas-filled shell demonstrated that much more development would be necessary before an effective concentration over the target could be obtained.

By then Haber had suggested that it would be more practical to discharge gas from cylinders, thus forming a cloud which would be carried by the wind over the enemy positions and he proposed the use of chlorine.[8] Manufacturing facilities were readily available and the gas could be carried in liquid form to the railhead where it would be poured into cylinders which would then be brought into the front line and discharged by specially-trained personnel. Although senior officers had grave doubts about the morality of introducing gas and a number of chemists other than Haber and his colleagues feared Allied retaliation, the idea became more attractive after rumours spread that the French had begun to use gas. Before the beginning of 1915 the *KWI* was asked to advise on the preparation of chlorine for war. Chlorine was already being made for commercial purposes and production was soon under way at the Bayer works at Leverkusen.

Falkenhayn, the new Chief of General Staff, after being assured by Haber that the Allies would be unable to retaliate, decided to use gas in support of an attack on the Ypres salient. Haber had already formed a special unit — No. 35 Pioneer Regiment — to operate the cylinders. It contained some of Germany's leading chemists, among them Otto Hahn who twenty-five years later discovered the possibility of nuclear fission, James Franck and Gustav Hertz (both future Nobel prizewinners), Wilhelm Westphal and Erwin Madelung.[9] On 2 April a full-scale trial was held well behind the Front Line; the discharge proved so effective that Haber and Bauer, who were supervising operations, rode too close to the cloud and were mildly gassed. In the following fortnight 5,500 heavy steel cylinders were hauled into position in the Front Line. The attack had to be postponed until the wind was in a favourable quarter for the discharge of the cylinders; that moment came on the afternoon of 22 April. The failure of the Army to exploit the surprise caused by the use of gas led Haber to assert that the operation was '*only an experiment*'. However, the military continued to be embarrassed about using gas and Falkenhayn was probably relieved when the High Command decided to move Haber's specialists to the Eastern Front to support the forthcoming offensive against Warsaw. Nevertheless the potential of gas as a weapon for breakthrough could not be ignored and occasional cloud gas discharges from cylinders continued to be made by the Germans in the west for the rest of 1915. But their scientists' prediction that the Allies were not in a position to retaliate turned out to be seriously wrong.

Allied Offensive and Defensive Measures

In a very short time the French and British were not only able to protect themselves against chlorine attacks but also to project their own chemicals across No-Man's-Land. The French set up the *Direction du Matériel Chimique de Guerre* later under General Ozil, an artillery officer; he became responsible for both the supply of chemical materials and for advising on offensive operations. As the core of French science lay in Paris, it was simple for him to rally the élite of the chemical world. Dr A. Kling, a physical chemist recently appointed Director of the Paris Municipal Laboratory, which for some time had performed a valuable task in detecting adulteration in food, drink and pharmaceutical goods, took charge of a team to investigate the effects of poisonous gases. Charles Moureu, an organic chemist and professor at the Collège de France, became chief scientific adviser for offensive operations. Responsibility for anti-gas measures was shouldered by Professor J. H. Vincent, Medical Inspector General of the French Army. Other luminaries were called upon to help, including Victor Grignard, a recent Nobel prize-winner for chemistry. An experimental ground for testing gases was established near the mouth of the Rhone within reach of one of the two French synthetic dye works and therefore capable of being turned over to make poison gases. Anti-gas equipment was tested at Satory near Versailles. On the operational side, the handling of gas cylinders was performed by two *Compagnies Z* — a motley collection of troops who were considered to be unsuitable for a more active combat role.[11] The less-fit, however, were eventually weeded out when a third company was formed.

The British effort in support of gas operations was at first directed by Colonel Jackson; he kept in touch with the Royal Society War Committee and the Commercial Advisory and Scientific Advisory Committee which counted among its members such experts as Baker and Thorpe, Beilby who worked for Castner-Kellner, the only British firm capable of making chlorine, W. B. Hardy a physiologist, and A. W. Crossley a chemist from University College London. With the introduction of more deadly gases like phosgene and mustard gas, other firms including the United Alkali Company, Brunner, Mond and Messrs Chance & Hunt became additional suppliers of war chemicals.[12] The job of the committee was to recommend the most suitable type of gas for use in a particular operation and the most convenient method of projecting it into the enemy's positions. Anti-gas measurers were supervised quite independently by Sir Alfred Keogh, Rector of Imperial College, who had been recalled to his old post of Director General of the Army Medical Service. Research on this aspect took place at the Royal Army Medical College at Millbank in London.

Unlike their French counterparts, the British scientists had no executive powers and experienced great difficulty in finding out what was happening at the Front. Communication between GHQ and London was spasmodic and did not improve. Luckily, an energetic young engineer officer, Major C. H. Foulkes, was appointed by the Commander-in-Chief as gas adviser and director of operations for the BEF.[13] Foulkes knew all about trench warfare but possessed no technical knowledge. However, he speedily mastered enough chemistry to enable him to direct the operations of the Special Companies that were formed to carry out chemical warfare. By mid-July 1915 seven of these companies were already in existence. Unlike the French, they were manned by chemists or chemical students from universities and technical colleges and scientists already serving in the ranks of the BEF.[14] In recognition of their unusual role all personnel were appointed to the rank of corporal. As strict secrecy was essential, the majority anticipated being sent to a safe and interesting job. In reality they found that not only was little use made of their scientific knowledge but that their main job was arduous and dangerous, for they had to carry the heavy gas cylinders into the front line and operate them.

A chemical warfare laboratory was set up in the field at the Lycée in St Omer near GHQ by B. Mouat Jones, an Oxford chemist then serving in the ranks of the London Scottish Regiment. The object was to collect information on the latest developments of the enemy and to carry out immediate analyses. The director of the Central Laboratory, as it was called, was William Watson, head of the physics department at Imperial College.

Protection of Front Line troops against chlorine was at first extremely rudimentary.[16] Both British and French began by covering the nose and mouth with a cloth or handkerchief soaked in a solution of bicarbonate of soda; urine was used when that was not available. Then gauze pads soaked in castor oil tied by tapes round the head were issued. Watson introduced a spray which neutralised chlorine with an alkaline solution. But it soon became vital that such improvisations should be replaced by a mask proof against other known gases and which enabled a soldier to carry out his combat role. The first British attempt was no more than a gauze veil impregnated with hyposulphite proposed by J. S. Haldane, the eminent authority on breathing apparatus in mines and brother of Richard (now Lord) Haldane. The second was a flannel hood or helmet partly designed by Watson. It was soaked in a solution of glycerine, hyposulphite and bicarbonate of soda and was fitted with a mica window, later replaced by celluloid enabling the wearer to see but not to shoot straight. Both masks were tested by Haldane, Mouat Jones and L. J. Barley another chemist in uniform. Haldane thought the hood was too uncomfortable to work in, but his two companions, after running round the Lycée cloister wearing this mask disagreed, not thinking much of the 'top scientist'.[17] This so-called hypo helmet was issued to all British troops by 6 July. It *was* uncomfortable to wear but at least it afforded better protection than the French equivalent.

The French went about the development of their mask or respirator in a less methodical manner and devoted far less attention to research. They relied on a muzzle or snout which extended over the chin; the gas was kept out by a pad covering the mouth and nose made of layers of muslin soaked in solutions of an alkali such as sodium sulphanite or thiosulphate.[18] As the mask took a long time to put on, a fabric mask called the M2 was issued; its improved features included a waterproof cover surrounding the celluloid goggles and it could be put on quickly; the major drawbacks were that it was not gas tight and could not be adapted to withstand new gases.

The first German mask, like that of the Allies, was simply a cotton waste pad soaked in sodium thiosulphate and potassium bicarbonate. But after the Allied retaliation Haber was put in charge of anti-gas measures and introduced a system which was far more effective than either that of the British or French.[19] He obtained samples of designs for respirators from a number of firms. From them he made a choice; the most acceptable was an impervious face piece made of rubberised cotton fabric (later replaced by leather when rubber became scarce in mid-1917). The wearer breathed through a drum containing pumice granules impregnated with potassium carbonate and coated with charcoal dust. It was proof against chlorine, tear gas, and even a very low concentration of phosgene. In late 1915 the eminent organic chemist Richard Willstaetter made the filter proof against the combined effects of both chlorine and phosgene. While the basic design of the German mask remained the same throughout the war, the filter contents were changed in response to the introduction of new variants of gas.

Like the French, the British accepted the fact that they must retaliate against the Germans but the Government decided to use gases *'which were as harmful, but not much more so, than those used by the enemy, though preparations and experiments might proceed for the employment of more deadly things'.*[20] Momentarily restricted to the use of chlorine discharged from cylinders, plans were made by Castner-Kellner for liquefying the gas for transport in the cylinders. Unanticipated difficulties arose when it was found that the chlorine leaked through the acetylene-welded joints and an efficient method of discharge had to be worked out.[21] Eventually a syphon tube was fixed inside the cylinder and when the valve was opened, the internal pressure forced the chlorine out through the tube in the form of a fine spray of liquid which was converted into gas at the point of emission, the discharge being similar to that of a soda water syphon. It was accompanied by a tell-tale hissing noise and a fall in the temperature which increased the density of the cloud (chlorine being heavier than air) making it cling to the surface of the ground as it was borne along by the wind.

By the beginning of June 1915 most of the difficulties with the cylinders had been overcome and the first test with chlorine was held at Castner-Kellner's witnessed by Foulkes and a number of staff officers, but surprisingly no scientists. The experiment proved that the gas would be effective over an area up to four hundred yards from the point of emission and that provided wind conditions were favourable, the enemy's gas masks would be unable to afford protection after half an hour's exposure. The infantry would be able to advance without protection behind the cloud several minutes after discharge had ceased. Production of the gas now went ahead and arrangements were made for Castner-Kellner to supply the French whose facilities for manufacturing chlorine were at the outset quite inadequate.

British First Use: Cylinders, Projectors and Mortars

Foulkes's Special Companies went into action for the first time at the Battle of Loos.[22] Zero hour had to be determined by the favourable condition of the wind. The attack was launched at 5.50 pm on 25 September 1915 after a massive artillery bombardment. Not surprisingly, the gas discharge was only partially effective. Some of the cylinders, which had been lying in the trenches for several weeks, could not be turned on because the connecting pipes had corroded; others were leaking and squirted out a brown liquid which saturated the ground in front of the British trenches; in some areas the wind was not strong enough to carry the gas forward. The enemy had been given some warning of the attack as the long discharge pipes attached to the cylinders had to be carried vertically through the front line trenches, making them visible to observers, and the German artillery retaliated sharply with a combination of gas and high explosive shell, puncturing many of the British cylinders. Nevertheless, many casualties were inflicted and confusion caused, but the British were unable to hold on to the ground gained despite a second attack made two days later. Like the Germans, British officers had expected that the enemy would be annihilated in the area covered by the gas cloud.

The remainder of 1915 and early 1916 were devoted to improving existing techniques and devising new apparatus for delivering gas against the enemy. Prevention of leakages from the cylinders was especially important as they naturally had a very disturbing effect on Front Line troops. A careful check was made on each cylinder, most of them being faulty in one way or another. It was decided to replace the flexible lead or copper pipes by rubber tubing through which the gas would pass before emission and better control was obtained by designing a pinch-cock or regulator. These improvements were suggested by Captain W. H. Livens (the twenty-five-year-old Special Company commander we met earlier in connection with flame-throwers; he had an engineering degree from Cambridge and his father was Chief Engineer of Ruston's Engineering Works in Lincoln. Livens was sent to collect the rubber tubing in England. Ignoring official procedures, he filled a Pullman car at Victoria Station with miles of rubber pipes and boxes of heavy gun metal castings. On reaching Boulogne, he personally telephoned the Quartermaster General for the immediate supply of twenty lorries — which he obtained. The readapted cylinders went into action successfully at the Hohenzollern redoubt a few weeks later.[23]

Livens had already given much thought to the possibility of projecting gas bombs and believed that the essence of chemical warfare was, firstly, to obtain surprise and, secondly, to saturate the target area with the maximum amount of gas.[24] But his train of thought was temporarily diverted by being required to design a flame-thrower. This device consisted of numbers of drums filled with oil, buried in the ground and ejected into the enemy lines by means of explosive charges. There was no apparent reason why such projectiles should not equally well be filled with gas. Livens and his father were thus encouraged to design and produce a portable projector to deliver gas bombs. This was simply a steel tube, three to four feet long, a quarter of an inch thick, and closed and rounded at one end. The recoil was taken by a steel base plate shaped like a Mexican sombrero. This apparatus was given the name of projector rather than mortar because GHQ did not want it to be classified as a gun for the purposes of supply, thus possibly hindering its production. It could, in fact, be produced in very large numbers quite cheaply. Tactically, it had a number of advantages over other trench weapons; it could be used *en masse* (on one occasion, one thousand were fired in one operation); it could be buried in the ground in quantity and concealed; all the projectors could be fired simultaneously. Batteries of twenty-five were usually sited a few hundred yards behind the front line from where they could be fired without accident to the troops. Bombs could be thrown up to a mile but, as they could not be accurately aimed, targets were usually confined to villages and defended localities.

The Livens projector was first used in its primitive form — a drum buried in the ground — in September 1916 and the steel projectors first went into action at Arras in April 1917.[25] There was much argument over the respective value of projectors and cylinders. Foulkes believed that cloud attacks were more effective, as they were silent, continuous, seeping into every nook and cranny, affecting many more troops than the projectiles. Several officers from the Special Companies disagreed, considering that not nearly enough projectors were made (some 140,000 by the end of the war) and that projector attacks were too few in number, allowing the enemy to readjust his tactics. From the British point of view, the projectors were much easier to set up and operate and less troublesome to the infantry in the front line. Moreover, the Germans did not fear cloud attacks once they were equipped with efficient respirators. Again, projectors were much less dependent on the wind and could ensure the '*sudden development of a high concentration of gas on the target*' which was where it was wanted.[26] The question was never resolved, as it was not possible to obtain reliable statistics; and evidence from prisoners of war was often highly coloured and unreliable.

The British were also able to achieve rapid concentrations of gas with the Stokes mortar; a four inch calibre model was developed for the purpose of firing gas bombs. They could be loaded so rapidly into one mortar that fifteen bombs could be counted in the air before the first to be projected had hit the ground.[27] As each shell contained two litres of liquid gas, very heavy concentrations could be put down by combined battery fire. Stokes mortars were also frequently used to fire smoke bombs containing red phosphorus. Smoke could be used tactically for a variety of purposes, but mainly to screen forward movement or as a feint to distract enemy attention, or it could cover small-scale operations such as wire-cutting or digging communication

TWI—H

trenches. Most of the research on smoke was directed by Richard Threlfall, chemist to the phosphorus-making firm of Albright & Wilson.

German Developments

Rather strangely, the Germans neglected the possibilities of the projector, though Nernst designed a mortar to fire gas bombs — a proposal which, for some reason, was quietly shelved — possibly because the General Staff believed that gas should be used for breakthrough rather than for attrition.[28] There was an attempt to use the *Minenwerfer* but the Germans never grasped the principle of using the projectors *en masse*. Towards the end of the war, they introduced a projector with a rifled barrel which was more accurate and had a greater range than the Livens. However, in order to achieve this superiority, the projectile had to be filled with pumice granules at the expense of phosgene to prevent the rapid dissemination of gas. Thus the effect of the sudden release of a large volume of gas was lost. Fortunately, they did not appreciate that the great advantage of the Livens projector was the ease with which it could be manufactured and its relative handiness compared with the heavy mortar.[29]

New Gases and Increased Toxicity

During the winter of 1915–16, Allied and German scientists strove to devise more toxic forms of gas capable of penetrating existing respirators. The main possibilities were phosgene, diphosgene, chloropicrin and hydrocyanide. The Allies favoured phosgene; the unsuspecting could inhale it without immediate effect and it was therefore difficult to distinguish between safe and dangerous concentrations; and it could be discharged from cylinders. The process for manufacture was no secret and, after tests by the chemist Georges Urbain in June 1915, the French decided to make it in bulk, though they were determined not to initiate it. As the British found it harder to produce than chlorine at the outset, an agreement was reached with the French that the latter should make good their deficiencies.

Meanwhile, the French devoted an excessive amount of time and effort in trying to produce hydrocyanide, despite the fact that it was patently impossible to get enough of it into a shell to produce an effective concentration for use in the field. The British were on the point of copying the French but were finally dissuaded, not least by the Cambridge physiologist Joseph Barcroft, who underwent a test of the gas in a respirator chamber in company with a dog. The dog quickly became unconscious but Barcroft felt no ill effects. The following morning the dog, which was awaiting autopsy, was found by the laboratory assistant alive and complaining that its belly needed filling![30] The British, as will be explained below, did manufacture chloropicrin, though it was not an easy compound to make, and put it into shell.

The Germans, with their greater knowledge of industrial chemistry, had no difficulty in manufacturing the above-mentioned gases and were the first to use a combination of phosgene and chlorine discharged from cylinders in an attack against the British in December 1915. Unfortunately the British hypo helmets were not impervious to phosgene and there were a large number of casualties in consequence.

Increased Protection

The necessity of providing protection against the more toxic gases had been appreciated by the Allies for some months as well as the need to make masks more convenient for combat; good visibility and gas proof eyepieces were important features. Following experiments by S. J. M. Auld, a chemist from Reading University, who had been investigating trench warfare diseases, the British introduced a helmet which was dipped in a solution of sodium phenate-hexamine; it was more effective against phosgene and hydrocyanic acid than the P helmet which had superseded the hypo helmet in the autumn of 1915.[31] The PH helmet, as it was called, was introduced in January 1916.*

However, research had already begun on a more serviceable respirator affording protection against known gases — the small box respirator, which was to become the standard gas mask for the British Army. The essential design was worked out by B. Lambert, a professional chemist who, on his own initiative, had submitted a design to the medical authorities at Millbank and to the Central Laboratory in France.[32] He appreciated that in order to avoid breathing in toxic gas, the air should be made to pass through as deep a level of absorbent material as possible. Absorbent granules acting as a filter rather than impregnated fabric was the answer. In its final form the box respirator consisted of a well-fitting mask of waterproof fabric with celluloid eyepieces, a nose clip and tube of rubber connected to the filter box which contained soda lime-permanganate granules. Manufacture of the first 'large' version began in January 1916 and of the 'small' version seven months later.[33] Production was extremely complex; the mask was composed of some thirty-five component parts, requiring a number of trades, while the end product had to meet a high standard of perfection for even a pinhole leak might cause the death of the wearer.

The small box respirator was also supplied to American, Italian and Russian troops, but the French preferred to use their own M2 mask. The driving force behind development and production of the small box respirator was forty-eight-year-old E. F. Harrison who had worked as a research chemist for the Pharmaceutical Society. He had to be rescued from the RAMC, in which he was serving as a private, and commissioned. According to Pope, he was '*one of the discoveries of the war*'.[34] He continuously exposed

---

* Horses were also fitted with this mask.

himself to toxic chemicals but ironically became one of the victims of the influenza epidemic in November 1918.

1916 — Developments on Both Sides

As the wind was rarely in the right quarter on the Western Front for the Germans to discharge gas from cylinders, they turned their attention to filling shell with phosgene. But they found that disphosgene, or trichloromethyl chlorosulphate, which they designated Green Cross was more suitable as it was safer for shell filling and did not require such elaborate preparatory measures for manufacture as phosgene.[35] Diphosgene was, however, less effective as it had a lower level of toxicity and slower rate of evaporation. Green Cross was first used against the French at Verdun on 22 June 1916 and against the British during the battle of the Somme. This was before the issue of the PH helmet and the M2. Cloud gas was no longer used against the British after August 1916 by which time the box respirator had come into service.[36] Cloud gas continued to be used against the French and the Russians. But cylinders went out of use altogether a year later. As with the British, this type of attack was always unpopular with the troops on account of the extensive preparations required and their dislike of having cylinders in the trenches. The scientists believed that cloud gas was ineffective against well-disciplined troops equipped with efficient respirators as adequate warning was usually given by the discharge of the cylinders (William Bragg had attempted to find a way of silencing them)[37] and the appearance of the gas, while the concentration of the gas diminished as it drifted forward.

The British also began to find that gas shell was more effective than cylinders especially when used against targets in woods and villages. On 12 June 1916 Jackson's committee declared that the *'essential feature of gas attacks is to produce a high concentration for a succession of short periods rather than a small concentration over a continuous period'*.[38] But development of gas shell was handicapped by lack of adequate research and manufacturing facilities, while some artillery officers were reluctant to acknowledge the importance of this means of delivering gas. The most important gas for use in shell and bomb developed in 1916 was chloropicrin. This was both asphyxiating and lachrymatory and the filter of the German respirator was not then proof against it. Trials took place at the experimental ground at Wembley in February 1916, but as the gas had never been made in England before (it was obtained by the action of bleaching powder on picric acid), a long period of development had to take place at Birmingham University and at the Lever Brothers Laboratories at Port Sunlight, eventually being manufactured by a Yorkshire firm — Messrs Ellison of Cleckheaton.[39] It did not become available for operations until 1917.

German Manufacture — Links Between Government and Industry

The close links of German government and industry clearly gave the Germans a strong advantage over the Allies. As soon as the French began using phosgene, Haber, whose important work on nitrogen fixation has already been described and who had been engaged in organising the development of respirators, was promoted from Sergeant-Major to Captain and put in charge of the chemical warfare supply section of the War Department. In effect, he became the sole technical adviser to the German Government on all aspects of chemical warfare, though he still was Director of the *KWI* which was now organised as a military establishment, most of the chemical research being conducted there, apart from field trials. Haber eventually commanded some two thousand personnel, including one hundred and fifty chemists. He was able to maintain close contact with GHQ in France and visited the front regularly, while in Berlin he dealt directly with the General Staff on matters concerning policy and supply.[40]

Haber's chemical section was the only branch of the War Ministry to be self-contained on account of the special nature of the work, the need for secrecy and the desirability of avoiding any delay with a weapon that was developing so rapidly. When, in the autumn of 1916, a War Bureau was formed to cope with the Hindenburg programme, the demand for gas shell was increased. This presented no difficulty to Haber and his colleagues as the necessary compounds were made by no more than ten firms, members of the *Interessengemeinschaft Farbenindustrie*, which were able to obtain for themselves an adequate supply of raw materials; it was therefore unnecessary for any gas to be manufactured in a Government factory. Firms were provided with information on the preparation of chemical compounds by the *KWI*, thereafter being given a free hand to choose the method desired. Interestingly, the chemical industry was very reluctant to reveal any of their own processes to the scientists working for the Government and even Haber was unable to see much of his own process for the synthesis of ammonia at the Badische Works.[41]

The Allied Response

Neither the British nor the French could match the direct approach of Haber with the military and with industry (not that the advice of Haber was always taken). The French at least had the advantage of a more centralised organisation, combining offensive and defensive measures, but General Ozil did not have the influence possessed by Haber and, apart from Kling, scientists in France were not encouraged to visit the Front. As described earlier, the British were beset with the division of the functions of supply and research and of offensive and defensive measures and no eminent scientist was given overall direction of research and applications, despite the pleas of

Frankland and Pope. Fortunately there were chemical advisers on defensive measures at Army level in France such as Harold Hartley and Barley, who were of a high calibre. Belatedly, the British Army recognised that chemical warfare had come to stay when a Director of Gas Services was appointed in March 1916. He was Brigadier General H. F. Thuillier, like Foulkes, an engineer officer. Thuillier took charge of the Special Companies, now organised into a Special Brigade under Foulkes, and the anti-gas organisation under Colonel S. L. Cummins a former professor of pathology at the Royal Army Medical College, who had been engaged on this work since gas began to be used.[42] The importance of developing new chemical weapons was acknowledged by establishing a testing ground at Porton on Salisbury Plain, which somewhat resembled parts of the Flanders terrain. Crossley, the Secretary of the Chemical Advisory Committee, became the first Superintendent. As might have been expected, relations between the scientists at Porton and headquarters of the Special Brigade were often strained, the Army, especially the artillery officers, who prided themselves on a knowledge of ballistics and explosives, accusing the scientists of being too theoretical, while the scientists maintained that the soldiers were too impatient.[43]

LOST — Mustard Gas

At the end of 1916, the Germans appreciated that the toxic substances so far used in battle were having a diminishing effect on Allied troops owing to improved gas discipline and the provision of respirators which gave better protection. Research was therefore directed to gases which could not be so easily detected or which had a delayed action. The most important substance given attention was dichlordiethyl sulphide. It was suggested by Lommel, a chemist in the Bayer works at Leverkusen, and Steinkopf, in charge of the synthetic section of the *KWI*, and given the code name LOST, after the first two letters of the chemists' names.[44] Dichlordiethyl sulphide was quite well known; it had been obtained by the English chemist, Frederick Guthrie, in 1860 and was more thoroughly investigated by the German chemist, Victor Meyer, in 1886 and by H. T. Clarke, a student of Meyer's in 1912.[45] The substance could be prepared either by the action of thionyl chloride on thiodiglycol or by the action of ethylene on sulphur monochloride or sulphur dichloride.

In order to produce a substance strong enough for military purposes, special care had to be taken to ensure that the chemical reaction took place at the correct temperature. In the Guthrie process pure sulphur monochloride decomposes above 100° Centigrade and boils at 138° Centigrade. The dichlorine decomposes above 40 degrees and boils at 60. Both sulphur monochloride and dichloride are reactive but sulphur monochloride is the more stable of the two. The Meyer-Clarke process consists of hydrogen chloride reacting on thiodiglycol. Provided all the substances are available, it is less complex than the Guthrie process. It was the method chosen by the Germans to produce LOST and the dye plant at Leverkusen could easily be adapted to produce it.

LOST was ideal as a battle gas; it had a high rate of toxicity of about the same order as phosgene and it was also a blistering agent, though the significance of this characteristic escaped the scientists until it had been used on operations. Its other qualities were that it only had a slight smell (that of mustard) and was less easily detected than other gases and, though producing no immediate sensations of discomfort, troops exposed to very low concentrations could be put out of action owing to the effects of the gas on the eyes and lungs. As the liquid had a low vapour pressure at atmospheric temperatures and reacted very strongly with water, it could remain for days on the surface of the soil and continue to produce a dangerous concentration of gas.

When the proposal to use LOST was submitted to the General Staff they asked, as was their practice, what were the chances of the Allies being able to retaliate. Haber replied that they should not use the new gas unless they were certain that the war would be over six months after its first employment.[46] The Germans appreciated that the Americans would soon enter the war which could not then continue for long and they had to use anything which might help to obtain an immediate decision. LOST therefore went into production and was put into shell marked with a yellow cross, from which it derived its operational name. It was first used at the outset of the third battle of Ypres, usually known as Passchendaele. In the British sector it caused 2,100 casualties of which no more than fifty to sixty were fatal. A week later a second shelling took place at Nieuport causing 2,300 casualties. The small box respirator gave adequate protection but the blisters on the bodies of men exposed to the attack were extremely painful and took a long time to heal. The characteristic of the gas to linger led to further casualties after the shelling.[47]

The Allies React

Although the new gas came as a surprise to the Allies, it was quickly identified. In fact, Moureu had already made a study of dichlordiethyl sulphide and the physiological effects were soon analysed by chemists in Paris.[48] This prompt reaction soon disposed of the possibility that the Germans had a weapon against which there was no antidote. The British called it mustard gas and the French Yperite after Ypres. In preparing to retaliate, the Allies were greatly handicapped as they were unable to utilise dyestuff manufacturing plant which could be easily adapted for warlike purposes. The French were first off the mark; at first they experimented with the German process but soon became hampered by the lack of ethylene chlorohydrin which was required as an intermediate material. So they reverted to the Guthrie process, discovering in due course that it was a mistake to carry out the reaction at too high a temperature, much better results being obtained at between 30° and 38° Centigrade. Another important detail which they discovered was that the reactants had to be stirred constantly. It took most of the winter of 1917/18 to assimilate all these aspects of the process and the actual manufacture of Yperite did not get underway before the end of May 1918. Eventually, six plants were in operation; the bulk of the supplies came from the *Usines du Rhône*. The French Army became the first of the Allied forces to employ the new gas operationally in June 1918.[49]

British attempts to emulate the Germans took even longer on account of their lack of both theoretical and practical knowledge in industrial chemistry and inadequate organisation to convert laboratory experiments into full-scale industrial production, thus amply justifying the prognostications of some scientists before the war.[50] But in the short term, failure was due to the Chemical Advisory Committee which, even at this late stage of the war, was unwilling to enlist all available chemists to work on chemical warfare problems. There was indeed public dissatisfaction with the way the Government had handled scientific policy, even to the point of employing '*the best scientists to give their advice and consistently ignoring the advice so forthcoming*',[51] while in private E. H. Starling, who had been chairman of the Royal Society Physiological Committee and had recently served in Italy on a technical mission, claimed that the use of dichlordiethyl sulphide had been discussed months ago but no attention had been given to the possibility of trying to make it. Further delays would occur as long as '*we have no head of the gas services in England and the offence and defence are under the direction of pseudo-administrative but really irresponsible committees*'.[52]

Churchill Steps In — The Chemical Warfare Committee

In October 1917, Winston Churchill, Minister of Munitions since that June, replaced the Chemical Advisory Committee by the Chemical Warfare Committee under Thuillier and brought in a number of leading chemists including Boys, Cushny, Donnan, Frankland, Pope and Soddy, so far excluded from offering advice on chemical warfare, and Quinan,[53] the engineer who had so expeditiously built the munitions factories. The first to investigate which was the best process for making mustard gas were James Irvine and his chief assistant, Walter Haworth, of the Chemistry Department of St Andrew's University.[54] They had already made important contributions towards the manufacture of synthetic drugs, as will be shown in a later chapter. At first Irvine tried the Meyer method but, like the French, realised that ethylene chlorohydrin would be difficult to obtain. He then switched to the Guthrie route but by September 1917 found that he did not have the requisite materials to proceed alone.[55] Other groups of chemists had by then been brought in from Bristol,

Cambridge and Manchester Universities to work on various aspects of the problem.

Pope, who was one of the new members of the Chemical Warfare Committee, now took the lead in research. In company with a colleague, C. S. Gibson, he tried to go a stage further than Irvine. On 17 January 1918, he reported to his committee that he had found the German method to be the best point of departure. But less than a fortnight later he had changed his mind and now recommended the adoption of Guthrie's method, using sulphur monochloride, the reaction taking place at temperatures between 50° and 70° Centigrade. In the following weeks, further experiments were made both by Pope and by the firm of Chance & Hunt but, in spite of advice from the French, the temperatures at which the reaction was made were too high, resulting in weak, ineffective batches of mustard gas.

British Wrangling Over Production of Mustard Gas

Meanwhile, industrial plants to manufacture mustard gas in bulk were being constructed in various parts of England. Threlfall was appointed to supervise the whole project. While the academic scientists favoured Guthrie's approach, the industrial chemists, on the whole, believed that Meyer's method was the best one. The only firm which, after several attempts, seemed to be capable of producing good quality mustard gas was Levinstein's, the Manchester dyestuffs manufacturers. They used the low temperature method recommended by the French under the direction of their scientific adviser, A. G. Green. This ascendancy, combined with the fact that the Levinstein family was not greatly liked by the scientific community, led to a good deal of acrimonious argument, confidentially during the war, and in public discussions on the chemical contribution when the war was over, the chief protagonists being Green and Pope.[57]

Thus, by the spring of 1918, the British Army had still to receive supplies of mustard gas for operational purposes and the various plants were turning out poor quality batches in the course of which a number of workers suffered from gas poisoning.[58] At last, in April, Quinan was put in charge of plant construction and manufacture of mustard gas. He closed down the original plant at Chittening near Bristol and began work on an entirely new plant at Avonmouth not far away. Yet even though Quinan must have known that the French and Levinstein's were using the low temperature method, he persisted in using the high temperature or 'hot' process and it was not surprising that his initial yields were disappointing. At length, after further advice from the French, the first satisfactory batches were produced at Avonmouth on 15 August and sufficient stocks had been accumulated to support the British attack on the Hindenburg Line at the end of September 1918.

As British production of gas-filled shell was subject to so much delay, the

Special Brigade relied on gas clouds discharged by cylinders and the bombs fired from the Livens projectors in the latter stages of the war. In the autumn of 1918 a system for the electrical discharge of large numbers of cylinders was developed. The idea, originally rejected by Foulkes, came from D. M. Wilson, a Special Company officer. It had the advantage of providing greater protection to the operators and avoided the possibility of gas eddying back towards the front line at low wind strengths. A barrage by one hundred electrically-operated cylinders was discharged for the first time at Robecq on 13 May 1918.[62]

Further German Developments

There was an operational difficulty in dispersing mustard gas after the shell had burst. Both the British and the Germans had to devise a shell case that would carry both mustard gas and high explosive. While the British abandoned their design because of the gas leaking into the explosive chamber, the Germans succeeded in making leakproof compartments. They first poured in the high explosive, then added the chemical filling. The noise made by the detonation, instead of the tell tale soft 'plop', was indistinguishable from an ordinary high explosive shell.[59]

The Germans made considerable use of mustard gas shell for the remainder of the war, particularly during their great offensive of March 1918 and found its characteristic of persistency especially useful when they were compelled to withdraw after the failure of the attack. They had also begun to use, to an even greater extent, quantities of shell filled with arsenical compounds which had been investigated several years earlier by the *KWI* on the suggestion of Emil Fischer.[60] These were diphenylchlorarsine (DA) known by the code name Clark, diphenylcyarsine (Cyan Clark) and ethyldichlorarsine (Dick) and all were contained in shell marked Blue Cross. Their chief characteristic was that the irritant action was delayed by about three minutes and it was anticipated that they would penetrate Allied respirators. In fact, these compounds caused such pain in the sinuses that troops would tear off their masks to seek more air and then became prone to breathing phosgene. But in order to disperse the particulate clouds formed by the gases an explosion just above the ground was necessary. This was never attained as an effective proximity fuse was not evolved in time.

The *KWI* even formed a particulate cloud section under Professor Regener, a skilful research chemist with experience in using an ultra microscope, but the results were not productive, partly because of the difficulty and novelty of the subject, and partly because of the lack of enterprise of the General Staff in developing this aspect of gas warfare.[61] Such lack of enthusiasm may well have been due to their fear of being unable to produce an efficient respirator if the Allies retaliated. The British did, in fact, decide to retaliate, after identifying Blue Cross. But once again they were handicapped by production difficulties. However, they did manage to produce small quantities of DA during the summer of 1918 but, like the Germans, never succeeded in solving the problem of effective dispersion.

The introduction of mustard gas, Blue Cross shell and the threat of particulate clouds, naturally demanded the modification of Allied respirators or the design of new ones. It was not until the last months of the war that distribution of a new small box respirator, called 'Green Band', and the *Appareil Respiratoire* (*ARS*), both of which were proof against particulate cloud, became possible. The Germans continued to modify their efficient filters but had some difficulty in devising a facepiece because of the shortage of rubber. The persistent nature of mustard gas demanded various forms of decontamination for clothing and equipment and treatment for burns and blisters.

United States Manufacture of Mustard Gas

The Americans were, of course, able to profit from the experience of the British and French in chemical warfare and took full advantage of the fact. No time was wasted in building plants for the manufacture of phosgene and chloropicrin at Edgewood by the Chesapeake River near Baltimore.[63] J. B. Conant, a twenty-four-year-old lecturer in chemistry at Harvard, now an Army major, was responsible for the development of mustard gas and, after consulting Pope, adopted the Guthrie method at Edgewood where the first batches were produced at about the same time as the British, though using rather less manpower.[64] (In World War Two Conant became one of the leaders of scientific research and helped to promote scientific liaison with the British.) In France the Americans appreciated that chemists of repute must work closely with the troops in the field. In the summer of 1918 a Chemical Warfare Service was formed under General W. L. Sibert, an engineer who had been involved in the building of the Panama Canal; it was responsible for both offensive and defensive measures. A chemical laboratory had already been set up under the supervision of Major Keyes from MIT.[65] Assisting him was G. N. Lewis, Professor of Chemistry at the University of California, later celebrated for being the first to produce 'heavy water', a vital ingredient for the operation of nuclear reactors. Lewis had earlier been attached to the Canadian Division and after the German offensive of March 1918 produced two masterly reports showing a *'military grasp of the situation not expected from a professor of chemistry'*.[66] Lewis was later put in charge of defensive measures.

Chemical Warfare on the Eastern and Italian Fronts

Gas warfare was waged not only on the Western Front but also on the Russian and Italian Fronts and, to complete this account, a brief mention should be made of these activities. As noted earlier, the Germans switched their gas troops to the Eastern Front in May 1915.[67] Between 31 May and 6 July there were three major discharges of chlorine mixed with bromine on the River Rawka forty miles west of Warsaw. A large number of Russians suffered casualties in the first attack due to the factor of surprise, but in the other attacks the Germans themselves suffered considerably on account of a change of direction of wind. For the remainder of the campaign, the Germans used quantities of gas-filled shell but it cannot be said that any significant success was achieved with chemical weapons.

As soon as the Germans began to use gas, the Russian GHQ put the distinguished chemist, Vladimir Ipatieff, in charge of chemical warfare.[68] Ipatieff had served on the pre-war Artillery Committee and had recently played an important part in modernising the technique of manufacturing explosives and improving the supply of munitions. On account of the lack of original Russian sources, we have to rely on Ipatieff's memoirs, which may well exaggerate the part he played, and the sparse information provided by Allied liaison officers.

After making a preliminary investigation, Ipatieff reported to his superiors that it would be possible to retaliate with chemical weapons against the Germans within *'four or five months'*.[69] Preparation of chlorine and other toxic compounds began immediately at several factories along the lines of the techniques employed by the German firm *BASF*. In a short while a number of plants capable of producing phosgene were built after experimental trials had been carried out by Professor E. I. Spitalsky. A War Chemical Committee was formed to provide technical advice and a small chemical plant put at its disposal for experiments. Liaison with the British and French was established. Dr Daniel Gardner represented the Chemical Advisory Committee in Russia and spent some weeks in Petrograd arranging the supply of British gas-filled shell to the Russian Army in March 1916. Gardner later reported that the British shell was used with *'great success'*.[70] Another British liaison officer went to Russia to give advice on the manufacture of phosgene. Little information is available on the effect of Russian gas attacks on the German and Austro-Hungarian armies apart from the fact that they were few in number. While it would be hard to confirm, it seems probable that Russian chemists were quite successfully integrated into the cumbrous war machine. Eventually towards the end of 1916 the supply of toxic gases was interrupted by the breakdown of the transport system. In order to ensure prompt delivery of war materials, Ipatieff organised a special section to ride on trains to ensure that they reached their destination. According to Ipatieff's own account, *'when there was a prolonged halt, pleas of station masters were brushed aside with the simple comment "On Ipatieff's orders". Before long the magic formula was repeated so often that everyone knew of me'*.[71] At least the story illustrates the inertia of Russian bureaucracy.

Parallel with offensive measures, research went into the development of an efficient respirator. As in other armies, improvised pads soaked in hyposulphide sodium were rushed to the troops under gas attack for the first time. As there were no further gas attacks after June 1915 for the rest of the year and for the winter of 1915–16, quite extensive development of a suitable mask could take place. The outcome was the Koumant-Zelinsky (KZ) mask which consisted of a rubber mask fitting closely to the face and a small filter which was attached to the face piece.[72] Although well-designed, in practice it was rather ineffective because the charcoal became warm quite quickly and became an impediment to easy breathing. Later, a mask on the German model was developed which proved to be more satisfactory. In order to overcome the Russian deficiencies, both the British and the French rushed supplies of gas masks to the Russian Front, including large numbers of PH helmets and small box respirators. But training in the use of this equipment was at best elementary, though Ipatieff sent follow-up teams to the front to study the behaviour of anti-gas equipment under operational conditions.

On the Italian Front chemical warfare on a large scale was impracticable on account of the mountainous nature of the terrain. Nevertheless quantities of chemical-filled shell were used by the German and Austro-Hungarian forces against the Italians on a number of occasions. In June 1916, shell filled with hydrocyanide was used at Monte San Michele resulting in heavy Italian casualties, but as the gas blew back on the Austrians, they too suffered from their own shelling. The most effective operation, however, was at Caporetto in the extreme north-west of what is now Yugoslavia. The mountainous terrain and deep valleys made the operation unique. It was decided to use the new rifled projectors devised by the Germans in order to achieve a powerful concentration which would provide an opportunity for the infantry to break through the Italian positions.[73] For the purpose, German specialist troops were put into Austrian uniforms and detailed to carry out the operation. The projectiles were filled with a combination of chlorine and phosgene and, although only small quantities were used, they had a devastating effect on the Italians. They had not been forewarned, were unprotected, and the mountain behind them prevented the gas from dispersing.

After the disaster of Caporetto, the British sent a mission to Italy with the object of providing technical assistance.[74] Frankland and Barley persuaded the Italian commanders to replace the French M2 mask, with which they had unwisely equipped themselves, with the British small box respirator. The entire Italian Army was in due course provided with these masks and when the Austrians used gas-filled shell in an attack on the River Piave in June 1918 the Italians suffered few casualties.

As for the use of gas by the Italians against their enemies, weather conditions militated against them as the prevailing winds blew from the north and the east.[75] Within the Ministry of Armaments and Munitions there was a chemical warfare department directed by Dr Villavechia and a staff of leading chemists. Some of the research and development work was farmed out to universities and colleges; the Institute of Pharmacy and Toxicology under the Royal University of Naples, for example, developed chloropicrin and trials were held at a proving ground at Nettuno. A large number of shells were filled with this substance in the period 1916–17.

Chemical warfare was thus by no means a negligible factor in land operations on the main European fronts. (British plans for using gas at Gallipoli and on the Egyptian and Mesopotamian fronts were never put into effect.) Its introduction by the Germans was a bid to end the stalemate on the Western Front. But before condemning the Germans for initiating a new form of warfare which many considered to be barbarous, there seems to be no reason to doubt that the Allies could equally well have introduced chemical warfare had they felt the situation demanded it. But chemical warfare failed in its original purpose and it remains a fact that apart from the Italo-Abyssinian and, currently, the Iran-Iraq wars, gas has never been employed in a major conflict. The experience gained in World War One may well account for the distrust in such a potent weapon. It is therefore worth while trying to summarise the misconceptions and the lessons to be drawn from the period 1915–18.

Gas Casualties[76]

There is a good deal of confusion over the numbers of casualties due to gas poisoning. This is mainly because it is virtually impossible to obtain reasonably accurate figures which can then be subjected to analysis. Casualty returns vary from country to country and are usually imprecise; in Russia, for instance, the total number of casualties will never be known, while there is reason to believe that the Germans under-estimated their casualties. The most authoritative account of chemical warfare between 1915–18 concluded that 'We shall never know how many were killed by gas, for throughout the war there were no accurate records of those whose death in action was directly attributable to this weapon'. Very approximately, there were 186,000 gas casualties in the BEF of which over four per cent were fatal; the French suffered some 130,000 casualties of which 17.5 per cent were fatal; the Americans had 73,000 casualties; and the Germans 107,000 of which five per cent were fatal. At least this demonstrates the ineffectiveness of the French respirators compared with those of the British and the German. Close study of the annual or monthly returns also makes it clear that the number of fatalities was greater in the period 1915–16 when cloud attacks were the order of the day whereas in the latter part of the war (especially after the introduction of mustard gas) the casualty rate was higher but there were fewer deaths. According to Haber, the German Army suffered its worst casualties at Loos in the first British cylinder attack, at Verdun in 1916 from the phosgene shells fired by the French, from the Livens drums in 1917–18, and from French mustard gas shells in the summer and autumn of 1918.

At the same time the number of civilian casualties should not be ignored, especially by those living in the battle area. Although gas attacks on the civilian population were not made deliberately by either side, many suffered as a result of cylinder discharges or gas shelling; the worst casualties were suffered by the French at Armentières in July 1917.[77] The business of filling shells was dangerous and caused severe casualties at Avonmouth and Chittening; these losses must be attributed to deliberate risks taken in order to adhere to the scheduled programme. German chemical firms refused to fill shells and the government had to build special plant for the purpose operated by military personnel.

Conclusions

As with the tank, the scientists who proposed the use of gas found it difficult to convince senior officers of the possibility of achieving surprise. In respect of the Germans, evidence now points to the probability that the General Staff never contemplated making a deep concentration after the first use of chlorine in 1915. The Central Powers did, however, have one outstanding success when surprise was gained in the attack across the Isonzo leading to the defeat of the Italian army at Caporetto.

Gas, in effect, was an unpredictable weapon on account of its dependence on suitable weather conditions and to which all the other details of an offensive had to be subordinated. Experience therefore led to the German preference for gas-filled shell over cylinder discharges and to the British adoption of the Livens projector — a weapon which was neglected by the Germans. Moreover, the use of gas-filled shell gave a certain degree of flexibility to gas operations for it could take the form of harassment or could be directed at specific targets like artillery positions. We have remarked on the value of mustard gas in defence and the Germans might have gained a further surprise with DA had they been more thorough-going in their field trials at Breloh on the moorland around Luneberg (where the German Army surrendered in World War Two). Hartley, who made a thorough examination of the German chemical warfare organisation after the war, believed that it was the weakest point in the German arrangements and that it illustrated '*the lack of confidence between the soldiers and the chemists*'.[78] Porton, though there were failures of communication between the civilian chemists and the military, at least '*produced more accurate information as to the relative value of different weapons*'.

Defensive measures against gas, on the other hand, resulted in much better cooperation between scientists and soldiers, Physiologists, like Barcroft, found a common ground for discussion with Army medical officers; in Germany, Haber, with his knowledge of industry, was able to build a good foundation for the production of anti-gas equipment. Only the French, though adopting a consistent approach for offensive measures, seemed to be indifferent to the protection of their troops against gas. Efficient respirators like the British small box respirator and the German mask and canister helped to give troops confidence that gas was something of which they need not be frightened, not that the element of fear could ever be entirely dispelled. But anti-gas training was a factor for bolstering morale and contributed heavily to the saving of life.

In introducing new gases like phosgene and mustard gas, the German scientists thought they would steal a march on the Allies. They underestimated the resilience of the British and French scientific communities in spite of the latter having inferior chemical industries to the Germans. Maybe the Allies had the edge over the Germans, first, because they allowed junior officers to exercise their initiative, making it possible for a young officer like Livens to develop his projector; secondly, because direct applications of chemical science, like filling shells with gas, were, under the pressure of war, more realistic than trying to develop more sophisticated techniques like particulate clouds for which long series of trials were needed. Again, like the introduction of the tank and the development of military aircraft, the primitive manner in which this new weapon was developed and operated was fraught with consequences for the future. New forms of warfare demanded from the military a new range of tactics for which they were quite unprepared. As in the case of submarine warfare, the generals, as well as the admirals, reluctantly had to acknowledge that scientists had a role in modern warfare.

The possibilities of chemical warfare were to occupy the minds of strategists from 1918 onwards while the threat of the indiscriminate use of gas, especially from aircraft, was to haunt the minds of civilians. Some of those who advocated chemical warfare went so far as to suggest that there was '*no comparison between the permanent damage caused by gas and the suffering caused to those who were maimed and blinded by shell and rifle fire*'.[79] They had the support of two of the leading thinkers on war. Fuller, the protagonist of the tank, wrote in December 1918, '*gas warfare is war by inundation of areas in place of the hitting of targets*', thereby going against war-time experience that cloud attacks were less effective than projectiles and shells, and claimed that '*several million casualties* [sic] *might have been avoided had their General Staffs been scientifically-minded enough to recognise the stupendous power of the chemist*'.[80] Eight years later, the critic of Western Front strategy, Liddell Hart, after another attempt had been made to prohibit poison gas by the Geneva Protocol of 1925, wrote that '*gas was preferable to high explosive — the paralysis or demoralisation of the enemy forces is as effective as, and more humane than, the slaying of them*'.[81] Yet this point of view never found favour with the governments of either side in World War Two (though by then more deadly nerve gases were in existence).

The possibility of retaliation, as amply demonstrated by World War One experience, and the need to prevent escalation, once one side had initiated the use of gas, were doubtless factors taken account of by General Staffs and which militated against their use.

7

Failure and Success at Sea

British Fire Control Failure

Representations to the Admiralty that the Pollen fire control equipment, described in Chapter One, should be given another chance from naval officers like Vice-Admiral Sir Richard Peirse, Inspector of Target Practice during the development of the Dreyer table and C. V. Boys, a prominent physicist and Fellow of the Royal Society, were ignored.[1] But after the naval actions in the early part of the war at Coronel, the Falkland Islands and the Dogger Bank, the limitations of the British fire control system and to a lesser extent the fire director were exposed. At that time only a few battleships were equipped with fire directors and manually-operated Dreyer tables. Henceforward gunnery officers had to revert to making corrections after spotting the fall of shot. In contrast, the Germans had no equivalent of the Dreyer table capable of mechanically plotting changes of range and bearing rates and guns had to be fired individually. But the Germans did have excellent stereoscopic rangefinders capable of obtaining a figure for even a smudge of smoke or other poorly-defined target.

Considering the great importance attached to defeating the German Fleet at sea, it is surprising that after the BIR was formed its ordnance sub-committee apparently never investigated fire control problems, even though it was headed by Percy Scott, the fire control expert now knighted and holding the rank of Vice-Admiral. Instead he concentrated on the improvement of '*anti-aircraft weapons of all kinds*' and was especially active in the defence of London from Zeppelin attack. Apart from Sir Richard Peirse, who joined the central committee in 1916, there was no comparable gunnery expert in the BIR. Dreyer served at sea until 1916 when he was appointed Director Anti-Submarine Division of the Naval Staff and it was only in the latter years of the war that he became Director of Naval Ordnance (1917–18) and then Director of Naval Artillery and Torpedoes (1918–19). Naturally he was prejudiced in favour of his own system.

The battles of the Falklands and Dogger Bank took place at ranges of about 20,000 yards, just as Pollen had foreseen, and often in poor visibility, added to which the Germans adopted zig-zag or evasive tactics. It now became a matter of urgency to increase the range of the fire director as far as the sights were capable of being adjusted. A super-elevation prism was fitted to the director sights and to the centre position sights of gun turrets. This new attachment was fitted to fire directors of the Grand Fleet in time for the battle of Jutland and probably without it the guns would have had little chance of hitting their targets.

It was equally important to adapt the Dreyer table to rapid changes of range and bearing as a result of German tactics. But installation of the fully-electrical Dreyer tables Mark IV, Mark IV* and Mark V took time while the Dryer table clocks did not have the advantage of Pollen's slipless drive. At least the range plots were extended to 17,000 yards and eventually to 24,000 yards, but the instruments were almost useless in bad visibility.

By the time of Jutland (May 1916), all the capital ships of the Grand Fleet were equipped with Dreyer tables, mostly manually-operated, and only two ships did not have fire directors. But in the critical stages of the action the operators of the Dreyer tables were severely handicapped by poor visibility when, according to a British account, only half a dozen salvoes could be fired at targets appearing briefly through the haze. There was '*totally insufficient time to admit of a rangefinder or even in some cases for a single range to be obtained by a rangefinder.*'[2] In such conditions the German fire control system had the advantage, though the German operators apparently tired more quickly than the British. Firing about a thousand shells less than the British from guns of no more than 12-inch calibre, the Germans blew up three battle cruisers — *Invincible, Indefatigable* and *Queen Mary*. On return to base, the German gunners were 'loud in their praise of the fire controls'[3] which, with the exception of those which had been completely destroyed, were still in working order.

Pollen was convinced that had the Grand Fleet been equipped with his integrating apparatus and improved Argo clock, British gunfire would have been far more effective. As it was, *Queen Mary*, the only ship with a Dreyer table and Argo clock, put out of action the battle cruiser *Lützow* with twenty-one direct hits and seriously damaged the *Seydlitz, Derfflinger*, and to a lesser extent, the *Moltke*.[4] Although an enquiry into the deficiencies of the Grand Fleet's fire control system was made after Jutland, all that could be done in the circumstances was to continue to improve existing apparatus. In 1917, for example, a typewriter was added to the Mark IV Dreyer table to identify ranges obtained by each rangefinder by marking on the paper a distinguishing mark for each one. The plotting officer was thus able to judge the relative performance of each rangefinder. Fittings were made to incorporate information both from consorts' gun range and from spotter aircraft. In 1920 Dreyer, still on the Naval Staff, ordered slipless drive to be introduced into the Dreyer table clock. The numerous improvements adapted from Pollen's original inventions over the course of the war and after undoubtedly entitled him to an award from the Royal Commission on Awards to

Inventors. Before the war he had received from the Admiralty around £13,660 for his services and a pledge to secrecy, and after a prolonged series of hearings the still disgruntled inventor received a further £30,000. It is worth noting that Scott only received £2,000 from the Admiralty for his fire director which was adopted by foreign fleets.

But there were other technical problems urgently demanding solution, especially the need for stabilised fire directors and gun turrets. During the Dogger Bank action, the British fire directors were virtually useless because of the rough sea. Such requirements had been anticipated eight years earlier by J. B. Henderson, Professor of Applied Mechanics at the Royal Naval College, Greenwich. He had studied under Kelvin and Helmholtz and was one of a handful of scientists specialising in the study of gyroscopes which until then had found few industrial applications. He had acquired practical experience with Barr & Stroud, the rangefinder makers, after leaving university. Henderson, on his own initiative, worked out a scheme for the electrical control of guns and turrets which attracted the attention of Jellicoe, then Director of Naval Ordnance.[5] Unfortunately the equipment of the small sloop provided for experiments was incapable of moving the gun fast enough to keep pace with the control gear or the roll of the ship and Henderson was forced to build a rolling platform in the laboratory at Greenwich to represent a ship carrying a 12-pounder gun. These experiments were ended by the war when the laboratory staff was dispersed and Henderson applied his knowledge of German on cryptanalysis in Room 40 at the Admiralty. Here he learned about the failure at the Dogger Bank and quickly appreciated that the electrical relay switch of his pre-war experiments, combined with optical control, could provide a solution. He was given permission to return to Greenwich and some of the former laboratory staff were recalled from the Fleet to help.

After the Dogger Bank action, Henderson devised a system of prisms which, even when the ship was rolling badly, would keep the target in view on the horizontal line of the trainer's telescope. It did this for long enough to enable him to set his instrument, which was synchronised with that of the layer. The device kept the target in view even when the roll was ten or twelve degrees beyond the horizontal. Henderson submitted his invention to the Admiralty in February 1915 and was instructed to make a prototype. This was installed and tested on the *Centurion* in July 1915. A revised version was later installed in the *Iron Duke* in March 1917 and Jellicoe recommended that the apparatus should be fitted to all warships as soon as possible. Seven instruments were required for each capital ship and one each for smaller types. Eventually the Fleet was equipped with the Henderson director gear. According to Beatty, however, it was difficult to manipulate, preliminary training with the Scott director being required. Nevertheless its great value was in a heavy roll, Beatty continued, '*by keeping the object in the field of view it greatly assists the trainer. This will be of special value in destroyers'.*[6] Only one ship was equipped with the new gear in time for Jutland.

For the remainder of the war, Henderson applied his inventive genius continuously to the development of gyroscopic and optical devices including bomb sights, compasses and the control of anti-aircraft guns and search-lights, though he later complained that he had found it '*very difficult to maintain sufficient enthusiasm to carry on inventing without apparent benefit and without official thanks or encouragement*'.[7] He was awarded £7,570 for his wartime inventions and for some ten years after the war was employed by the Admiralty in developing a more sophisticated version of his director firing gear.

Meanwhile, improvement of fire control tables was left to the discretion of individual ships, but the lack of apparatus to cope with poor visibility continued to handicap the Grand Fleet on the few occasions when it came into contact with the enemy. Better results were obtained on the introduc-tion of aerial spotting by kites, balloons or aircraft, but these measures were soon counteracted by the enemy's extensive use of smoke screens. After a light cruiser action in November 1917, in which the British ships pumped shells into the smoke without hitting anything and suffering considerable damage from German fire in return, the Navy decided to investigate the idea submitted to Admiral C. E. Madden, second-in-command of the Grand Fleet, by Lieutenant J. S. Dove, a young watch-keeping officer serving on the *Royal Sovereign*.[8] Although he had only recently learned how to operate the Dreyer table, Dove appreciated that vital minutes might be saved by mechanically transmitting changes in bearing from the fire control instru-ments, located for better protection in the bowels of the ship, to the fire director above. He had failed to attract the interest of Captain Dreyer who had now become Director of Naval Ordnance after serving in the *Iron Duke* at Jutland.

Nonetheless, in company with Lieutenant H. Clausen, an RNVR electri-cal engineer serving on the *Benbow*, Dove designed an apparatus called the Gyro Director Training Gear by which it became possible to fire at an invisible target whether it had temporarily been observed or whether it was only a shape on the horizon. The two officers began to develop their apparatus in rather primitive conditions on board ship at the end of December 1917 and, six months later, had an equipment ready for testing. After successful trials, the Gyro Director Training Gear was installed on battleships, battle cruisers and monitors for the remainder of the war.

The Admiralty now recognised that in order to defeat German tactics such as zig-zagging and smoke screens, the process of computing range, bearing and deflection would have to be greatly accelerated, mainly by automatic control. After the war, Admiral Beatty was instrumental in setting up a committee to work out new methods of fire control; among its members were Dove and Clausen and the leading technical assistant of Pollen, Harold

Isherwood.[9] About the same time the Admiralty was persuaded to build a Research Laboratory at Teddington under the new Director of Scientific Research. Here it was possible to study a variety of gunnery problems such as electrical transmission and gyro stabilisers and a rolling table was erected to simulate the performance of a gun turret in rough seas.[10] To some extent this satisfied the often-repeated demands of J. J. Thomson that the Navy should have its own physical laboratory.

Torpedo Propulsion

The tactic of zig-zagging mentioned above was induced by recent improvements in torpedo propulsion. Hitherto torpedoes had been driven by the energy stored in cold air. But as the speed of warships increased and countermeasures against torpedoes grew more effective, as will be described later, it became necessary to improve the performance of these weapons nine years before the war. Several proposals for generating steam to increase their speed were considered by the British, but the one eventually to win favour with the Admiralty was the brain child of Sydney Hardcastle, a watch-keeping lieutenant who was posted to Chatham in 1904 to supervise torpedo maintenance.[11]

Appreciating how necessary it was to increase the range and speed of the contemporary torpedo, Hardcastle decided that it would be possible to use compressed oxygen to burn paraffin fuel, '*the product of combustion*' as the patent described it, '*together with the steam generated by the heat of combustion constituting the working medium of the engine*'.[12] The instrument operating the system was called a continuous pressure generator. After experiments conducted in strict secrecy over the period 1905–08, the original high speed range of the Whitehead torpedo was quadrupled and its original speed up to 4,000 yards increased by about eighty per cent. High speeds of about forty-five knots could now be maintained over a course of 4,500 yards.

Hardcastle's 'heater' torpedo made its debut in the naval manoeuvres of 1912 when cruiser commanders were astonished to find that their ships could be torpedoed in *daylight* — a practice which had been abandoned some years before. Hardcastle's invention thus gave the British Fleet a valuable lead over the Germans but it took some time before its significance was properly appreciated, mainly because of the cautious policy underlying the prescribed tactics for destroyer attacks. By the end of the war, daylight attacks on German naval units had been made on eight occasions. The device was found to be superior to anything possessed by the French or the Americans and was made freely available to them.

The high speeds which could now be attained by torpedoes demanded improvements in gyroscopic control of the weapon. It was usually obligatory to manoeuvre the attacking ship to a position at right angles to the target before firing the torpedo thus wasting precious minutes. In order to improve the chances of a successful attack, H. J. Maskell, chief draughtsman of the Torpedo Factory at Greenock, devised a special clutch for the gyroscope which rectified the gimbal rings and wheels, so aligning the torpedo to the correct orientation at any position in space. It was now possible to fire a broadside at a target steaming athwart at twenty knots. From 1913, Maskell's invention was fitted to all torpedo gyroscopes. His superior declared that it was '*a real masterpiece of the inventive faculty*'.[13] Like Hardcastle, he was in due course rewarded by the Royal Commission on Awards to Inventors.

Direction Finding

Early in the war, the Royal Navy established a need to detect wireless signals transmitted by ships on wave lengths exceeding 5,000 metres. The problem was considered by the physicist W. Duddell, a member of the Royal Society War Committee and an expert designer of precision instruments. Before the war he had investigated the arc system for generating continuous waves and he now designed a ten foot square aerial which would be much handier in a ship than the larger Bellini-Tosi aerials then used for maritime navigation. Work was transferred from Duddell's laboratory in London to the NPL where, under the direction of Glazebrook and one of his assistants F. E. Smith,[14] experiments were carried out with the Duddell aerial.* In March 1915, wave lengths from 2,200–9,000 metres could be picked up and the direction of the sending station (as far away as Strasbourg) fixed within a few degrees. Sea trials with the aerial took place in April and the aerials were installed in five battleships shortly afterwards. It was now possible to pick up ship's signals in the Heligoland Bight.

At the same time, an extensive land-based system of direction finders began to supply valuable information to naval and military intelligence. The architect of these installations was H. J. Round, one of Marconi's team of engineers engaged on experimenting with improved types of valve. In September 1914, Round had suggested to the Director of Military Intelligence that direction finders should be used to locate enemy wireless transmitters.[15] He was seconded as a lieutenant to Military Intelligence and, in 1915, built up a network of valved direction finders behind the Western Front for the purpose of pin-pointing transmitters based in Germany. Round improved on current systems in which two stations were used (the first two were near St Omer and Abbeville) after finding that a more accurate fix could be obtained with groups of three stations.

After the onset of trench warfare, long range wireless communications became less important to the German General Staff, and Round was recalled to England to organise a second network to enable the Naval Staff

---

* Duddell, aged forty-five, died in November 1917 having literally worked himself to death on secret experimental projects.

at the Admiralty to detect signals sent out by German ships, submarines and aircraft from which their positions could be located. They were known as 'B' stations; six were immediately erected along the East Coast and one on the coast of Flanders to sweep the whole of the North Sea. After U-boat attacks spread into the Atlantic, five more 'B' stations were established in Southern Ireland to cover the South-West approaches. All these stations were administered by the Admiralty but were under the technical control of Round. Three more stations were built in South-East England for the use of military intelligence. A further six 'B' stations were set up for the detection of enemy naval signals in the eastern Mediterranean.

Another type of apparatus was required for the interception of ciphered naval, diplomatic and commercial signals traffic. The Admiralty had one station assigned for this purpose at the beginning of the war but the information provided was soon supplemented by three amateur wireless enthusiasts — Russell Clarke, a member of the pre-war wireless telegraphy committee, Leslie Lambert (later well known as the broadcaster A. J. Allen) and Colonel B. Hippisley, a Somersetshire squire, who had picked up German signals on their sets. Their services were accepted by the Admiralty and they were installed in the coastguard station at Hunstanton near The Wash.[16] Round took over their post and built four more 'Y' stations, as they were called, in South-East England.

The way in which the 'B' and 'Y' stations worked was as follows. When an enemy ship in the North Sea, and later in the West Atlantic made a signal, its bearing was taken by each 'B' station and telegraphed to Room 40 in the Admiralty. Here corresponding lines were at once laid down on a large chart. The intersection of these lines gave the position of the ship when it made the signal. The 'Y' stations intercepted coded signals from German naval headquarters to surface ships and submarines and vice versa. These were also telegraphed to Room 40 for decoding by a small group of German-speaking and classical scholars and mathematicians[17] who had been recruited by the Director of Naval Education, Sir Alfred Ewing,[18] in order as the First Lord, Winston Churchill, wrote 'to penetrate the German mind and movements and make reports'.[19] As is well known, they were given invaluable help by the most secret code book of the German Navy, retrieved by the Russians from the cruiser Magdeburg, sunk in the Baltic in August 1914, and handed over to the British.

In due course, Round improved the reception of the 'B' and 'Y' stations by equipping them with more powerful valve amplifiers. It became possible, for instance, to intercept German shipborne buzzer signals on the 200 metre wave length from Flamborough Head and Aberdeen. Interception which before the war had only been possible on freak occasions at night now became the norm. By May 1915 it was possible to track U-boats across the North Sea — the margin of error being approximately twenty miles from a central point. In the Atlantic, however, it is unlikely that fixes were obtained under a fifty mile radius. It was also possible to track Zeppelins heading for the British coast; in both cases interception was often facilitated by the bad wireless discipline of the Germans. (Twenty-five years later, during the Battle of Britain, with far more sophisticated coding machines and wireless apparatus, it was still possible for British Intelligence officers to intercept German Air Force signals and so to discover the intended targets of the bomber force.)

The Germans began to use direction finding at about the same time as the British and built a network along the north German coast line into occupied Belgium. According to a post-war study, the Germans believed the British system was superior to their own and if so, this may have been due to the much wider base line enjoyed by the British stations giving them greater accuracy. The Germans, of course, were well aware that the British were using direction finders and attempted to deceive them by transmitting spurious signals — a ruse that did not pass unrecognised by the staff of Room 40.

Its Use in Intelligence

There is no doubt that British Naval Intelligence was greatly helped by direction finding, though much of what was later described by this name was, in fact, the outcome of cryptanalysis — an activity which it was essential to keep absolutely secret. The importance of direction finding increased when the Germans intensified their U-boat campaign and the 'B' stations often fixed the position of a U-boat when cryptanalysis could not provide an immediate answer. Unfortunately, the Naval Staff were slow in recognising the value of cryptanalysis. If physicists and chemists were incapable of understanding the problems of war, why should university lecturers or classical scholars? Yet there is now sufficient evidence to show that the efforts of this highly original team in Room 40 helped, first, to deprive the High Seas Fleet of its advantage of being able to strike unexpectedly and, secondly, by providing invaluable information on the movements of U-boats when the Navy at last reorganised itself to meet this threat.[20]

But the organisation and operation of the 'B' and 'Y' stations depended on the remarkable talents of Round and Russell Clarke. While Round devoted himself to improving the location and reception of enemy signals, Clarke, who had a good knowledge of German in addition to his technical and inventive abilities, was responsible for dealing with German counter-measures against the interception of their signals. In this 'war of the wave lengths' it was impossible to prevent messages being received but reception could be made as difficult as possible (1) by varying the wave length at short intervals; (2) by making messages as short as possible, so that unless receivers were already tuned accurately on the proper wave length, part of the message would be lost or be very corrupt by the time tuning had been completed; (3) by varying the intensity of transmission; (4) by transmitting the message mechanically so rapidly that it could not be read by ear. Clarke managed to find a remedy for every unexpected move. According to J. B. Henderson, he was '*a thorough physicist, skilled artificer and most ingenious inventor*'.[21] In his well-equipped workshop at his home, he continually improved his apparatus. '*Room 40's success*', continued Henderson, '*depended on the reception of practically all the German wireless waves which reached our coast, of all wave lengths and all intensities and having them accurately reported. If the Room is reckoned to have been a success then a considerable measure of that credit is due to Russell Clarke*'. Unhappily Clarke, exhausted by the strain, died soon after the war and was unable to enjoy either the financial award made to him by the Government or public recognition of his services, as the existence of Room 40 was to remain secret for some years.

Round, however, was publicly credited soon after the war with providing information of the sailing of the High Seas Fleet on 30 May 1916 by Admiral Sir Henry Jackson who was First Sea Lord at the time.[22] Jackson ordered the Grand Fleet to sea and to engage the enemy in what was to become known as the Battle of Jutland. But Jackson was unable to disclose an outstanding example of the misunderstandings and poor relations between the Naval Staff and Room 40. The Germans had tried to mislead British Intelligence by indicating by wireless that their flagship had not sailed on the morning of 31 May. While Room 40 was aware of the deception and that the German Fleet had already sailed, the Naval War Staff was not. As a result of erroneous information passed to them, the two British commanders, Jellicoe and Beatty, commanding the main body of the Grand Fleet and the battle cruisers respectively, made their rendezvous in the North Sea dangerously late, losing several hours of daylight that might have changed the course of the battle.[23]

Round continued to develop his system and in 1917 introduced rectifying and amplifying valves for the 'Y' stations and in certain cases new circuits with shielded transformers which maintained the required accuracy. From 1916 to 1918 a group of three continuous-wave direction finding stations operated without ceasing from Aberdeen, York and Lowestoft. They were fitted with automatic clockwork searching devices for the changing wave lengths used by the Germans. In January 1917, Round was awarded the Military Cross and received commendations from both Admiralty and War Office. On 17 April 1918, the former stated that '*during the last three months Round has done very good research work and has produced and erected apparatus for the Intelligence Division of the Naval War Staff which has been of the greatest value and has directly assisted naval operations*'.[24] Some months later, the War Office reported that '*It would be difficult to exaggerate the value of this officer's inventions which have made the whole system of WT intelligence possible*'.[25] Round was also responsible for developing several other specialised and highly secret items of equipment, including a transmitter for secret agents operating overseas and a short wave wireless telephony set for use in high speed motor launches.

Improvements in the relations of the Naval War Staff and Room 40 were not achieved until May 1917, at the height of the battle against the U-boats. The value of the cryptographers was then acknowledged by designating them Section 25 of the Naval Intelligence Division and the information from German signals became much more accessible. At about the same time, cryptography began to be taken more seriously in other theatres of war. A team from the Admiralty was sent to Italy to intercept and evaluate the wireless traffic of the Austrian and German naval units in the eastern Mediterranean. Additional 'Y' stations were set up to support these activities. Little is known of how much intelligence was passed to the French whose main naval effort took place in the Mediterranean, but the French direction finders may well have had greater success in locating U-boats than their cryptographers. The final vindication of the British code breakers came in 1919 when an entirely new unit was formed from the few members of Section 25 and War Office Intelligence staff still serving and put under control of the Foreign Office.[26] Under the guise of the Government and Cypher School the cryptographers were to apply the lessons learned in 1914–18 to even greater effect in 1939–45.

Wireless Communication Between Ships

The tactical control of naval ships at sea by wireless telegraphy, demanding uninterrupted transmission and reception, took longer to achieve than direction and position finding. Research aimed at the changeover from spark to continuous wave thereby making possible frequent changes of wavelength, reduction of interference and, at the same time, producing sets that were not too complicated for sailors to operate. The essential component was de Forest's high vacuum or thermionic valve, given to Colonel Ferrié in 1914 but not available for operational use until 1915–16.

German valve development was not far behind the American and possibly ahead of both the British and the French.[27] The impetus came from Robert von Lieben and the *Telefunken* Company. In 1913 *Telefunken*'s chief engineer, Alexander Meissner, began work on a high vacuum tube with greater amplifying powers than the '*soft*', gas-filled valve such as Round had devised; he produced his first transmitter early in 1915. But many physical and mechanical problems had to be solved before the valve was ready for service.[28] While *Telefunken* and Siemens took care of the engineering side, the physical problems were solved by several of the best physicists, including two Nobel prize-winners — the fifty-year-old Wilhelm Wien who had made an extensive study of wave lengths and sixty-four-year-old Karl Braun, inventor of the cathode ray tube, who had received his Nobel prize jointly with Marconi.

In contrast, British naval wireless telegraphy at the outset of war was inadequately served by the small staff at HMS *Vernon* which, in addition to experimental work, had to train wireless operators for the Fleet.[29] Some months after the war had started, the total scientific staff still numbered only two under H. A. Madge, though C. L. Fortescue, Professor of Physics at Greenwich, an early co-worker with Madge, was persuaded to help with supervising experimental work at *Vernon* on a part-time basis. J. J. Thomson, who for some years had shown a keen interest in naval wireless, then proposed that Gilbert Stead, one of the assistants at *Vernon*, should work full time on valve research at the Cavendish with its better laboratory facilities.[30] This soon had a healthy effect on naval wireless development which had been badly needed.

In April 1915, Fisher, the First Sea Lord, informed Churchill that there was '*conclusive proof*'[31] that German submarines were transmitting and receiving signals at distances of three hundred miles by day or night; it was '*vitally necessary*' that British submarines should be able to do the same. '*If this is true*', replied Churchill, '*it is very discreditable.* Vernon *has not worked out well in this war*'.[32] As a stop gap for the high vacuum valve, the Fleet was equipped with Poulsen arc transmitters which were capable of generating continuous waves and by 1916 were more reliable than the spark transmitters.[33] Trials by the Grand Fleet using the Poulsen sets that autumn were '*most satisfactory*'[34] and resisted enemy jamming. Most of the major units of the Fleet were being equipped with Poulsen apparatus by the end of 1916.

Meanwhile the experiments at the Cavendish under the direction of J. J. Thomson, supported by research at the Royal Naval College, King's College, London and the Royal Holloway College, and examination of the latest French Audion valve at *Vernon* led to the development of three '*hard*' transmitting valves in mid-1917. Manufacture was in the hands of British Thomson Houston, the Rugby electrical firm which became the main valve supplier to the Royal Navy, with supplementary orders fulfilled by General Electric, the firm's American partners. Even so, '*soft*' valves, such as the helium-filled valve devised by F. Horton of the Royal Holloway College, continued to be used for the rest of the war and in the opinion of some naval scientists gave as good value, when performing satisfactorily, as the '*hard*' valves. Manufacture of many of these '*soft*' valves took place at the factory of Osram Robertson.

All this research took place under extreme pressure, yet as Fortescue commented, '*it was interesting to note the extent to which we reached at times the limits of knowledge. A lot of the work done on the valve was really almost pure research and the valve actually produced was a good example of pure research running in parallel with its immediate application*'.[35] The importance of '*pure*' research was belatedly recognised by the Admiralty in August 1917 by the creation of a separate signals division and a little earlier by the transfer of wireless and underwater sound telegraphy from *Vernon* to the Signal School, Portsmouth where there were more ample facilities for research.

Submarine Detection: Hydrophones

On account of the lack of knowledge of the physical properties of sea water, the velocity of sound under water, or the effect of temperature and salinity, submarine detection required even more fundamental research than wireless communications. At the same time the need for countermeasures against the U-boat became more compelling as the underwater threat increased. Consequently little attention had been given either to developing submarine tactics or to countermeasures against submarine attack. As we have seen, experiment was left to the initiative of enterprising officers and the first in this new field was Captain C. A. McEvoy, on the staff of *Vernon*, who began to investigate the possibilities of using hydrophones for underwater detection as early as 1896.[36] By 1909 a naval committee was studying the possibility of submarine signalling apparatus, but the only outcome was the purchase of two types of microphone developed by the American Submarine Signal Company and its British offshoot. Known as the Harvey-Gardner hydrophone, it was installed in a number of ships and was the only instrument capable of detecting the noisy engines of U-boats when they made their debut in 1915.[37]

The shock of war had by then caused the Admiralty to set up a small experimental station for developing hydrophones at Hawkcraig Point. This establishment was put in charge of Commander C. P. Ryan, a somewhat unorthodox naval officer who had developed a strong interest in wireless telegraphy for which he had abandoned his career. But on the outbreak of war he returned to the active list and devoted himself to the introduction of hydrophones. He had no scientific training and was further handicapped by the lack of any serious study on the propagation of sound underwater, apart from some theoretical work by Rayleigh and the mathematician Horace Lamb (author of '*Hydrodynamics*' 1895) and several practical experiments such as the measurement of the velocity of sound in the water of Lake Geneva in 1827 and the velocity of explosion waves in the sea by Richard Threlfall and John Frederick Adair in 1888. The existing apparatus for submarine signalling or for listening for underwater sounds was extremely rudimentary.

Nevertheless, by the summer of 1915, Ryan had succeeded, with the help of a small band of RNVR officers, in designing and making both moored and portable hydrophones which were operated from the shore and used for the detection of hostile submarines.[38] In fact, propellers of large vessels could be detected under favourable weather conditions at distances of ten to twelve miles in the Firth of Forth. He went on to devise an acoustic device placed near a minefield; when the engines of a U-boat were picked up by the instrument the minefield could be activated from the shore. This magnetophone, as it was called, was an ordinary telephone receiver in which the vibrations of the diaphragm were translated into minute electrical impulses and transmitted along a cable to the shore. During 1916 magnetophones were installed in the minefields protecting the anchorages at Invergordon and Scapa Flow.

Quite rightly, Ryan gave priority to the development of portable submarine detection apparatus for use on board ship. He was responsible for evolving two useful devices. One was a simple diaphragm dangled over the side of a ship by an operator wearing headphones. The other was a more complicated two-directional hydrophone based on a design by Professor J. T. McGregor Morris and his assistant A. F. Sykes of East London (later Queen Mary's) College — an instrument which gave reasonable results in terms of sensitivity and directional accuracy. Early in 1916, Ryan began to design directional plates or hull-fitted microphones to be attached to submarines. It was possible, with a hydrophone on each side of the vessel, to obtain the approximate bearing of a ship, utilising the soundscreening properties of the submarine hull. The respective tones of the hydrophones were established by Lieutenant Hamilton Harty, the conductor of the Hallé Orchestra, who used to sit among a pile of steel hydrophones tapping each one with a small hammer and arranging them in pairs as 'port low' and 'starboard high' pitch. The hydrophone circuit simply consisted of a battery, transformer, two way switch and earphones. The operator determined the bearing of the enemy vessel by comparing the intensities of the sound received by the pair of hydrophones. Fitting of submarines did not begin until 1917 by which time the design had been further improved. Two versions were designed for surface ships.

The leading members of the BIR panel responsible for submarine detection were Sir Ernest Rutherford, the celebrated physicist, Sir Richard Paget, a barrister with an interest in audition among other scientific problems and W. H. Bragg, X-ray specialist and crystallographer, whose son's work on sound ranging has already been described. Rayleigh and Lamb were encouraged to continue their theoretical studies, for it was agreed that more fundamental research was required before efficient types of apparatus could be evolved. In November 1915 the panel sent three young scientists to Hawkcraig to work on sound receivers and to analyse the predominant frequencies in the sound spectrum of ships.[39] They were A. B. Wood and H. Gerrard, both students of Rutherford's at Manchester who were later joined by Professor F. L. Hopwood from St Bartholomew's Hospital, London. Their study of frequencies proved to be more difficult than anticipated because of the varying resonances in diaphragms and microphones. On one of his visits to Hawkcraig, Paget, who was a keen musician and had a skull note G sharp when he tapped his head, suggested listening underwater with both ears. He was taken out to sea in a small boat and while a submarine circled in the vicinity leant over the side of the boat, his legs held down by a sailor, and immersed his head in the water. When he came up he tapped his head and ran up the scale to the required pitch which was duly noted by the sailor. Nothing came of this ingenious experiment and even attempts using more sophisticated apparatus failed to detect any dominant notes produced by submarine engines.

Wood and his colleagues did, however, attempt to improve the accuracy and robustness of the Morris-Sykes hydrophone which, however, was unable to distinguish between sound coming from ahead or astern, but these, too, were unsuccessful. Rutherford also designed a portable microphone which had good bi-directional properties. However, by the winter of 1915, Rutherford appreciated that little progress was being made, largely because of the lack of scientific direction from Ryan who seems to have developed a feeling of resentment that the civilian scientists were interfering with his work. In contrast, more progress was being made by the French Navy in acoustic devices. After complaints had been made to the Admiralty by BIR, Bragg was appointed Resident Director of Research at Hawkcraig while a number of scientists at Birmingham and Manchester were asked to solve problems relating to sound analysis and the behaviour of metal diaphragms either when vibrating in air or when in contact with water. Also outside the Establishment, Rayleigh and Lamb contributed further theoretical studies on underwater acoustics. The growing importance of scientific aid for submarine detection was emphasised by Admiral Jellicoe during a conversation with Threlfall who visited Scapa Flow that autumn.

But the academic approach of Bragg and his colleagues was in sharp contrast to the pragmatism of Ryan, whose aim was to reduce fundamental research to a minimum and get the '*hardware*' into operation as soon as possible. Then there were obstacles encountered by the scientists, such as their inability to obtain equipment with which to carry out experiments and, probably even more important, the lack of contact with naval staff who had actually been in action against the enemy. However, by the end of 1916, the Admiralty was more aware of the need to concentrate on the U-boat threat. An Anti-Submarine Division was set up in Whitehall and it was decided to move Bragg's group to Parkeston Quay at Harwich where there were better laboratory facilities and workshops, submarines with which trials could be carried out and, above all, as Bragg informed Rutherford, '*direct contact with the officers on active service. It is the thing that I have always felt myself was the greatest essential to any approximation between science and the Navy*'.[40] These contacts were derived from the crews of the flotillas under Admiral Sir Reginald Tyrwhitt, then operating in German coastal waters.

The work at Parkeston concentrated on improving the direction-finding capabilities of the portable hydrophone and this led to the invention of a uni-directional hydrophone as a result of observation and analysis by Bragg. He appreciated that in symmetrical hydrophones the diaphragm could not distinguish between sound striking its front or its back, therefore the instrument was bi-directional. The answer lay in making the instrument non-symmetrical so that only one side of the diaphragm could be activated by the sound waves. This was done by fixing a screen or baffle plate in the water in front of one of the diaphragm faces. After painstaking work with various baffle plates, one, devised by Hopwood, in which a hollow disk of xylonite was partly-filled with lead shot, was found to be the most satisfactory, though it was still far from perfect. With it, it was found possible to locate a submarine at four miles range. A number of these hydrophones were used by submarine chasers such as drifters and other small craft as well as by a few submarines.

An even more difficult problem, and one which was never satisfactorily solved, was how to eliminate noise, like water rushing past the hydrophone, ship's engines and propellers, all of which interfered with efficient reception while the search vessel was moving at some speed. These noises distorted the distant engine beats of a U-boat and, in addition, made the task of listening even more exacting. A partial solution was to employ a reliable electric amplifier to magnify the weak signals picked up by the hydrophones. Such a component was devised in due course by the French, who had put some of their best physicists on the job, and it became available late in 1917. It is worth noting that French research on amplifying valves had been centralised under the *Radio-télégraphie Militaire* and dealt with both naval and army requirements.

Their best listening device was invented by Lieutenant G. Walser of the French Navy in 1917.[41] It consisted of two steel blisters, one on either side of the ship's hull, and three to four feet in diameter. The blisters were covered with a large number of small diaphragms and resembled a magnified fly's eye. The sound from an external source was brought to a focus inside the ship and the direction determined by the position of this focus, the sound being conveyed to the listener by means of an adjustable trumpet-like system. Bearings could be obtained within a few degrees and the operator could also determine when the hunting vessel was directly above the submarine. The French intended putting Walser gear into most of their patrol vessels but were unable to do so before the war ended. The Walser gear was not adopted by the Royal Navy, one reason being that British naval architects disliked having holes cut in ships' hulls!

When the Allies began to devote greater efforts to hunting U-boats, as opposed to trapping them in minefields, hydrophones were required that could function accurately in rough seas and did not compel the hunting vessel to stop so that hydrophones could be used. (The instruments in use at the end of 1916 could only function properly if the vessel carrying them was stopped and if the sea was calm so avoiding water noise.) One way of dealing

PLATE 18. Fritz Haber, in charge of German chemical warfare, on a visit to the Western Front. The respirator carried by the soldier was a standard issue. *Imperial War Museum.*

PLATE 19. Sir William Pope, Professor of Chemistry at Cambridge. Member of the Explosive Committee of the Board of Invention and Research and of the Chemical Warfare Committee which played a part in the development of British mustard gas. *The Royal Society*.

PLATE 20. The British small box respirator. *Imperial War Museum*.

PLATE 21. French 'Tampon P2' respirator. It consisted of three separate gauze layers covered by muslin or similar fabric and was impregnated with alkalis before issue. Used in the autumn of 1915, it preceded the M2 mask. *Imperial War Museum.*

PLATE 22. German leather respirator. The horses are also fitted with masks for breathing. *Imperial War Museum.*

PLATE 23. Livens projectors on the Western Front. Electric leads are being fitted and drums loaded. *Imperial War Museum.*

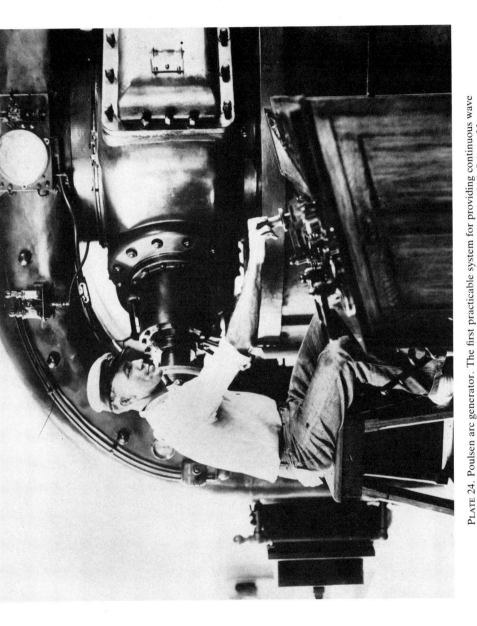

PLATE 24. Poulsen arc generator. The first practicable system for providing continuous wave wireless telegraphy and was installed in battleships of the Grand Fleet in 1916. *Science Museum Library*

PLATE 25. Hydrophone watch, Otranto barrage 1917. The crew are being trained in using hydrophones developed at Hawkcraig. In the foreground a sailor is dunking a 1915 non-directional portable general service hydrophone. Two portable directional hydrophones are suspended from the boom in the background. The hydrophones were connected to the earphones of the listeners by the electrical boxes on the deck which contained batteries and transformers. *Imperial War Museum.*

PLATE 26. Burney's paravane, for cutting mooring wires of enemy mines, being hoisted overboard. *Imperial War Museum.*

PLATE 27. Synchronised Vickers machine gun, designed to fire through a propeller, on test bed. *Imperial War Museum.*

PLATE 28. Wimperis low altitude drift bomb sight fitted to all British seaplanes, flying boats and airships on U-boat patrol. *Public Record Office.*

PLATE 30. British sound locating trumpets with observer listening with stethoscope for approaching aircraft, 1917. *Public Record Office*.

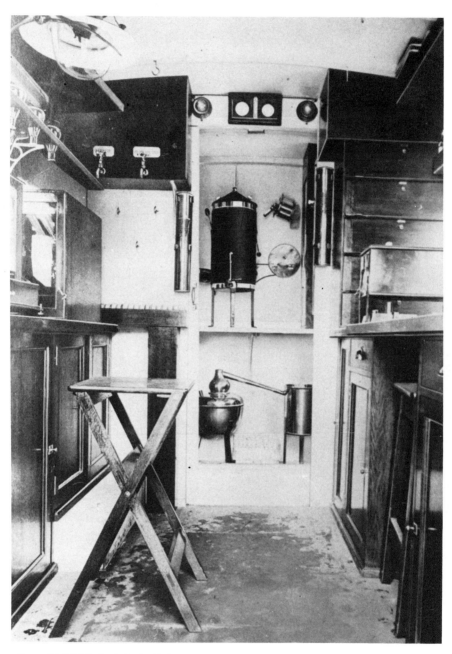

PLATE 31. Mobile Pathological Laboratory on the Western Front. *RAMC Historical Museum, Aldershot.*

PLATE 32. British oxygen mask being fitted on a pilot. *Imperial War Museum*.

with the problem was to tow a hydrophone in a container behind the searching vessel. Although some members of BIR doubted whether this system would be practical because of vibration from the towing cable and from the accompanying noise from the towing ship's propellers, a number of experiments took place during 1916–17.[42] One of the most promising schemes was the '*fish*' hydrophone invented by G. H. Nash, a versatile electrical engineer from the Western Electric Company. Before turning his attention to submarine warfare, he had invented a scrambler to safeguard messages exchanged between field telephones on the Western Front, although it was later superseded by the Fullerphone already described.

Nash worked directly for the Anti-Submarine Division; his main problem was to discover how to tow a hydrophone through the sea at speed without background water noise interfering with the reception of the instrument. The next stage was to obtain good reception without having to stop the ship's engines and, finally, to enable clear reception in a fairly rough sea. His '*fish*', streamlined like a torpedo, had wooden ends, wooden ribs and stringers, and sides made of thin sheets of German silver. The interior, filled with water, contained two microphones electrically directed from the towing ship and able to provide bearings of a submarine. After some abortive attempts, Nash claimed to have solved all the problems he had set himself.[43] At the end of April 1917 the Navy ordered 136 sets after successful trials. The Nash Fish began to be used on North Sea patrols early in 1918.

By this time new types of U-boat were quieter than their predecessors of two years earlier, especially when operating at slow speed. There is no evidence that the Nash Fish contributed directly to the destruction of a U-boat, though it certainly possessed harassing value and the chief technical officer of the Anti-Submarine Division declared after the war that he thought it was '*the most successful chasing device*' to have come out of the war.[44] Several other towing devices were put into operation following the Nash Fish. One was a wooden container called the '*Porpoise*'; this was the brainchild of Ryan and benefited from the comprehensive experiments with baffles to make it uni-directional.[45] It was rotated by a small electric motor, the operator's telephone receiver being short-circuited whenever the hydrophone motor was running, so that its noise did not disturb listening. Another towed device was called the '*Lancashire Fish*', after the Lancashire Anti-Submarine Committee under Rutherford. It contained three microphones in the vertices of a wooden equilateral triangle but it was never used during the war.[46]

American entry into the war produced a fruitful exchange of ideas and improvement in detection equipment after the meetings between British, French and American scientists in mid-summer 1917. With its penchant for looking to the electrical and communications industry for advanced technology and to the physicists in the universities for theoretical knowledge, the NRC (the American military research organisation) was already producing workable acoustic gear.[47] Even by the autumn of 1917 some of these devices were ready for testing on British warships, ranging from portable listening tubes (the C or CS tube) to the Multiple Velocity (MV) tube which was a hull-mounted binaural device modelled on, and better than, the Walser gear. There was also a towed hydrophone, not unlike the Lancashire Fish, triangular in shape with a microphone at each corner called the K tube. American scientists had already begun to cross the Atlantic to seek operational experience. Among them was Max Mason from the University of Wisconsin who had been responsible for developing the MV tube. He spent some weeks touring British naval research establishments acquainting himself with the latest techniques. But he and his colleagues had much to offer in return. They had discovered that rubber was far less prone to distortion than steel in diaphragms; it was an innovation that would be valuable in underwater experimental work in between the two world wars. The American hydrophone, in contrast to the British, was non-resonant with a broad frequency response, and had the advantage of reproducing sounds more accurately though the British instruments had a longer range.

In the opinion of some British naval officers with first hand operational experience, American standards were less rigorous than the British, trials being conducted in ideal conditions with elderly and noisy submarines as targets.[48] Nevertheless the CS tube was found to be useful at short ranges and over five hundred were installed in British ships. The K tube could pick up signals at a distance of sixteen miles and certain features were incorporated in British hydrophone designs. The MV tube was useful at ranges from five hundred to two thousand yards with the chaser steaming up to 20 knots.

What contribution did hydrophones make towards the sinking of U-boats? Only six shore-operated hydrophone stations were set up during 1915–16, mainly on the East Scottish coast. Sixteen stations came into operation around the rest of the British Isles from 1917 to the end of the war as a result of the efforts of the Anti-Submarine Division. Their effective range varied from about three miles on calm weather to about half a mile in rough. How effective they were is not known, but they must have been a deterrent to the enemy and enabled anti-U-boat patrols to operate more efficiently. Shore-controlled minefields, using hydrophones and magnetophones, were established from mid-1916 onwards, mainly off the Belgian and French coasts and off the Shetland Isles. Two U-boats were definitely sunk, two possibly sunk and two damaged. Of course the same results might have been achieved if hydrophones had not been used.

A considerable anti-submarine task force was built up during the war from available sloops, drifters, motor launches and even yachts and paddle steamers. Many of these vessels were equipped with built-in or portable hydrophone systems. After directional hydrophones became available, hunting flotillas of fast motor boats were formed to operate in the English Channel. But their value was limited by the small number of depth charges they could carry. Towed hydrophones came into service late in 1917. According to Admiralty statistics, in only fifty-four out of 255 encounters between patrol vessels and U-boats did hydrophones play a part. In the final months of the war four U-boats were definitely sunk after hydrophone contact, the majority being pursued after a visual sighting had been made.[49]

Offensive Measures Against Submarines

Extensive minefields were in fact the most effective anti U-boat measure. But the weapon with the greatest future potential was the depth charge developed by the Royal Navy since 1907. This underwent many improvements both in construction and in projection during the war.[50] The usual method of dealing with a U-boat was by dropping the depth charge over the side of the patrol vessel on the line of the target. But unless the attacker was on the course of the U-boat or very close to it, it was difficult to hit. What was required was a square of influence in which depth charges could operate as follows. One depth charge would be dropped on the line of course, one on either side, and one in front. The depth charge was actuated by water pressure at the required depth. If mortars or projectors were to be used to throw depth charges, the setting of the fuse, which was a delicate instrument, would have to be safeguarded.

In the spring of 1917, Sir John Thorneycroft, the marine engineer and shipbuilder, was asked by the Anti-Submarine Division to solve the problem. Thorneycroft designed a new type of thrower with two separate chambers. In the first, the ignition of the cordite took place and the gases produced by the comparatively slow combustion of the fuse were drawn into the second chamber where they were allowed to expand at a slow rate and pressure. This controlling of the fuse made it possible to throw the depth charge without premature detonation. Thorneycroft completed his design within ten days without recourse to help from any naval department. The new projector satisfied the Navy and instructions were issued that the device should be fitted on all submarine patrol vessels. A total of 2,760 depth charge throwers was made.[51]

The improvement achieved through the throwing of depth charges is demonstrated by the fact that in 1918 twenty-two U-boats were destroyed by this weapon, compared with six in 1917 and only two during the first two years of the war.[52]

Developments in Other Countries

There is no need to dwell on the development of German hydrophones as the Germans were not threatened by Allied submarine activity to the same extent.[53] Like the British, however, their acoustic apparatus owed much to American design. Examination of two U-boats captured with the acoustic gear still more or less intact revealed a system of microphones attached to each side of the pressurised hull so that the whole submarine acted as a sound collector, but the boat had to remain absolutely silent while listening for enemy vessels. Like the Allies, the Germans used portable detection apparatus dropped over the ship's side, but they do not seem to have experimented with towed hydrophones on the '*fish*' model to any extent.[54]

Development of Echo-Ranging

Instead the Germans made great advances in improving the performance of their submarines, especially in reducing engine noise. Detection of these new vessels by hydrophone became even more difficult. To the Allied scientists the answer seemed to lie in the development of echo-ranging rather than passive acoustic gear. Practical applications of underwater signalling had been tested for some years before the war, principally in the United States, for navigational purposes. The Submarine Signal Company had begun to meet the demand for the provision of warning systems around shoals, wrecks and other kinds of hazards and had advanced into the communications field by engaging R. A. Fessenden, the wireless pioneer and contemporary of de Forest, to develop an underwater morse code transmitter.[55] Fessenden devised what was virtually the first transducer — an instrument capable of transmitting and receiving underwater sound. Successful trials of his apparatus took place in Boston harbour in June 1914. The Admiralty was sufficiently impressed as to purchase a set and required the Torpedo School at Portsmouth to develop it as a communications system between destroyers and submarines. By then, war commitments restricted installation of the apparatus to submarines only.

Another aspect of underwater acoustics was the use of ultrasonic waves for echo detection; the sinking of the *Titanic* after hitting an iceberg in 1912 stimulated scientists to investigate the possibilities mainly in England and Germany. It was Fessenden, however, who was the first to succeed in obtaining an echo from an iceberg in April 1914. Echo detection was taken up by the BIR in the latter stages of the war for the purpose of shore-based equipment and an attempt was made to copy the successful Einthoven recording galvanometer being used on the Western Front. Four sound ranging stations were set up on the East Coast by which it became possible to fix quite accurately the position of minefields laid off the Belgian coast and on, 23 March 1918, the positions of monitors bombarding Zeebrugge were fixed.

In France, a young Russian chemist, Constantin Chilowsky, had proposed an ultrasonic echo-ranging system after the tragedy of the *Titanic* and had turned his interest to the possibility of submarine detection when U-boats began to harry Allied shipping.[56] Chilowsky submitted his idea to the French government, and no more than one month later Painlevé had passed it to the physicist, Paul Langevin, for consideration. Langevin had been a student of Pierre Curie and had also studied at the Cavendish Laboratory where he had got to know Rutherford and other well-known British scientists. He was now engaged in war service in the French Ministry of Marine's Signal Department. Although at first sceptical about Chilowsky's idea, he invited the Russian to join him in Paris. Experimental work began in Langevin's laboratory in the *École Municipale de Physique et Chemie Industrielles* in Paris in March 1915.

Langevin wanted to use magnetostriction and piezoelectricity, which he had studied under Curie, for his ultrasonic wave lengths but there were no suitable valve amplifiers then available. Instead he had to use a mica-dielectric transmitter.[57] High frequency power was generated by a wireless telegraphy arc transmitter. The instrument was unable to receive as well as transmit and a carbon microphone was specially designed for this purpose. At the end of 1915 the first successful underwater signals were transmitted across the Seine just below the Pont National. In 1916 experiments were moved to the naval base at Toulon and signals were transmitted and received at a range of two kilometres; echoes were obtained from the sea bed and from an armoured plate suspended in the water at a distance of two hundred metres. Although these results were encouraging, they were not as good as those achieved by Fessenden with his passive sonic oscillator before the war.

Early in 1917, Langevin, who had by then parted company with Chilowsky, being temperamentally opposed to one another, began to experiment with quartz crystals obtained from a Parisian optician. If cut in the appropriate way, they could be expanded or contracted by electrification; and conversely, when stretched or compressed mechanically they produced an electric charge. Thus an alternating electric potential applied to a quartz crystal causes it to vibrate and these vibrations produce sound waves. So, by suspending a quartz crystal in water and applying it to a pulse of alternating current of appropriate frequency, the crystal will be made to vibrate and communicate to the water a pulse of sound waves of the desired length. This is transmitted through the water and is reflected by any obstacle. If the obstacle is sufficiently large, an echo will be received on to the quartz which sent out the transmission. The echo creates a weak pulse of alternating current which can be detected by electrical instruments.

Langevin was greatly helped in the development of his transducer by being able to use the new eight valve amplifier designed by the *Radio-télegraphie Militaire*. This was able to magnify the weak piezoelectric charges without masking them by self-generated noise within the amplifier. At last, in April 1917 (when Allied and neutral ships were being sunk by U-boats on an unprecedented scale), Langevin tested his first quartz transmitter in a laboratory tank. The beam, resonated at 150 kilocycles per second, was so powerful that fish were killed in its path and an unpleasant sensation was felt by observers putting their hands in the water in the vicinity. But the voltage was far too high and there was difficulty in obtaining supplies of suitable quartz. Langevin had to revert to a compromise design. It was, in effect, like a box formed by two steel blocks with slivers of quartz sandwiched in between; one of the steel faces being in contact with the water. He chose a transmitting frequency of 40 kilocycles anything lower would have increased the range but would have led to a corresponding increase in the size and weight of the transmitter.

Sea tests off Toulon began in February 1918 and Langevin had the satisfaction of obtaining clear echoes from a submarine for the first time; he found he could receive signals up to a range of eight kilometres. Even so, Langevin could not compete with the accuracy obtained by the Walser passive acoustic gear which could register the exact moment when a submarine chaser and its prey crossed each other's path. A commission now had to recommend to the French Navy whether or not the experiments should be continued. One of its members was Maurice de Broglie who, it will be recalled, was the French scientific liaison officer with BIR; he had been following the submarine detection experiments closely. Doubtless due to him, a favourable verdict was given leading to the installation of sets in fast patrol boats, many of which were already fitted with Walser gear. But the war was over before any results could be obtained.

The British did not learn about the French echo sounding experiments until told by de Broglie in May 1916, though more detailed information was obtained shortly afterwards when the mission led by Pope visited laboratories in Paris under the guidance of de Broglie.[58] Rutherford had already attempted unsuccessfully to obtain signals with quartz using an ordinary telephone head piece. So the British responded with alacrity to an invitation to visit Langevin in Toulon later that summer. In the meantime, Chilowsky came to London and provided the BIR with an extensive report on what the French had done. On the strength of it, it was decided that the BIR should duplicate this research and that R. W. Boyle, Professor of Physics at Alberta University in Canada was put in charge of the work. Similar difficulties to the French were experienced in obtaining signals on ultrasonic wave lengths and much time spent in experimenting with various transmitting and receiving techniques used in wireless telegraphy without success. In November 1916 when it was reported that the French work had come to a halt, it must have seemed unlikely that a practical apparatus would ever be obtained to use against the U-boats. But research persisted and W. H. Eccles, a member of the BIR and a pioneer designer of wireless telegraph stations, joined forces with Boyle. During the critical spring of 1917, when the U-boat appeared to be unbeatable, further valuable exchanges of information took place between Langevin, Boyle and Eccles. Langevin's breakthrough in April justified continuation of British research.

Like the French again, this was hampered by the lack of suitable quartz. A source of supply was tracked down to a warehouse in Bordeaux, belonging to a manufacturer of crystal spectacle lenses and chandelier pendants. After being brought to London the quartz was cut into thin slices for the transmitters by a firm of tombstone makers in Lambeth. On 30 October 1917, Eccles reported to the BIR that he and Boyle had transmitted their first signals at a range of nearly a mile using a quartz transmitter only fifty square centimetres in area.

Boyle wanted to make a practical instrument which could be used operationally as soon as possible. He therefore did not try to copy the '*Langevin sandwich*' but developed a separate quartz transmitter and receiver. In March 1918, using a prototype at Harwich, he found he could obtain echoes from a submarine at a range of 500 yards. This set could only be used outside the ship. It would be much more convenient to have a set installed in the bottom of a hull. Boyle next built an inboard set, the transducer being encased in a retractable, cylindrical canvas-covered dome projecting under the hull of a trawler. Echoes were received with the first of these sets at distances of six hundred yards, later ranges of up to three thousand yards being obtained. These results coincided with the signing of the Armistice in November 1918; the first set was fitted into a patrol boat early in 1919 and operators were trained to use it. Had the war continued, the Royal Navy would have been the first of the Allied navies to operate ultrasonic sound ranging equipment. For reason of security this was now called Asdic (Anti-Submarine Division*ic*) after the Admiralty department that had commissioned the research. It remained a closely-guarded secret throughout the inter-war years until the purpose of the acronym was explained by Churchill, once more First Lord, in November 1939.

The British and American navies had begun to cooperate in hunting U-boats in the latter part of 1917. It did not take long for the Americans to appreciate how ineffective were the hydrophone systems then in operation. A scientist from the General Electric Company attached to the US Fleet reported that '*Three thousand British vessels used in submarine work are relatively of little value in overcoming the submarine menace . . . there were from one to five submarines passing through the English Channel every day. The fact is that they are placing mines at the mouths of practically every important habour on the British coast*'.[59] The only solution would be to press ahead with ultrasonic detection techniques.

The Americans became aware of Franco-British ultrasonic research during the exchange of naval scientific matters in June 1917 and at once formed groups to study the problem. No time was wasted in drawing on the talent available in universities and industry and also in the new Naval Experimental Station at New London. For a short time, the vanguard of this body of research was a group of physicists from Columbia University, New York. J. H. Morecroft, Professor of Electrical Engineering, was appointed to direct underwater ultrasonic development and immediately left for France to consult Langevin. Meanwhile, Sir Richard Paget visited the

American group and convinced them to switch research from the '*Langevin Sandwich*' to the British model of quartz transducers. Another research group concentrating on high frequency oscillators was formed at Schenectady by the General Electric Company, while on the West Coast the San Pedro Submarine Committee, under G. E. Hale of the NRC, devoted itself to analysing the behaviour of quartz transducers modelled on the '*Langevin Sandwich*'.

Much work was done in investigating Rochelle salt as an alternative to the scarce mineral quartz. It had long been known to possess piezoelectric activity and not long before had been used by the Curies. But it was very soluble in water and difficult to cut and grind to the required size. Special techniques had to be developed to grow crystals on a commercial scale and to design appropriate tools for converting this fragile substance into a practical seaworthy device.

Operational trials took place at Nahant and New London on the East Coast in the autumn of 1918 using quartz transmitters and Rochelle salt receivers. Ranges between four hundred and six hundred yards were obtained. So far, the transducers had been suspended from C-tubes hung over the side of a vessel. The problem of enclosing the apparatus within the hull of a ship was never satisfactorily solved during the war; one proposal to put a Langevin transducer into a steel box fixed to the hull by a spider-like metal framework came to nothing as poor echoes were obtained.

Altogether the Americans had achieved a good deal in the short time they had been engaged in the development of such a complex subject and it would provide them with a useful foundation of knowledge for post-war experimental work. The rapid advances made were due to good communications between naval establishments and commercial laboratories and especially to the flow of up-to-date information provided by the scientific attachés in the European capitals.

Underwater Protection of Warships

It is time to consider some of the defensive measures introduced to minimise the effects of explosions from torpedoes and mines on ships' hulls. Naval actions in the Russo-Japanese War had shown that it was possible for a warship to remain afloat after being hit by a torpedo, provided such vital areas as ammunition magazines, boilers and engines were adequately protected; one Russian warship equipped with a thick longitudinal bulkhead had survived several Japanese torpedo attacks.[60] Profiting from this knowledge, the Admiralty had provided new battleships of the *Dreadnought* class with similar protective bulkheads. But this extra protection made the ship heavier and slower and the cost was increased. It was necessary to discover how much damage was inflicted by explosions from torpedo attack against the hull of a target ship. The old battleship *Hood* was selected for the experiments which took place near the Beaulieu River in Hampshire and off Spithead in the first half of 1914. They took the form of exploding charges of wet gun cotton underwater at selected point along the sides of the hull. In a review of the tests held in September it was concluded that the most effective protection would not be obtained from longitudinal bulkheads but from an armoured bulkhead which would keep water out of the boiler room behind it, while the ship should be divided into a number of filled or empty compartments which would minimise the effects of an explosion. Further experiments were not possible because of the war, but the arrangements of bulkhead protection and compartmental sub-division which had already been adapted in the *Queen Elizabeth* class were embodied in the *Royal Sovereign* class.

In the meantime, the sinking of three elderly British cruisers off the Belgian coast by the torpedoes of a U-boat that month, followed by two more cruisers and an old battleship by the beginning of 1915 and the sinking of a battleship by a mine in the same period, demanded an urgent solution to defending ships against underwater attack. On 21 October 1914 Tennyson d'Eyncourt, the Director of Naval Construction, who it has been seen was shortly to apply himself to designing the first tank, suggested that a portable structure could be quickly developed for the protection of warships under-water.[61] It would be made of steel plates and angles firmly secured to the hull and sub-divided into watertight compartments about twenty feet apart which would serve to detonate a torpedo at a reasonably safe distance from the hull. Further protection would be given by an enclosed space between this structure and the side of the hull but allowing the sea to enter and so enclosing the ship by a water belt. This would prevent fragments flying out of the centre of the explosion from piercing the hull — an effect which the recent *Hood* experiments had shown it was necessary to stop. D'Eyncourt suggested that four old cruisers of the *Edgar* class should be fitted with this system and tested.

Although the idea of fixing a portable bulge to the side of a battleship was not novel in naval construction, the arrangement of airtight and water-filled compartments was original. Both the First Lord (Churchill) and the First Sea Lord (Prince Louis of Battenberg) were in favour of trying it out, Churchill stating that the *'whole subject was of supreme urgency and importance'*.[62] The first two ships were converted in about three and a half months and were tested at sea in April 1915. In spite of the unwieldy attachments, their speed and general handiness did not seem to be greatly affected and the other two ships were subsequently fitted. Similar arrangements were fitted to slow-moving monitors used for coastal bombardment.

The effectiveness of the bulges was not put to the test until June 1917 when the *Grafton* (one of the *Edgar* class) was torpedoed in the Mediterranean from a distance of only thirty yards. Although quite considerable damage was caused to the hull and there were some casualties in the sick bay, most of the blast was absorbed by the bulge and the vessel was able to reach the nearest port under her own steam.

At the same time, the possibility of incorporating bulges in the design of warships was being considered.[63] Before any decision could be taken, theoretical experiments were necessary to discover the minimum size of the bulge and the distance it should project from the hull. Bertram Hopkinson, the Professor of Mechanical Engineering at Cambridge, on the strength of his knowledge of explosives, was asked to determine a law of comparison for high explosives used against ships' structures in underwater attack. Experiments took place both in the laboratory and on a small scale model of a merchant ship fitted with bulge protection. The results seemed to confirm Hopkinson's law of comparison for high explosives i.e. that *'if the linear scale between a model and the full-sized steel structure be taken as $1 : n$ the effect of detonating charges of explosive in the weight ratio of $1 : n^3$ against the model and the structure respectively will be similar, provided the relative distances of the charges from the structures are kept in the ratio of $1 : n'$.* If this was correct, it would be possible to reduce the width of the bulge by using materials capable of absorbing the shock of the explosion.

The best material appeared to be steel tubing which absorbed shock better than baulks of timber and probably could reduce the critical distance of the explosion from the hull by about fifty per cent. These assumptions were tested in large scale models using a charge of 400 pounds of TNT. The force of the explosion was, in fact, largely absorbed by the closely-packed tubes which were crushed flat upon the side of the ship. Hopkinson's law of comparison was thus vindicated and when new ships were designed the width of the bulge was modified so as to reduce the increase of beam and retain the vessels speed. In the case of one battleship — *Ramillies* — the loss of speed due to bulge addition amounted to less than one knot at full speed.

The effectiveness of the tubing was demonstrated in October 1917 when the monitors *Erebus* and *Terror* were torpedoed within a few days of each other off the Flanders coast. *Terror* survived an attack by three torpedoes; most of the explosion was contained by the bulge and, despite water penetrating through holes in the ship, it was beached for temporary repairs and eventually towed back to Portsmouth. *Erebus* was struck by an unmanned electrically-controlled torpedo carrier steered with a wire going back to the shore, while directions for steering were signalled by wireless from an accompanying aircraft.[64] Again, the explosion was contained by the tubes and buoyancy chambers; casualties were confined to the immediate vicinity of the explosion.

Paravanes

Other forms of protection against mines and torpedoes were investigated early in the war and even before. From 1912 Rear Admiral E. E. Villiers

RN, who became Commander-in-Chief Nore, had experimented with anti-torpedo nets fitted to ships like an apron.[65] Such a system was both cumbersome and dangerous as it was possible for a mine submerged some feet below the water level to become entangled with the netting. (German mines were usually moored at depths varying from six to thirty five feet below the surface.) In January 1915 Villiers began to tow wires attached to the bows of a ship which would swing outwards in the shape of the letter 'V' and sever the moorings of a mine with special cutters. He used booms or underwater kites to keep the wires and cutters in a stable position. They were found to be clumsy and ineffective. Similar methods were tried out by the Russian Navy.

An alternative idea was suggested by Commander C. D. Burney, a twenty-seven-year-old RNVR officer (and son of Vice-Admiral Sir Cecil Burney), then commanding the destroyer *Velox*. Burney invented a torpedo-shaped body fitted with stabilising vanes called a paravane.[66] Two paravanes were towed, one on either side of a vessel from a point as far forward and as low down as possible. The wires moved in a horizontal plane slightly below the level of the vessel's keel. The outer end of the wire was kept in position by the paravane which had to be kept at a constant depth slightly in excess of the draught of the ship and at as great a distance as possible. While the paravanes were being towed, the wires formed a wedge-shaped protective element advancing before the ship, the distance from one paravane to the other being about two hundred feet.

The action of the protective gear was simple. The paravane towing wires fouled the mooring wire of any mine which might strike the vessel but passed over any mine which was too deeply anchored. The speed of the vessel caused the mine and its sinker to be deflected down the 'wedge' and away from the vessel until the mine reached the paravane. On the head of the paravane and forming part of the towing bracket, were jaws carrying specially-designed cutter blades. The mine mooring wires on striking these cutters were speedily severed. The sinker dropped to the bottom of the sea while the mine floated to the surface well clear of the ship where it was visible and could be destroyed by rifle fire.

Burney submitted his proposal to the Admiralty in February 1915 but it was not until the following October that he received permission to develop it. For this purpose he was attached to the *Vernon*. Like other impatient inventors, Burney found it irksome working under official supervision and the Admiralty came to the conclusion that he was '*temperamentally incapable of cooperating with any existing system and that if any results were to be obtained from his ideas he must be permitted within certain limits to work by himself*'.[67] Actually, setbacks in development led to the appointment of Dr B. P. Haigh, an electrical engineer from the Royal Naval College, as consulting designer to the paravane department.[68] The main trouble lay in the towing wires. These were subjected to violent vibration and had to be renewed after only a few hours at sea. Haigh was able to reduce the vibration and fatigue in other parts of the towing apparatus. (In 1939 he was responsible for designing the first reliable towed sweep for magnetic mines.)

Paravanes, known by the code name Otter, began to be fitted to merchant ships from mid-1916 onwards. The German minelaying campaign reached its climax in 1917; mines accounted for eighty-six merchantmen in the first half and forty-four in the second half of that year. By 1918 the Allied minesweeping operations had been considerably improved, only eighteen vessels being sunk in that year to the end of the war. Most mines were laid around the East and South-East coasts and frequently only ten miles out from the coast, where it was too shallow to operate paravanes. So the majority of mines were destroyed by conventional minesweeping methods. Estimates by the Director of Merchant Shipping at the Admiralty of the value of paravanes were more conservative than the claims presented to the public.[69] Mine moorings were cut on twenty-four occasions by paravanes operated by merchant vessels. Their value increased, of course, when ships had to move out of swept channels and they were therefore more useful to naval ships operating in waters where minesweepers were unable to carry out a search. In such cases the paravane, equipped with a special oscillator to enable it to maintain its depth at high speeds, was a warship's sole protection against mines. An outstanding example of their value was when units of the Italian Navy were able to make a successful attack on the Austrian Fleet at Durazzo by penetrating a minefield with the aid of paravanes.

Burney was also encouraged to develop the paravane as a method of attacking submarines. An explosive charge of 300 pounds of TNT was fitted to the paravane and detonated by an electric current transmitted through the core of the towing wires. Safety devices were inserted in the firing circuit to prevent accidental firing. Again, only moderate results were obtained, five U-boats being confirmed as being destroyed by explosive paravanes. As already noted, the majority of U-boats were destroyed by depth charges and mines. Burney nevertheless received some acclaim for his invention. After the war he entered Parliament, at the same time renewing his interest in technology by forming a company which built the short-lived but successful rigid airship *R 100* in the 1930s.

8

'Tumult in the Clouds'

Before the war little thought had been given to the possibility of equipping aircraft with armament to enable them to fight for the gathering of information about the enemy that was considered to be their primary military function. All the major European powers had carried out tentative experiments in fitting machine guns and bombs to aeroplanes and airships and there had even been several proposals enabling machine guns to fire through the blades of an engine's propeller. The principal restricting factor was the weight of any quick-firing gun after installation and its effect on the stability of the fragile machines of those days. Armaments carried in the aeroplanes that went to war in the autumn of 1914 were therefore restricted to carbines or grenade-throwers arranged to suit the convenience of the pilot. Weight was also the main obstacle in fitting aircraft with wireless, added to which was the danger of fire; and no more than a handful of aircraft were fitted with transmitters, mainly in the French and German air services, permitting pilots to communicate with a ground station at limited range.

Synchronisation of Machine Guns

By the beginning of the spring of 1915, however, the need for superiority in the air had already been recognised. Most aeroplanes at that date were driven by engines installed behind the pilot (known as pushers), but there was soon no doubt that greater power and manoeuvrability could be obtained by having a tractor engine in front. In the latter case, the problem arose of firing a fixed machine gun without damaging the propeller blades. In order to overcome it, experiments were made with a gun mounted on the top wing of a biplane, the pilot firing it by remote control. For the time being, responsibility for protection devolved upon the observer/gunner firing a moveable light machine gun from the rear.

The French were the first to use a system whereby plates were fitted to the blades of a propeller deflecting any bullets striking the latter. This crude device enabled the fighter ace, Roland Garros, early in 1915 to destroy a number of German aircraft before he was forced down behind the German lines, apparently after his aircraft had been damaged by shots from the rifle of a reservist guarding the railway near Courtrai. Garros was unable to destroy his plane and it was examined by Anthony Fokker, the enterprising Dutch aircraft designer and manufacturer working for the Germans.[1] Fokker (or more likely his colleague, Heinrich Luebbe, a weapons expert) quickly appreciated that he could improve on the French deflector system by synchronising the firing of a machine gun with the revolutions of the propeller. He devised a system whereby the gun was fired by a thumb push on the control lever of the engine, cams attached to the propeller shaft permitting fire only when the bullets were able to clear the propeller. It is not known how much Fokker was aware that his proposal had already been patented by the German engineer, Franz Schneider, in 1913 but had failed to attract any notice. A demonstration was laid on for senior German air officers after only a few days. Within eight months of Garros's capture, the formidable combination of the Fokker monoplane and the synchronised machine gun had gained air superiority for the Germans over the Western Front. It is no exaggeration to say that it had as revolutionary an effect on air warfare as had gas on trench warfare.

An interrupter gear* had been pigeon-holed by the British War Office before the war as being too complicated and expensive and the secret of Fokker's success remained undiscovered until April 1916 when an undamaged gear was retrieved from a crashed aircraft in France.[2] The gear was soon copied by RFC engineers and, at about the same time, another model was suggested by Vickers for its machine gun. But the first, and temporarily the most effective, proposal for a synchronised gear came from a Russian naval officer and pilot, Commander Victor Dibowsky, a member of the Russian liaison mission in London. Dibowsky had appreciated the need for a machine gun firing through the propeller when flying on the Eastern Front and on his own initiative had conducted experiments with a Vickers machine gun in Moscow. A model and drawings which he had brought with him were shown to F. W. Scarff, a forty-year-old engineer/artificer warrant officer serving in the RNAS armament section.[3] He had a flair for invention and had already devised a bomb sight and a ring mounting for an airborne Lewis gun. After a quick examination, he realised that Dibowsky's model could be improved (it was essentially similar to the Fokker gear) and following a couple of weeks' development the new apparatus was successfully tested at the RNAS experimental station on Grain Island in February 1916.

Development of the Scarff-Dibowsky gear coincided with the entry into service of the Sopwith 1½ Strutter fighter in which pilot and observer sat behind the engine. The pilot fired a Vickers machine gun equipped with the Scarff-Dibowsky gear while the observer covered the rear with a moveable

---

* The main difference between interrupter and synchronised gears was that the former prevented the gun from being fired when the propeller blades were in the line of fire, while the latter positively fired the gun when the propeller blades were *not* in the line of fire. Both terms tended to be used indiscriminately.

Lewis gun. At first some pilots disliked aiming their aircraft at an enemy plane but soon appreciated how useful it was to be able to attack the enemy in the 'end-on' position. The device enabled the British air service to regain air superiority over the period of the Battle of the Somme during the summer of 1916.

The increasing sophistication of aerial combat stimulated technological development. At the end of 1916, Harry Kauper, then working for the Sopwith Aircraft Company, invented a new kind of interrupter gear, capable of operating two machine guns mounted side by side providing a much greater volume of fire.[4] This gear superseded the Scarff-Dibowsky gear in the summer of 1917. The French, in the meantime, had developed a gear to operate with the Hispano-Suisa aero engine installed in the Spad fighter, also used quite extensively by British pilots.

But it was found that the mechanical gear tended to fail when an aircraft dived at high speeds; the cam became erratic and caused an irregular rate of fire. Time was also wasted in readapting gears when installing them into new types of engine. Even the latest Sopwith-Kauper gear tended to become clogged with oil except when operating in very low temperatures. A hydraulic system, in which power was transmitted by waves in a fluid like oil, was introduced in 1917 by George Constantinesco, a Roumanian mathematician, engineer and designer who had settled in London and before the war had applied his invention to rock drills used for mining.[5] Constantinesco had recently been working on an ultrasonic sound transmitter for the BIR and before that had acquired some notoriety by suggesting a system for keeping the troops warm in the trenches. After seeing his rock drills in action, officers from the War Office and MID encouraged the 'mad Roumanian', as he was nick-named, to develop his wave transmission proposal. The waves enclosed in a tube were transmitted by the piston of the engine; each impulse was absorbed by a spring which returned into place for the next impulse to push it forward again, so ensuring that each shot passed through the blades of the spinning propeller. Although Constantinesco began development in February 1916 nearly a year elapsed before the prototype became available. It was manufactured by Messrs Dorman, the engineering firm, one of whose directors was Walter Haddon, Constantinesco's employer, but did not come into general service until October 1917. The gear became standard equipment for the RAF by the end of the war and proved to be more popular with pilots than any of its predecessors. It was also adapted by the American and Japanese air services towards the end of the war. Although Constantinesco was handsomely rewarded by the Government for his invention (he gave a substantial sum from it to Roumanian Red Cross workers), he maintained that greater use should have been made of his talents.[6]

By 1917, both sides were flying in formation on the Western Front and tactical schemes for aerial combat were being worked out. In the 'dog fights' which occurred, instant and concentrated fire was necessary. Engagements between aircraft usually took two forms: a direct shot after the enemy had been taken by surprise and a deflection shot when an enemy plane passed through the firer's sight for about one twentieth of a second. With the normal Vickers it was impossible to fire more than three shots in that time. Both English and French technicians began to search for an effective speeding-up system for their automatic guns. In England, Dibowsky was encouraged by senior officers of the RNAS to find an answer after he had examined the Sopwith-Kauper gear and concluded that the volume of fire could be increased merely by using one gun instead of by the two with which it was equipped. After seeing demonstrations in France he improved the firing lock on the Vickers gun, finding that he could then fire up to 1,150 shots a minute provided the gun did not jam.[7]

Gunnery experiments for the Air Force were usually carried out at the RNAS Armament Works in Battersea. It was after seeing or hearing Dibowsky's gun being tested that the second-in-command of the establishment, Major G. W. Hazelton, was inspired to look for an improvement. Hazelton, an Ulsterman, had been trained as a railway engineer, but he had an inventive turn of mind and in peace time had published a specification for a two-stroke engine.[8] In September 1917 he set himself the task of doubling the rate of fire of a Vickers machine gun, then only capable of firing five hundred rounds per minute. He already had to his credit a proposal for synchronising the Lewis gun — a much harder requirement than synchronising the Vickers — because the former's rate of fire was slower and intermittent. Hazelton overcame the problem and his modified gun was installed in several small types of aircraft, including a seaplane. His solution for speeding up the Vickers was to make a cylinder which was attached to the barrel casing of the gun; its function was to utilise the propellant gases, supplementing the recoil of the barrel by acting on a piston attached to the muzzle of the barrel. Costing no more than seven shillings, the invention increased the gun's rate of fire from five hundred to one thousand rounds per minute. It was now possible to fire six shots in one twentieth of a second so increasing the chances of hitting the enemy plane by almost one hundred per cent. A number of Vickers guns were hastily adapted for use in France in time to meet the German offensive of March 1918. The Air Inventions Committee believed that Hazelton's was probably the '*most meritorious invention during the war in connection with aerial gunnery*'.[9] Dibowsky failed to get his somewhat similar device accepted and this illustrates the lack of coordination on research that so often caused duplication of effort.

Machine Gun Sighting

Improving the accuracy of fire was equally important, especially for the Lewis gun. No provision for an accurate sight seems to have been made before the spring of 1916 when Yves Le Prieur, the officer responsible for

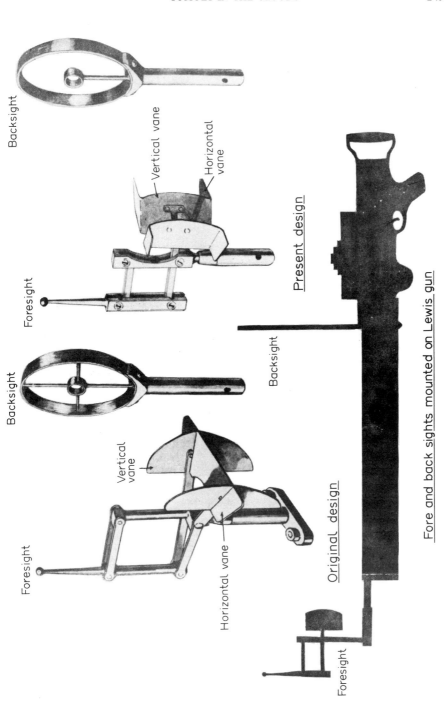

Backsight

Vertical vane

Horizontal vane

Foresight

Present design

Backsight

Backsight

Vertical vane

Foresight

Horizontal vane

Original design

Foresight

Fore and back sights mounted on Lewis gun

8.1 Arrangement of Norman universally-jointed sight for use on the moveable Lewis gun mounted on aircraft. *Public Record Office.*

introducing the French Navy's fire director, demonstrated a sight with a wind vane corrector at RFC headquarters on the Western Front.[10] Some of these sights were introduced but were found by most pilots to be too complicated. One of them was Major Geoffrey Norman, a pilot serving with No. 18 Squadron and before the war a mining engineer. According to him, the need for a quick-setting accurate gunsight had become 'desperate' in the summer of 1916; until then when taken by surprise, the gunner had to adjust his weapon manually to the estimated speed of the enemy aircraft. Norman made a wind vane in the squadron workshop. This vane actuated the foresight on the gun's muzzle in such a way that the bead was always offset by a certain amount from the normal line of sight in the direction of the line of flight of the firer's machine. The amount of the offset was to the distance between the fore and back sights in the ratio of the average speed of the firer's machine to the velocity of the bullet. The foresight aligned to the fixed back sight thus gave a correct line of sight when firing from an aircraft at a fixed target. The sight was universally jointed so that it could be used in elevation, depression as well as in deflection. The firer aimed by aligning the ring of his back sight with the bead of the foresight, aiming ahead of the target (as with a shot gun), so that it always appeared to be flying straight towards the bead. Gunners learned how much to allow for deflection very quickly by practising on model aircraft. Firing usually took place at ranges between one hundred to two hundred yards.[11]

In September 1916, while on leave in London, Norman showed his invention to Bertram Hopkinson and Mevill Jones, lately Professor of Aeronautics at Cambridge, and now experimenting with gun and bomb sights at the Aircraft Armament and Gunnery Experiment Establishment at Orfordness. Although they did not altogether approve of the principle of aiming off the target, they decided to adopt the Norman gun sight and it came into service in January 1917 and was the main Lewis gun sight for the remainder of the war. German air crew seem to have had nothing like it.

Bomb Sights

The expansion of aerial combat tended to overshadow research on methods of accurate bombing from aircraft. The first British experiments took place at Farnborough, Eastchurch, and the Experimental Wing of the Central Flying School at Upavon. One of the earliest 'bombing' trials was supervised by the young physicist G. I. Taylor, who was a member of the scientific team at Farnborough recruited from Cambridge in 1914. He and Mevill Jones were asked to improve on the French steel *flechettes* or darts designed to be dropped on troops from aircraft. As these small missiles lacked the necessary aerodynamic qualities, a number of experiments became necessary. The final test was to measure the area of distribution when discharged from the plane. A piece of paper was stuck to each dart in the ground with the object of photographing the distribution from the air. Just as the photographer was about to ascend, a cavalry officer rode up to ask what was going on. When told, he gazed at the darts and exclaimed '*Damned good shooting, what!*'. Taylor recalled that the darts were never used, '*not apparently for the reason we had originally raised as an objection, namely that missiles descending vertically would have a much smaller chance of hitting a standing man than the same weight of bomb going off on contact with the ground and throwing its fragments horizontally. The reason we were given was that darts were regarded as inhuman and could not be used by gentlemen.*'[12]

Later, more serious studies on bomb sights were initiated at Upavon by an Oxford chemist, Robert Bourdillon, who had designed a bomb sight while serving as an intelligence officer on the Western Front. His request to transfer to the RFC to elaborate his invention was granted and he was allowed to recruit a few of his scientific friends from Oxford to help him. One of them was Henry Tizard, then serving as an artillery officer in Ireland. He was soon to direct experimental work at Martlesham and before the Second World War was to have a profound effect on military science by supervising the introduction of the British radar early warning system. Bourdillon's device depended on operating a stop watch in conjunction with the sight to calculate the distance from a reference point on the ground to the target. The method depended on flying straight up or down wind and when anti-aircraft fire became troublesome, it was no longer practicable to use.[13]

More interest was being shown at that time in bombing by the RNAS which had bombed targets in Germany from September 1914 and would shortly be assigned to the attack of surfaced submarines. Further, attention had recently been drawn by a few percipient officers to the possibility of bombing communications targets like the Rhine bridges from the air thereby, perhaps, accelerating the end of the war in France. Such targets demanded very accurate bomb sights and one submitted to the Aeronautical Committee of the MID was rejected as being '*too elaborate for practical warfare conditions*'.[14] A thirty-seven-year-old RNAS officer who refused to accept this sort of argument was H. E. Wimperis who had served as an apprentice with Armstrong-Whitworth's and was later an engineering adviser to the Crown Agents. Before transferring to the Air Service he had worked for J. B. Henderson at Greenwich on fire directors.

Wimperis's drift bomb sight, as it was called, depended on the air speed as read on the air speed indicator to which was added or subtracted figures for height and wind velocity through the means of a vector linkage. This enabled the bomb-aimer to adjust his bomb sight for wind speed and direction, machine speed and height and, at the same time, keep his sight on the target. Wimperis had worked out the problem by February 1916 and submitted his proposal to the head of the Armament Section of the RNAS. In May 1917, the growth of bombing tasks required that the sight should be combined with a compass containing a separately rotatable bearing ring and three lubber's marks, making it possible to bomb off the line of flight and also to solve navigational problems. The instrument was called the Course Setting Bomb Sight and was first tested by the RNAS the following August. As we have seen, a determined effort was being made that summer to overcome the U-boat threat and the new sight was fitted into the American-built Curtiss *Large America* flying boat then coming into service for use on anti-U-boat patrols. The sight was ideal for attacking a fleeting target.[15] It was later ordered by the Americans for use in their naval aircraft and won praise for being *'without question the best British bomb sight'*[16]; after the war it was manufactured in large quantities in the States. It was used by US Army bombers to sink the German battleship *Ostfriesland* off the coast of Virginia in the historic bombing trials held in 1921.

Continuous Wave Sets for Aircraft

Communications between aircraft and the ground and between aircraft in the air were of equal importance to weapons since reconnaissance and cooperation with the artillery were the main tasks of the Air Force throughout most of the war. At the outset, neither side had made any provision for developing a suitable light wireless set for aircraft, proof against engine noise when being operated. The first squadrons sent out to support the BEF had only one machine fitted with a French Rouzet spark gap transmitter weighting 100 pounds; its signals were hardly audible beyond forty miles.[17]

Fortunately for the RFC, Marconi's had already set up an experimental establishment at Brooklands, not many miles from the Royal Aircraft Factory at Farnborough, where some of the scientists from Cambridge were working on wireless including R. Whiddington. The whole of Marconi's staff were at once seconded to the RFC.[18] Several of them were to become key figures in developing airborne wireless and included J. M. Furnival, Robert Orme (a friend of Hippisley and Russell Clarke, the pioneers of direction finding for the Navy) and C. E. Prince, who had been Round's assistant before the war, and had been responsible for developing valves for use by the Services and the Post Office. Before joining the RFC he had commanded two Marconi cavalry stations in the Westmoreland and Cumberland Yeomanry. Prince immediately appreciated that the current system of spark transmission should be replaced as soon as possible by the triode valve for transmission and reception. He was lucky in having a receptive, technically-minded commanding officer, Major H. C. T. Dowding who, twenty-one years later, would become first Commander-in-Chief Fighter Command at the time when radar was being introduced for the Air Defence of Great Britain. In April 1915, Dowding formed No. 9 Squadron which conducted the first serious experiments in air to ground communication by wireless telegraphy. As wireless for the RFC was administered by the Royal Engineers, Prince found it difficult to obtain equipment for his work, having, as he recalled, '*to beg, borrow or steal instruments or apparatus due to there being no proper experimental establishment*'.[19]

While he began to develop his valve transmitter, primarily for morse but ultimately for telephony, a few squadrons on the Western Front were doing as best as they could with the spark transmitter or a signalling lamp, the latter being usually more popular as it was less susceptible to break-down.[20] In time, a cadre of wireless officers was built up capable of operating the instruments and confidence in wireless gradually grew. It was first used extensively in France at Festubert in May 1915; pilots observed the battle and reported progress by wireless. Although the attack failed to develop, contact was successfully maintained between air and ground. It was the genesis of the contact patrol, the purpose of which was to provide information on the rate of advance. Greater use of wireless was made during the preparations for the Battle of Loos in September 1915; about twenty aircraft spotted for the guns working in conjunction with some sixty ground stations.

By this time, progress was being made with a continuous wave airborne transmitter using the Round valve.[21] The first successful experiment was made in April 1916 when signals from a 20 watt transmitter in a small airship flying over Wormwood Scrubs were picked up at Aberdeen 400 miles away. But although the soft valve had good power-handling qualities it was extremely temperamental and demanded skilful handling. For example, valves usually had to be heated before flying in order to reduce the vacuum and were provided with a thin tubular extension known as the 'pip' containing a crystal of asbestos or other mineral. But when airborne, the valve often became too hard to oscillate and a small electric heater was designed to warm the regulating 'pip'.[22] The alternative, as in the Navy, was to persevere with developing and producing a hard valve which was more reliable and easier to manufacture, though in some respects it was less sensitive than the soft valve. A programme for research was initiated for military and naval aircraft, that for the former taking place at the newly formed Wireless Experimental Establishment at Woolwich and for the latter at Eastchurch, Cranwell and at the physical laboratory of Imperial College. A major contribution was made at Imperial College by leading scientists such as O. W. Richardson and F. Horton from London University,[23] G. Stead from the *Vernon*, R. Whiddington from Farnborough and G. B. Bryan from the Royal Naval College. Practical experience of valve manufacture was provided by S. R. Mullard. Just before the end of the war, this group evolved a high vacuum receiving valve (the R5) which had better amplifying capability than some of its more powerful predecessors.[24] Post-war investigation confirmed that the Germans had not produced anything better. Unfortunately it came too late to be used on operations.

Inevitably, replacement of spark by continuous wave transmitters and of soft by hard valves took time. Only in the autumn of 1918 was it possible to install continuous wave transmitters in certain types of aircraft, as, for example, spotters for the Grand Fleet and for monitors bombarding shore batteries and anti-submarine patrols.[25] A few night bombing squadrons were also fitted with the new sets.

Introduction of Wireless Telephony

Meanwhile, Prince was concentrating on the development of wireless telephony for air to ground communication and vice versa. He appreciated that information would be sent back much faster by this means than by morse and would radically improve army–air cooperation. Something of the struggle he had to get his ideas accepted emerge from statements supporting his claim that he was the first to introduce wireless telephony for aircraft. *'Wireless telephony'*, he wrote, *'has proved an affair of the greatest importance and magnitude in the world . . . moreover its initiation was not official but was the result of intense personal struggle for its existence and recognition'.*[26] His post-war award from the Air Ministry was £650, later grudgingly increased to £1,000!

In February 1916, at St Omer, he demonstrated the possibility of speaking from the ground to a pilot in an aircraft to a party of senior officers headed by Kitchener. Conditions were hardly favourable as the pilot had to battle through a snow storm while he spoke to the Field Marshal who had reluctantly put on a pair of head phones. However, the party was sufficiently impressed to demand the installation of wireless telephony for inter-aircraft communication as soon as possible.[27] This was a complex task. Not only had a transmitter to be developed which was proof against engine noise, vibration and forms of aerial disturbance, but also the equipment for voice communication, in particular a flying helmet incorporating microphone and headphones. A remote control system had to be provided to help the pilot to tune or adjust transmission separately from the main instrument in his tiny cockpit. At that time there were no fixed aerials, a long wire being trailed behind the machine and reeled in rapidly when there was an emergency. A cartridge aerial was introduced before the end of the war enabling an aerial to be slipped instantly when combat seemed imminent.

No suitable transmitter for wireless telephony could be produced before early 1917. When it appeared it was used mainly by squadrons engaged in home defence.[28] They were controlled by six ground stations in the London area, transmitting within a radius of 50–100 miles on 450 or 700 metre wave lengths. Only two squadrons were equipped with wireless telephony on the Western Front and flying over the enemy lines was prohibited in case a set was captured and copied by the Germans.[29] The possibility of communicating with tanks from the air was considered, one squadron being assigned for experiments. But the difficulties in designing a suitable aerial for the tank and of obtaining audible reception were never overcome.[30] Some bombers were equipped with wireless telephony receivers so that they could be directed to suitable landing grounds on returning from a raid.[31]

While the major advances in aircraft wireless sets were made by electrical engineers like Round and Prince, several academic scientists were asked to improve the reliability of continuous wave transmission. Among them was J. S. E. Townsend, first Wykeham Professor of Physics at Oxford who, after becoming a lieutenant in the RNAS, returned to his laboratory to design a wavemeter or tuning coil.[32] Drawing on a pre-war friendship with Paul Langevin, he made frequent visits to Paris and became an invaluable source of information on French military wireless developments. But delays in development prevented his wavemeter from coming into service until late in the war. A. B. Field, Professor of Mechanical Engineering at the Manchester College of Technology, developed a high frequency alternator much lighter than anything *in use by the British Government*[33] *and as far as we know by any of the Allied governments*'. The prototype was mass-produced for supply to the Admiralty and to the Russians. Field and a colleague, E. P. Taylor, went on to design a 200 watt alternator for use in military aircraft and, finally, produced a design for a propeller-driven alternator along the lines of a French model. The only aircraft capable of operating this alternator was the powerful Martynside fighter with a four-bladed propeller but which arrived in France too late to be flown in action. A wind-driven generator was brought out by the electrical engineering firm of British Thomson Houston and was used by home defence squadrons equipped with wireless telephony.

The extensive use of wireless at sea and in the air led to a crisis in the production of components, especially valves which demanded very special-ised craftmanship, in 1918. That May a small inter-service committee was formed and made responsible for assigning priorities and ensuring the correct distribution of equipment between the Services.[34] Members included experts like Eccles the naval scientist and Furnival, Prince, Mullard, Orme and Whiddington representing the Royal Air Force. They had a salutary effect on standardising equipment. At the same time coordination of wireless research improved after the creation of the RAF, being concen-trated at Biggin Hill in Kent where experiments in the location of aircraft by sound had begun to take place.[35] The Air Ministry also took over wireless research at Cranwell and at Imperial College.

In the final stage of the war, when operations on the Western Front again became fluid, wireless at last began to come into its own and '*the wing and squadron link was of great assistance owing to the constant rapid moves of units and the consequent disorganisation of telephonic and telegraphic com-munications*'.[36] Spotting and contact patrols normally operated at wireless ranges up to fifteen miles. At sea, aircraft operating with the Grand Fleet (from the improvised carrier *Campania*) could only transmit signals in the early years of the war, but by 1917 reception became possible at ranges of just over one hundred miles. In the spring of 1918, seaplanes were being phased out and aeroplanes were coming in. For these smaller machines, continuous wave sets were essential and had replaced all spark instruments that summer. Normal reception was limited to one hundred and eighty miles but occasionally signals could be heard at a distance of three hundred miles.[37]

Surprisingly, considering their advanced technology, the Germans failed to surpass this effort. Evidence of their inability to keep pace with the Allies was discovered in special instructions issued by the German Army on the Western Front in June 1918 to the effect that special care should be taken to salvage as much equipment as possible from crashed Allied planes as '*the enemy has secured a distinct advantage in his successful use in aeroplanes of continuous wave apparatus which possess great superiority over the spark apparatus. It is of the greatest importance for us to salve enemy wireless equipment of this discription . . . as we have not so far been successful in constructing a continuous wave wireless apparatus for aeroplanes which can work without certain disadvantages*'.[38]

Rotary Engines

As the need for specialised fighter aircraft grew, greater insistence was placed on their performance, especially on their ability to climb quickly and to make fast low-level attacks. The British had not made any significant advances in aero engine design, apart from the Green engine at Farnborough, and tended to rely on British versions of French engines.[39] However, early in 1916, British pilots discovered that their planes were no match against the fast and highly manoeuvrable Fokker.

Before the war experiments had been made by the French with an air-cooled rotary engine which revolved around a stationary crankshaft. It was considered to be superior to the stationary engine as it was light, easy to maintain, and usually started at once; but it was handicapped by its rather low performance, then being about 130 horse power. The most promising rotary engines came from the works of Clerget and Le Rhône.

Walter Bentley, a twenty-seven-year-old engineer who had switched from railways to the infant motor car industry and was already acquiring a reputation as a car designer, had appreciated the advantages of aluminium over steel components in motor engines and in 1914 had fitted a small car with aluminium pistons which had given a useful boost to horse power.[40] After joining the RNAS he suggested that rotary engines, making use of light alloy components would be more suitable for aeroplanes than the heavy Rolls-Royce and Sunbeam engines then in service. In 1916, Bentley was encouraged to improve on the Clerget model by making it more powerful and adaptable to military requirements. The Bentley Rotary 1 (BR1), as his first 150 horse power version was called, was fitted in the Sopwith Camel with which RNAS squadrons in France and Belgium were equipped in May 1917.

It was capable of climbing to around 17,000–18,000 feet, even reaching heights of 25,000 feet and far outpacing the Clerget engine. German pilots soon learned to respect the Camel and in June 1917 one of the new high altitude Zeppelins was shot down by fighters equipped with the BR1 engine. Following upon these successes, Bentley was asked to design a BR2 version of 230 horse power at the end of 1917. It was fitted into the Sopwith Snipe fighter but only two of these squadrons were in action before the end of the war. Subsequent analysis confirmed that the SE5, designed by the Royal Aircraft Factory and equipped with the French Hispano Suiza engine, was a better performer and shot down more enemy aircraft than the fighters powered by the BRs 1 and 2. At the same time, Bentley could not claim to be entirely original in his use of aluminium cylinders as research at the NPL and elsewhere had been taking place for some time. Nevertheless, his engine helped considerably to reverse German air superiority in the last two years of the war. The later development of the static radial engine meant that the rotaries were not needed. The German air service made much less use of rotary engines, possibly because they required large quantities of castor oil for lubrication and this was an item in short supply due to the Allied blockade.[41]

Incendiary Weapons Against Airships

The development of the long-range Zeppelin airship capable of bombing London or Paris from bases in Germany, if not on the scale predicted by Wells in 'War in the Air', was threatening enough to provoke studies on anti-aircraft weapons in England and France. Further point was given to the need for research by the appearance of rigid airships, in addition to small airships, at German army manoeuvres and by the regular passenger-carrying flights by airships across Germany. A form of incendiary shell which would ignite the inflammable hydrogen gas contained in large bags within the envelope for lifting the airship seemed to be the answer. But surprisingly little seems to have been known about the detailed design of the Zeppelins outside Germany and it was erroneously believed at the time that there was a layer of inert gas between the outer cover of the airship and the gas bags, produced by exhaust gases extracted from the engines. It was therefore necessary for the shell to have a fuse delicate enough to detonate on penetrating the fabric, otherwise it could pass through the envelope without harm.

Experiments were carried out at Woolwich at the behest of the Master General of Ordnance by W. R. Hodgkinson with an incendiary shell filled with thermit, composed of ferric oxide and aluminium.[42] However, when actually confronted with the possibility of aerial attack, the British decided to rely on small bombs or explosive darts (the latter developed by the French). Some years before the war, a bomb had been developed for the

RNAS by the inventor, F. M. Hale, then General Manager of Explosive Trades Ltd, a small powder manufacturing company which had been taken over by Nobel Dynamite Trust.[43] Hale had designed a grenade discharged by a rifle which had attracted attention among arms dealers and which, together with the Mills bomb, was used extensively on the Western Front.

The bomb, two pounds in weight, was approved for use in naval aircraft by Commander Murray Sueter and fulfilled two most important requirements, namely that it should be safe to handle and carry in an aircraft, and that it should explode on impact with the ground. Hale's bombs, with delayed detonators, were used to attack Dusseldorf on 8 October 1914 when a German Army airship was destroyed in its shed. Flight Lieutenant R. A. Warneford RNAS brought down another German Army airship in flames off the Belgian coast in June 1915, using a Hale's bomb. Two months earlier, a German naval airship, already crippled by anti-aircraft fire, was despatched by darts over the Thames estuary. Filled with yellow phosphorous, these missiles were showered out of sealed containers. They were invented by Commander Francis Ranken, a naval engineer who had joined the RNAS. However, darts were soon superseded by explosive bullets.[44]

The Zeppelin raids over London, the East Coast and Midlands had shaken the civilian population although the actual damage done was virtually negligible. After a series of quite sharp raids in the autumn of 1915, attacks were stepped up again in the summer and autumn of 1916. The Zeppelins had proved to be much less vulnerable than expected and were able to climb rapidly out of range of intercepting fighters and anti-aircraft guns. Much discussion took place on the best weapon to use against these monster aircraft, the War Office eventually concluding that guns would have to be supplied with explosive or incendiary ammunition, several types of which had already been submitted by hopeful inventors. But an important objection had to be overcome as the British Government had signed international agreements banning these armaments at the St Petersburg Declaration of 1866 and the Hague Convention of 1899, while the Hague Convention of 1907 had stipulated that armaments causing unnecessary suffering should be prohibited.[45] On the other hand, the Germans had, in the opinion of the Allies, initiated the use of chemical weapons and flame-throwers and it was alleged that the Austrians had used explosive bullets against Serbian troops. Moreover, the killing of civilians in the air raids further justified the use of more deadly types of ammunition while it was argued that they were intended to destroy aircraft rather than inflict harm on the crews manning them. The War Cabinet therefore had no hesitation in permitting their use on 13 July 1916, but only against airships raiding the homeland, for the War Office believed that if the Germans captured pilots equipped with that kind of ammunition on the Western Front they would '*murder*' them.[46] At the end of 1916, Haig asked whether the ban could be rescinded so that incendiary bullets could be fired at observation balloons over the Western Front, but permission was not granted. The use of explosive or incendiary bullets against heavier-than-air machines was authorised after the *Gothas* started raiding southern England. However, the problem now arose that it was dangerous to fire these bullets through propellers.

The most promising type of explosive bullet, believed to be superior to the Austrian variety, was invented by J. Pomeroy, an Australian engineer, who had twice submitted his design to the War Office and once to the BIR and to the US Army before it was finally accepted by MID in September 1915.[47] By then Pomeroy had become a bankrupt as he had been required to pay for most of his experimental work. His bullet had a hollow in its nose containing a charge of dynamite which exploded on impact. Pomeroy bullets fired in Lewis guns came into service at the beginning of September 1916 and the inventor's persistence was vindicated when a German Army Zeppelin was set alight over London three nights later. After the war, Pomeroy was awarded £25,000 tax free for his invention.

A combined explosive-incendiary bullet was devised by F. A. Brock, a director of C. T. Brock the well-known firework makers, who, apart from being thoroughly acquainted with explosives, exercised his inventive talent on such varied subjects as toxic gases, smoke screens and optical instruments. He was killed while taking part in the Zeebrugge raid with the intention of capturing a German range finder.[48] The characteristic feature of his bullet was that it could ignite and explode after penetrating the double fabric of the Zeppelin (normal bullets exploded on impact). In September and October 1916, two German airships raiding London at Potters Bar and Cuffley were set on fire with Lewis gun ammunition containing one-third Brock bullets. Another air-to-air missile was a rocket designed by that prolific French inventor, Yves Le Prieur. It was tried out on a British naval seaplane but the rockets caught alight too quickly after leaving the plane, endangering the pilot. However, the RFC seemed to have had more confidence in this weapon, firing it from the fast Nieuport Scout at tethered observation balloons.

Experiments were also made with '*sticky*' phosphorus compositions. J. F. Buckingham, owner of a small engineering works in Coventry, who was an experienced chemist, developed a flat-nosed phosphorus bullet which was approved for use by the Royal Flying Corps.[49] Its first success was the destruction of a German aircraft over Belgium on 22 February 1916. On account of their high sensitivity, incendiary-explosive bullets were not fired through the propeller but were restricted to the swivelling Lewis gun firing to the rear or over the wing.

By the end of 1916, British fighters, making good use of their new armament and fitted with the more powerful rotary engines, had established a marked ascendancy over the Zeppelins operating at altitudes of 12,000 to 13,000 feet. But little had been done so far to improve the effectiveness of the anti-aircraft guns, and members of the Air Board, like Lord Curzon and

Lord Sydenham, were irked at what they believed to be the slowness of MID in providing suitable weapons to defeat the Zeppelin menace, noting that French anti-aircraft guns had already shot down a German Army airship near Verdun in February. A possible solution was soon provided by the ubiquitous Richard Threlfall, a director of the phosphorus-making firm of Albright & Wilson, who had communicated to the BIR a proposal (subsequently passed to the Air Board) for a phosphorus-filled bullet or shell. Sydenham immediately authorised experiments with the comment that a shrapnel shell bursting within sufficiently close proximity of the target to be fatal *'ought to appeal to the anti-aircraft gunner who so far has been a rather helpless person'*.[50]

As Threlfall was busy with the provision of smoke screens for the Navy, experiments were entrusted to his son, a pilot then on sick leave from the RNAS. Phosphorus was put into both anti-aircraft gun shells and machine gun bullets. The former proved to be very effective against airships as they could penetrate two layers of fabric leaving 'a smear of phosphorus which continues to burn for quite long enough to ignite fabrics causing a large enough fire to ignite any explosive mixture of hydrogen which may happen to pass through the hole a few seconds later'.[51] After tests against model airships and balloons, the Ordnance Board was sufficiently confident in March 1917 to authorise the supply of the new projectile for the 13 pounder quick-firing gun which was then considered to be the best anti-aircraft weapon. The bullets took longer to perfect as they tended to explode prematurely. But by the spring of 1918 they had become superior to other types of incendiary ammunition, being more destructive, longer-ranged, and proof against the cold at high altitudes. Threlfall's varied military research was rewarded by a knighthood. In contrast, German feelings about the inventor of the phosphorus bullet were vehemently expressed by an airship crewman who later exclaimed *'Had we caught the man who invented that bullet we should have gladly burned him in a stream of burning hydrogen'*.[52]

Yet, in spite of their casualties, the German Navy's reaction was to lighten their airships by increasing the lift and reducing the size of the gondola. A new class of rigid airship, introduced in the spring of 1917, flew at altitudes of 16,000 to 20,000 feet, thus rendering obsolete the entire British air defence system. In the remaining months of the war, only two more Zeppelins were shot down by aircraft in raids over England and none by anti-aircraft fire. Yet the necessity for the airships to operate at extreme heights imposed a severe handicap on their operations as navigation became more dependent on wireless instructions and bomb aiming became more difficult.

Improved Control of Anti-Aircraft Defences

By the autumn of 1917, however, the Germans had largely replaced the vulnerable, slow-moving airships by the *Gotha* bomber, causing new problems for the air defences. That June, twenty *Gothas* dropped about ten tons of bombs on London in daylight and escaped unscathed. Yet another reorganisation of guns and searchlights had to be made. Similar bombing attacks increased on the Western Front causing a growth of anti-aircraft artillery and an auxiliary wireless reporting system to provide information on the routes of enemy planes. New techniques were demanded not only for estimating range and altitude of a moving target but instruments for both early warning and location of the enemy raiders in order to get defending aircraft in the most favourable position and to alert guns and searchlights. Scientists were needed to advise on predictors and sound locating apparatus. In France, German air bases were within easy range of Paris, the centre of the war effort and the *École d'Écoute des Avions* was established early in the war at the *Institute Aérotechnique* of the University of Paris under the well-known physicist Jean Perrin.

In contrast, British anti-aircraft research was more a process of improvisation depending on a handful of individuals. Early in 1916, Horace Darwin and Sir Alexander Kennedy, the electrical engineer responsible for advising on gun sights, appreciating the need for training anti-aircraft gunners, induced MID to set up a small research section to investigate problems of height and range finding.[53] They asked A. V. Hill, a promising young physiologist from Cambridge then serving with the infantry as a musketry instructor, to organise a scientific party. Hill assembled some of his academic friends, a mixture of elderly dons and young graduates, either mathematicians or electrical engineers, who were able to calculate trajectories and fuse curves. It was called the Anti-Aircraft Experimental Section, or informally as '*Hill's Bandits*' and became responsible for the development of height and range finders and for experiments on the ballistics of anti-aircraft guns and the location of aircraft by sound.[54]

The section went through the usual difficulties of having to convince the military that a handful of civilians in uniform could contribute to solving operational problems. Trials with height and range finders began at Northolt near London but just as the naval scientists had experienced difficulty in obtaining a submarine for experiments, so Hill had a struggle to obtain an anti-aircraft gun. Eventually he obtained the use of a six-inch naval gun mounted on a monitor at Great Yarmouth. The gun was equipped with a primitive sight invented by Commander A. (Barmy) Gilbert, RN. According to Hill, the trials were so '*devastating for the official range table, on which the sight was based*'[55] that the team was moved to the naval gunnery school at HMS *Excellent* where further sight corrections could be made.

At the same time, Glazebrook offered the facilities of the NPL for experiments on the burning of fuses and on electrical gearing for height and range finders which was supervised by E. H. Rayner, one of his staff. Theoretical work on the behaviour of fuses was taken on by Professor W. J. Goudie at University College London as well as at Woolwich. Karl Pearson, Professor of Applied Mathematics at the Francis Galton Laboratory, University College, became responsible for computations and preparation of charts for range tables, allowing Hill's section to concentrate on practical gunnery experiments.[56] The effect of wind speed and barometric pressure on the behaviour of shells and fuses also had to be studied and valuable information was provided by the Meteorological Office which was increasingly being called upon to improve weather forecasting for operations on the Western Front. E. A. Milne, a Cambridge undergraduate and later a Fellow of the Royal Society, devised a method by which consideration could be given to the varying pressure acting on a shell in order to determine its effect on fuse behaviour. Milne's section also made analyses of the effects of upper-air wind velocities on shell bursts. Gunnery officers made wind corrections after observing positions of burst in order to make the necessary allowance in their calculations before re-sighting their guns.

The predictor currently in use in the British Army for laying a gun on a flying aircraft consisted of two instruments to measure both lateral and vertical deflection. The respective velocities moving in a horizontal and in a vertical direction were recorded by a universally-jointed pivoting sight kept trained on the target by means of a gear which was connected to a kind of speedometer indicating the rate of angular movement of the sighting means. The gun was laid according to this rate. In order to estimate the range, each instrument was provided with a number of scales calibrated for selected ranges, or alternatively, a change speed device was interposed.[57] The effectiveness of this predictor depended entirely on obtaining the correct range and, even more, on the skill of the operators. The equipment was designed by J. E. Wilson, a civil engineer, and W. E. Dalby. Professor of Mechanical Engineering at Imperial College and associated with naval predictors. It was brought into service in 1916. Alternative forms of predictor or height finder were proposed at a later stage of the war but were all superseded by an electrically-operated predictor invented by the French engineer, M. F. Brocq. This was used with the three-inch twenty hundred-weight anti-aircraft gun which had replaced the 13-pounder as the most effective anti-aircraft weapon.

Anti-aircraft gunnery was virtually an unknown subject demanding the acquisition of skills in getting the best out of fuses and predictors. It was not long before Hill was asked to provide what became known as the Travelling Ballistic Party to visit anti-aircraft detachments on the Western Front, provide instruction and make reports on the behaviour of guns, fuses and predicting instruments. This detachment went to France early in 1918 and was so well received that GHQ asked that the tour should be extended, and even suggested that a permanent scientific party should be based in France to do this kind of work.[58] Later Hill, justifiably, claimed that this was the forerunner of the operational research sections formed to evaluate weapons and make scientific analyses of operations that proved to be so useful in World War Two and were taken up by the British and American Services.[59]

Sound Location of Aircraft

The development of night bombing required the coordination of guns and searchlights and it was essential that the latter should be provided with some means of locating an invisible target. Hence the introduction of sound locators with which Hill's *'Bandits'* were also closely associated. The science of acoustics was relatively new, the most recent research being carried out by Lord Rayleigh some years before the war. Preliminary studies were therefore initiated by C. Jakeman of the NPL leading to the construction of a number of trumpets with mouth pieces ranging in diameter from eighteen to thirty-nine inches. An assessment of their value was made by E. A. Milne.[60] Much larger trumpets, which were connected to the ears by stethoscopes, were devised by Perrin and by American scientists, one produced by the latter being eighteen feet long with a diameter across its mouth of four and a half feet. Its designer claimed that sound was magnified three times compared with an unaided ear. But however sophisticated these instruments became, their effectiveness depended on eliminating background noise. This included the noise of guns when a barrage was being fired and the whistling of the wind in the trumpets, while the noise of enemy aircraft engines was often too faint to be picked up. A detachment from Hill's section went to Rochford in Essex to test Jakeman's apparatus under operational conditions but no spectacular results were obtained. Nevertheless, for lack of more effective apparatus, development of the British trumpet type of sound locator went ahead. After the war it was claimed to be *'superior to that of any other nation and* [was] *adopted practically unchanged for general use by the Americans'*.[61] Operating personnel, who were required to have above average powers of concentration, were trained at the Royal Engineer School of Electric Lighting at Stokes Bay and learned how to cooperate with searchlights and air patrols.

Other less practical systems of sound location were given a trial. One was devised by an RE officer, Lieutenant G. M. Moubray, who believed that the sound of approaching aircraft could be picked up and measured by listeners sitting at the bottom of shafts dug at various depths.[62] A number of these shafts were dug in the British Fifth Army area in France in 1918 but were overrun by the Germans in the March offensive; it is unlikely that any information of value was lost. Another instrument was the Baillaud paraboloid mirror. This also seems to have met with little success but it led, after the war, to the construction of immense concrete mirrors overlooking the Romney Marsh; they were intended to pick up the sound of aircraft crossing the Channel.

A quite independent line of research was taken by W. S. Tucker, the inventor of the microphone used by the sound ranging sections in France.[63] Tucker believed that his electrical instruments could be adapted to give warning of enemy aircraft approaching the British coast at distances of

twenty miles and over. Encouraged by Professor Hugh Callendar, Professor
of Physics at Imperial College, he set up a laboratory at Imber Court near
Esher in Surrey which was administered by MID.[64] In the autumn of 1918 he
evolved a disk or wheel, twenty feet in diameter, on which were mounted a
number of Tucker microphones operating in conjunction with a galvanometer. Tucker believed that his apparatus would register aircraft sounds despite
artillery barrages and other noises and '*enable accurate location to be carried
out*'. The apparatus was erected at Joss Gap on the Isle of Thanet to listen
for movements of enemy aircraft across the North Sea. However, it was
found that the microphones were so sensitive that they picked up too many
superfluous noises while reception was often impeded by the pounding of the
surf on the nearby beach. A proposal, which might have been more effective
but which was never put into operation, was the installation of Tucker's
microphones on an airship patrolling some miles off the coast. The comments of air defence headquarters on these experiments to Admiral Bacon,
the Comptroller of MID, aptly summed up the situation on 21 October 1918.
'*If it is possible to obtain an instrument that can be depended upon only to
reciprocate to the sound of aerial engines, a great advance in the anti-aircraft
defences will have been obtained*'.[65] A satisfactory answer was not found
until seventeen years later when it was discovered that aircraft were susceptible to radiolocation, leading to the revolutionary development of radar. It
is worth recording that A. V. Hill, along with Tizard and Wimperis, because
of their experience of war science, were members of the committee set up to
introduce it for the defence of the United Kingdom.

Helicopters and Pilotless Aircraft: A Look to the Future

Some indication has been given of the scientific and engineering developments that under the stress of war converted the primitive aircraft of those
days into formidable fighting machines. Yet there were other inventions that
appeared to be too revolutionary at the time to justify any large allocation of
resources. Several years before the war, for example, proposals were
received by the British Government for aerial torpedoes or pilotless aircraft.
One idea submitted to the Ordnance Board in 1913 was rejected on the
grounds that the electrical propulsion system would be unlikely to lift the
aircraft.[66] Even so, the possibility of pilotless aircraft was seriously considered by the Royal Aircraft Factory in 1914. Two years later, another
proposal was submitted by an anonymous naval officer for a pilotless aircraft
to carry either explosives or '*short grappling lines*' to bring down night-flying
Zeppelins. Even if found to be inaccurate, it was believed that the moral
effect would deter the enemy. The distinguished naval aviator, Commander
E. R. Samson, the first pilot to take off from a ship and a pioneer of wireless,
now in charge of air defence on the East Coast, offered the opinion that '*with*

the knowledge of wireless control in the position it is, it seems a distinct pity that the idea should not be put in hand at once'.[67] In Germany, a proposal was made for an aerial torpedo to be launched from a Zeppelin, but it ended up by being converted into a pick-a-back monoplane to be launched from a giant bombing aircraft. As for the fate of the British proposal, after being neglected for some years after the end of the war, it was resurrected in the late 1920s in the shape of the Larynx bomb-carrying guided weapon.[68]

More attention was given to the possibility of building a helicopter based on the proposal of Louis Brennan, educated at Melbourne University, who had invented a guided torpedo as early as 1884 which was rejected by the Admiralty but adopted by the War Office as a standard form of harbour defence.[69] Brennan's design for a flying machine supported by rotors and powered by a Bentley rotary engine was taken up by the MID in 1916 after being dismissed by the War Office. Although capable in theory of ascending and descending vertically and having an endurance capacity of three hours, it was not until the autumn of 1918 that its potentiality as a spotting aircraft in support of ground or naval artillery began to be appreciated. This was in spite of development being supervised by the scientific advisory bodies including such an unconventional character as Wilfrid Stokes, the mortar designer. It was left to Admiral Bacon to pronounce two months before the war ended that Brennan's design was *'without doubt the most important of all inventions that has been under consideration for the last year. The time has almost arrived when the helicopter will be started building. It is possible that it may revolutionise all accepted aeroplane design'.*[70] But after prolonged trials, the Brennan helicopter was abandoned in 1926 in favour of the Cierva autogiro, although it had shown itself to be an adequate weight-lifter and had flown briefly in the open on seventy occasions.

In the end the devices that could satisfy immediate practical problems like the synchronised machine gun, gun sights and bomb sights were the ones which, quite rightly, were given priority. Even though Churchill, as Minister of Munitions, could write in October 1917 that *'Dominating and immediate interests of the Army and Navy have overlaid air warfare and prevented many promising lines of investigation from being pursued with the necessary science and authority'*,[71] in fact, ideas *were* put into practical shape by engineers of the stature of Mervyn O'Gorman, Horace Darwin, Bertram Hopkinson, Prince and Wimperis among others. By mid-1918, high altitude fighters were in operation, wireless telephony as well as wireless telegraphy were being used by fighters and bombers, and bombs weighing 3,000 pounds could be discharged mechanically from aircraft compared with the 20-pounders dropped by hand in 1914.

9

The Unseen Enemy

In the South African War the British Army suffered a greater number of deaths as a result of disease than by enemy action.[1] This was no exception to the prevailing rule as in other contemporary conflicts, such as the Cuban and the Russo-Japanese wars, disease also took a heavy toll. But at least the practice of medicine was being transformed from *'an observational and empirical craft into a scientific calling'*.[2] It was at last in a position to provide the military with the means to overcome the great scourges of earlier campaigns such as dysentery and enteric fever which had deprived armies of so much of their cutting edge.

Sir Alfred Keogh and Preventive Medicine

Improvements in the health and sanitation of the British Army were begun by Sir Alfred Keogh, Director General of the Army Medical Service from 1905 to 1910. Keogh served in South Africa and this experience had taught him that much of the so-called *'wastage'* of war could be avoided by preventive medicine, a corollary of which was scientific research. Keogh founded an Army school of sanitation, extended the Royal Army Medical College at Millbank and substantially improved relations between the Army Medical Service and the medical profession by commissioning investigations on tubercular disease, cholera and Malta fever. Keogh retired in 1910 to become Rector of Imperial College, South Kensington but was reinstated in his old appointment at the War Office in October 1914 at the request of Kitchener on the understanding that he should be granted exceptional powers. Haldane, who as Secretary of State for War had encouraged Keogh's timely reforms, assured Kitchener that he was *'one of the best organisers I ever knew'*.[3] Unfortunately the *'wastage'* that Keogh was determined to prevent was only too prevalent in the early months of the war and hundreds of soldiers were sent home from the Western Front for trivial ailments. Nevertheless, neither Keogh nor Lord Esher, a close friend of Kitchener, were able to convince the latter that the Director General of Army Medical Services should become a member of the Army Council.

At the outbreak of war the medical department was far too preoccupied with administration to concern itself with the startling new problems relating to disease and surgery that arose either in trench warfare or in the so-called *sideshows* in the Middle East and Africa. Fortunately, the Government had set up the Medical Research Committee in 1913, after the passing of the National Health Insurance Act two years earlier, providing it annually with funds for the specific purpose of extending medical knowledge. The committee was headed by Lord Moulton who, it will be recalled, later became responsible for the supply of explosives. Among its members were Christopher Addison, instrumental in setting up the MID, and distinguished professors of medicine from the universities such as Clifford Allbutt and Gowland Hopkins, while the Army was represented by Sir William Leishman, Professor of Pathology at the Army Medical College.[4] As the committee had hardly begun work, it was relatively easy to apply itself to warlike instead of peaceful medical problems. However, the War Office was not obliged either to seek its advice or even to use it if accepted, and had it not been for Keogh, with a foot in both the scientific and military camps, most of the studies it commissioned would never have been given practical application.

A Shortage of Anaesthetics and Drugs

The first major problem encountered by the Services was how to overcome the acute shortage of local anaesthetics and drugs that occurred in the autumn of 1914. This was due to the dependence of the British drug industry on both imported raw materials and manufactured products from overseas, especially Germany. At the end of that year, the National Health Insurance Commission, which was responsible for the supply of drugs, asked the Royal Society War Committee for help in suggesting alternative sources of production. The young official representing it was John Anderson, who had experience of chemical research and who would be even closer associated with scientific affairs in World War Two when he became responsible for the British share in the development of the atomic bomb. The Royal Society immediately made contact with scientific departments of universities and technical colleges, thirty-two of which responded favourably.[5]

Two local anaesthetics were urgently required.[6] One was novococaine, a synthetic chemical of German origin built by a number of complex chemical processes; the second was beta-eucaine also previously obtained from Germany; a third drug called orthoform-neu was also unobtainable through normal commercial sources. Dulcitol, a form of sugar used in bacteriological work, was another substance in short supply.

Much of the stop-gap production that now took place was done in the modern laboratories of St Andrew's University under Professor James Irvine mentioned earlier in connection with mustard gas. Luckily there were some postgraduates still engaged on research and, with the help of a handful of largely untrained assistants working day and night, over a hundredweight of milk sugar was converted into dulcitol during a period of ten weeks and satisfied the immediate requirements of the Government. Further quantities of dulcitol were prepared in October 1915; the process was speeded up and about one fifth of a ton of milk sugar was converted into dulcitol in the course of five weeks.[7]

A stock of novococaine was synthesised in the same laboratory during the summer of 1915, about sixty workers producing over twenty kilograms of the compound diethylaminoethanol which was offered to the Government at cost price. As a result, a much quicker process was evolved and the laboratory at St Andrew's made regular assignments available to government departments.

The synthesis of orthoform-neu required the preparation of pure lactic acid and the bacteriological sugars, glucose, galactose, and sorbitol. All this production was made possible by having a first class laboratory, a research endowment fund through which materials could be purchased, and the provision of an adequate number of research scholarships and fellowships for science students. But the way in which the work was expedited was entirely due to the outstanding powers of leadership displayed by Irvine and to his *'remarkable ingenuity of thought and technique'*.[8]

Beta-eucaine was urgently required in 1915 and the Royal Society arranged that some seventeen laboratories should collaborate to produce the anaesthetic. The laboratories most heavily engaged were at Sheffield University and at Imperial College. It was at the latter that a less time-consuming and more efficient means of production was discovered by S. B. Schryver, Professor of Biochemistry with the assistance of A. T. King and F. A. Mason, a research chemist. By using acetal instead of paraldehyde as an intermediate process they were able to obtain higher yields.[9] Over 216 pounds (representing over three million doses) were made by the improved method and supplied to the Services. Large scale commercial production was subsequently undertaken by six pharmaceutical firms. British manufacture of beta-eucaine now became freely available.

The Treatment of Wounds: New Antiseptics

Great progress was made during the war in the treatment of wounds. In the first place the introduction of civilian operating theatres at casualty clearing stations and field ambulances provided the opportunity to operate as early as possible and for prompt treatment of wounds. Secondly, great advances were made in the development of suitable antiseptics. It was soon discovered that wounds, caused largely by fragments of shell, quickly became subject to serious infection due to anaerobic bacteria lurking in the well-manured soil of Northern France and Flanders. Army surgeons, who had found it comparatively easy in the Boer War to deal with bullet wounds received on the '*clean*' South African veldt, were now faced with entirely new problems. The biochemists and pathologists came to their aid.

At first it was believed that dirty lacerated wounds could be sterilised by powerful antiseptics. In fact antiseptics like carbolic acid proved to have limited success and experiments began to be made with milder antiseptic solutions.[10] One school of thought led by Sir Almroth Wright, who had also had experience of conditions in South Africa, exploited what was termed '*physiological*' methods, the treatment consisting of encouraging a free flow of lymph into the wound for which purpose hypertonic salt solutions were employed. This method led to the packing of septic wounds with tablets of solid salt with or without the addition of sodium citrate. Wright, assisted by a number of his trained pupils from St Mary's Hospital, Paddington, including the future discoverer of penicillin Alexander Fleming, set up a pathological laboratory at Boulogne where they carried out a series of experiments on recently-inflicted wounds.

Other pathologists, however, decided to investigate the germicidal action of hypochlorites which were usually used for the purification of water but rarely for surgical purposes. Hypochlorite preparations came to be accepted both by the Allies and the Germans and Austrians as being the most satisfactory antiseptic solutions. In Britain several investigations were supported by the MRC. One took place at Edinburgh University, being carried out by a team under Professor Lorrain Smith. It devised a combination of bleaching powder and calcium borate which was called 'eusol' in the form of a solution and as a powder 'eupad'. Both forms proved to be exceedingly efficacious in the treatment of septic wounds.

A somewhat similar and equally successful solution was worked out by H. D. Dakin who had left England before the war to do research at the Rockefeller Institute in the United States. He at once returned home and was invited to continue the investigations begun by the American biochemist Alexander Carrel at a French military hospital in Compeigne.[11] In company with a group of French pathologists under Dr Daufresne, Dakin devised a hypochlorite solution containing no boric acid but a mixture of carbonate and bicarbonate. These solutions were known as '*buffer*' solutions indicating their ability to reduce the actual change of reaction due to the addition of either acid or alkali. Dakin's and his French colleagues' solution saved '*many hundreds of lives and thousands of limbs*'. Later in the war Dakin developed another form of disinfectant known as chloramine T. This substance, although of quite a high germicidal value, was almost non-toxic; it was particularly useful in dealing with wounds involving the mouth and it was also an efficient drug in ridding chronic meningococcus carriers of their infection.

In September 1916, arrangements were made by the MRC with the Admiralty for Dakin to go out to the Dardanelles to advise on the disinfection of hospital ships.[12] The crowding of large numbers of cases in these vessels, many of them suffering or convalescing from enteric fever or dysentery, led to much secondary infection during the voyage. The process of generating hypochlorites by the electrolysis of sea water had long been known and Dakin installed on the Cunard liner *Aquitania* (used to evacuate wounded direct to England) a simple plant for this purpose using the ship's current. His system produced disinfectant which practically abolished cases of secondary infection and was also extremely economic in carbolic acid and cresol. The *Aquitania* used the same electrolytic tank during World War Two and the ship's medical officer confirmed the efficacy of the disinfectant solution which it continued to provide.

Certain synthetic dyes, such as crystal violet, malachite green and brilliant green came to be used as antiseptics due to the need for substances of low toxicity but of high antiseptic potency for disinfecting wounds. The MRC sponsored the development of what became known as acriflavine by C. H. Browning of the Bland Sutton Institute of Pathology at the Middlesex Hospital.[13] Browning discovered that while the action of other dyes used for antiseptic purposes was diminished by the presence of blood serum, that of acriflavine was actually increased, even to five times its potency in water. It was also harmless to the tissues even in strong concentrations and therefore had great therapeutic value in various infections. Special arrangements had to be made for its manufacture in the small British synthetic dye industry, Levinstein's of Manchester, already mentioned in connection with the production of mustard gas, being selected to provide supplies for the medical services.

Wound and Surgical Shock

Not only was the antiseptic treatment of wounds greatly improved but great advances were made in coping with wound shock and surgical shock — conditions that arose out of loss of blood from effective circulation. The technique of blood transfusion to treat such cases was enormously improved by using the citrate method so that blood could be stored for use *in vitro* and provided according to types. These studies, mainly conducted by Rendle Shaw, a physiologist from Bristol University, were combined with a number of administrative improvements such as '*warming up*' wounded men before an operation and using gas and oxygen instead of ether — measures that probably saved tens of thousands of lives. According to MRC reports, the results obtained at the Casualty Clearing Stations were transformed by the progress made during the war in these matters.

Enteric, Dysentery and Typhus

How did medical science assist in the prevention of disease? One of the most devastating diseases in former wars had been enteric fever. In South Africa, Almroth Wright had carried out the first inoculations against typhoid fever but only on a small and quite inadequate scale with the result that the Army Council decided to suspend the practice of inoculation until further evidence had been gathered. For some years before war broke out in 1914 Sir William Leishman, Professor of Pathology at the Royal Army Medical College, carried out a programme of research. In August 1914 all the arrangements for inoculating the BEF had been made but no compulsory order was issued and only about twenty-five per cent of the troops agreed to be inoculated. But after the stabilisation of the front in October 1914, typhoid fever, carried by refugees, broke out on quite a large scale. Leishman, who had become adviser in pathology to the BEF, now had to persuade the troops that it was in their best interest to be inoculated. Before the end of 1915, nearly ninety-eight per cent of British troops had agreed to be inoculated with the result that there was a significant drop in the number of cases of typhoid. It was estimated that vaccination had reduced the chance of contracting the disease to about one tenth. The writer of Leishman's obituary for the Royal Society claimed that '*Had casualties in the British Army from enteric fevers been on the same scale as during the South African War, 900,000 troops would have been invalided and 130,000 would have died. That the total cases were 1/45th and total deaths 1/100 of these figures is in part due to improvement in army sanitation, but there are good reasons for believing that the greatest factor in the protection from epidemic extension was afforded by the inoculation of almost the entire personnel of our armies. For this achievement, Leishman must be accounted to have been one of our most successful generals in the Great War*'.[14] Jean Vincent, up to the war head of the bacteriological laboratory at Marseille, performed a similar service for the French Army.

As it happened, there were more outbreaks of paratyphoid than typhoid in the first year on the Western Front and the possibility of including paratyphoid bacilli in the prophylactic inoculation had to be considered. In 1916, after a brief period of experiments, a new triple vaccine called typhoid-paratyphoid (TAB) became available for the British Army and proved itself to be efficient in controlling paratyphoid as well as typhoid fever.

An important contribution towards the diagnosis of enteric fever was made by the first Oxford Professor of Pathology, Georges Dreyer, who had gone to France to serve in the RAMC with the rank of honorary major.[15] There was a difficulty in that most soldiers had already been inoculated (when this had at last been accepted) so that the old methods of serum diagnosis became unreliable. However, before the war Dreyer had worked out a system of using standardised '*dead*' cultures which enabled diagnoses to be made even in triply-inoculated patients provided that regular observations were made at intervals of five days. With the assistance of the MRC, a laboratory was established in Dreyer's department at Oxford from which standardised emulsions, together with the requisite outfit for carrying out the tests, were supplied free to all military pathologists. Much valuable information about the course and diagnosis of the different forms of enteric fever resulted from the widespread use of this standard method which had the advantage that the observations of different workers were strictly comparable.

In addition, investigation of enteric fevers and other diseases was greatly helped by equiping motor vans as mobile bacteriological laboratories (the first was actually a holiday caravan) and attaching them to a clearing station close to the front.[16] The medical officer in charge had a car, enabling him to go to any place in the area where his services were needed. The role of these officers was threefold. First, they examined all kinds of morbid products from hospital wards, thereby contributing to the diagnosis of enteric fevers and other epidemics on the medical side, and of the various kinds of infection that attack surgical wounds. Secondly, they examined contacts in cases of infectious fever both among the troops and in the civil population. Thirdly, they investigated new forms of diseases that appeared among the troops in order to discover their causes and the means of prevention. Typical examples of two of these units on the Western Front related to cases of poisoning by noxious gases, trench fever, gas gangrene, the lice problem, venereal disease, and the bacterial examination of water supplies.

Unhappily, the careful precautions relating to ensuring inoculation and good hygiene were not observed to the same extent in the Dardanelles. Although there was little typhoid, there were a large number of cases of paratyphoid.

The other historic disease which always affected military campaigns was dysentery; and once again it proved less easy to overcome than some of the other diseases.[17] A number of cases were reported on the Western Front during the winter of 1914–15, but this was only the prelude to a major outbreak which took place before the battle of the Somme. Its increase was attributed to the arrival of troops from the Middle East and India. No effective prophylactic inoculation against bacillary dysentery was discovered during the war although research was conducted. Prevention therefore had to be confined to hygienic precautions and to the search for carriers.[18] A number of centres were established in England where troops returning from the Mediterranean could be segregated and observed. The MRC provided laboratory assistance at these centres and organised courses of instruction in protozoology for the numerous workers who were comparatively unversed in the subject. A mass of detail was accumulated and analysed; the results were published in reports on amoebic dysentery and bacillary enteritis. Never before had there been an opportunity to study the tropical forms of dysentery in England and many new facts were brought to light.

One useful drug for treating amoebic dysentery was introduced by Henry Dale, Director of the Wellcome Physiological Research Laboratory, and a future President of the Royal Society and chairman of the Scientific Advisory Committee to the Cabinet in World War Two. It was called bismuthous iodide, Dale discovered that carriers of amoebic dysentery, who had long been treated without success with emetine administered hypodermically in the normal way, could be freed from infection by use of the new drug which, unlike emetine, could be given orally.[19]

Typhus fever — a scourge of military campaigns in the past — did not affect British and French troops (apart from the British medical units in Serbia) so much as the Germans and Austrians on the Russian and Balkan fronts.[20] Throughout the war there were catastrophic epidemics of typhus fever, usually spread by lice, affecting both those armies and the civil population. In Poland some 40,000 people died. In Serbia the number of cases ranged from 100,000–135,000, the death rate rising to sixty per cent.[21] It was therefore imperative that research should be devoted to diagnosing this louse-borne disease with the object of identifying the virus that caused it. Some years before the war W. James Wilson, a Belfast pathologist, had discovered that the serum of patients suffering from typhus contained a bacillus belonging to the *proteus vulgaris* category which was a pointer towards diagnosis; his findings were published in one of the medical journals.[22]

But Wilson's discovery was probably unknown to two pathologists, Edmund Weil, in charge of the 5th Mobile Epidemiological Laboratory in the Austrian Army, and one of his colleagues named Arthur Felix.[23] In 1915, it became a matter of urgency for them to try to discover the causal agent of typhus as it was feared that it might emerge on the Silesian Front as it had already done in Serbia, Russia and Poland. In September 1915, they isolated from the urine of several patients strains which were, unknown to them, similar to those identified by Wilson. They named the culture X19 and later discovered that the serum of practically all cases of typhus fever agglutinated X19 while the controls were consistently negative. They concluded that X19 either played some part in the causation of typhus, or was a constant secondary invader. The so-called Weil–Felix reaction became a valuable form of diagnosis for suspected cases of typhus fever at the Robert Koch Research Institute in Berlin.

A culture of X19 was given to a British Army doctor after the Allied entry into Jerusalem in December 1917 and was passed on by him to a young Australian doctor, Neil Hamilton Fairley, working in a military hospital in Egypt.[24] Fairley confirmed that the Weil–Felix reaction was, in fact, useful in diagnosing typhus fever, but rejected the notion that X19 was in any way a causal agent of the disease; its virus still remains to some degree an immunological puzzle.

In the meanwhile, Weil and Felix had been forced to abandon their laboratory in the Ukraine following German reverses and the Russian revolution. After loading all their records and research products onto cattle trucks, they made a hazardous rail journey to Prague; the only thing that prevented their precious baggage from being looted was the dire explanation that it contained cultures of typhus and cholera. After the death of Weil from typhus in Palestine in 1922 all the records of his wartime work mysteriously disappeared and Felix, who later became a British subject and Fellow of the Royal Society, never located them.[25]

Gas Casualties

There were a number of other applications of medical science in trench warfare which must now be mentioned briefly. The treatment of casualties from gas poisoning was something never faced before or even contemplated by service doctors and pathologists.[26] Not that the symptoms of gas injury were unknown as they were well defined in the literature of occupational diseases, but the duration and concentration of a gas cloud and how to escape from it were aspects about which knowledge was acquired as the war progressed. The severity of the illness depended on the amount of gas inhaled and its concentration. Most troops recovered quickly but those badly gassed developed severe inflammation of the lungs. Violent spasms of coughing, retching and vomiting aggravated the strain on the heart which was being deprived of oxygen because of the inflammation of the bronchii and air sacs. After three or four hours the sick reached a critical phase from which they recovered after sleeping, or deteriorated further. In the latter event, death followed swiftly due to heart failure caused by pulmonary oedema, a drowning of the lungs in fluid released within them. The inhalation of phosgene did not cause spasms and so was more insidious than chlorine. Its inflammatory action was more localised and took a little longer to develop; otherwise it was more dangerous.

Rapid evacuation of casualties, fresh air and absolute calm were essential but hard to implement in the early days because the motor ambulance and casualty clearing system were still being developed. If anything, the German treatment of gas casualties was more advanced than the Allies as they were already using oxygen cylinders in the summer of 1915. Drugs such as atropine to reduce spasm and the secretion of fluid were used during 1915–16. But the victim's best chance of survival lay in good nursing; drugs were merely adjuncts of varying degrees of usefulness.

The delayed action of phosgene, used from 1916 onwards, meant that most gas casualties could be treated at the CCS.[27] If the patient survived the first twenty-four hours and was able to avoid pleurisy, he was likely to survive and would be capable of resuming light duties. Treatment still continued to depend on the use of a few drugs, venesection and oxygen — the latter administered over a lengthy period offered the best hope.

After mustard gas was introduced in the summer of 1917, the incidence of lung injuries gave way to first and second degree burns often accompanied by severe inflammation of the throat and (less often) of the lungs.[28] Conjunctivitis was the commonest injury. It was treated by boracic washes or colloidal silver in aqueous solution and disappeared entirely in ten days to a fortnight. Blisters were treated by keeping them asceptic, covering them lightly, and avoiding friction. The famous painting called '*Gassed*' by Sargent in the Imperial War Museum showing a file of blinded soldiers helping each other along to the CCS after a bombardment by mustard gas shells is a moving, though rather sentimental, record of one aspect of the horror of modern warfare but it necessarily omits the sequel of the recovery of most of the men within a fortnight. Nevertheless, mustard gas made heavy demands on scarce resources at the Front, such as water, clothing, clean gauze and medical attention — so creating unexpected difficulties.

Nephritis and Trench Fever

In the case of gas casualties, medical science offered no outstanding advances in knowledge. But there were other diseases of an epidemic nature in trench warfare on the Western Front which eluded clinical investigation. One of them was known as trench nephritis,[29] though it was also encountered in the rear areas of the battlefield. The symptoms affected the kidneys, being indicated by an appearance of albumin in the urine. Nephritis had been experienced by troops in the American Civil War; it attacked other ranks rather than officers and, curiously, not Indian troops. It made its first appearance in the spring of 1915, reaching its peak that July. A very complete study of cases reaching England was made at St Bartholomew's Hospital, London and the chemical pathology of the urine was elaborately investigated in France. But no microbe was discovered and efforts to transmit the disease to animals were unsuccessful.

After another bad outbreak in the winter of 1916–17, the MRC convinced the medical authorities in the BEF that a more vigorous analysis of the disease was overdue.[30] In Feburary 1917, a Nephritis Committee, composed of senior medical officers, asked the MRC for help. Hugh Maclean, in charge of the biochemical laboratory at St Thomas's Hospital, London, who had a special interest in the analysis of urine, was given a temporary commission in the RAMC and sent to Étaples to set up a small laboratory for analysing cases of nephritis. Maclean's letters to William Fletcher, Secretary of the MRC, provide a graphic description of the Army's indifferent attitude to biochemical research. On arrival in France, Maclean found that no accommodation had been made for his laboratory. Undeterred, he eventually found a small wash house at the back of one of the general hospitals which he used until a larger building had been erected. In such unpromising conditions he began to examine the first batches of men who would eventually total 40,000 before they went up to the front. His object was to discover whether they had any previous kidney trouble; such a scheme he believed was '*the only one to throw light on the condition*'. It had actually been suggested a year earlier by the MRC but ignored by the Army doctors.

It was also, incidentally, a monumental survey of the kidney condition of young Englishmen of the time.

Before the end of April 1917, Maclean had won the reluctant approval of the Nephritis Committee and, equipped with a card index, he began his daunting task. Early in July, he had examined 18,000 men and reached the tentative conclusion that nephritis was due to a mild form of kidney disease. But further examination led Maclean to reject this theory in favour of one that it was a louse-borne disease. He reached this deduction in August 1918 after a particularly trying period in which his laboratory was nearly totally destroyed in an air raid, he himself only escaping injury by leaving the building a few minutes before the bomb fell. Further examinations of troops who had suffered from nephritis were made in London and the results published in the medical and scientific literature. The MRC later asserted that Maclean's work *'proved that "clinical" guesses at prognosis and the right treatment for nephritis cases were almost meaningless; he had worked out definite tests, based on measuring the degree to which the kidney can perform a definite task, by which a real estimate of existing damage can be done, and both prognosis and treatment guided'*.[31]

Somewhat akin to trench nephritis was a novel disease, called trench fever after examination of a small number of cases in the winter of 1915.[32] The symptoms were recurrent fever with a cycle of about five days; the sickness was identified by outbreaks of spots, vomiting and headaches and an enlarged spleen. Further examination by a pathologist working at a hospital in France proved that it could only be transmitted by blood transference. This was proved by injecting the blood from an active case into volunteers for the experiment and these examples further showed that the infecting property resided in the corpuscles and not in the serum. But no visible parasite could be found in the blood. Eventually, the British Trench Fever Committee and an American Army Commission proved to their mutual satisfaction that the disease was louse-borne and therefore completely preventable by delousing.

Malaria and Bilharziasis

The most serious disease encountered by troops operating in the eastern Mediterranean, Mesopotamia and German East Africa was malaria. Macedonia was the theatre of operations that suffered more casualties than anywhere else. Attention to quite recent military history should have provided a warning for in the summer of 1855 the British Army was suddenly prostrated by a serious outbreak of malaria in the Crimea.[33] In October 1915 the British and the French decided to land at Salonika in order to try to prevent the Serbian armies from being cut off by the Bulgarians. The vortex of the fighting was in the low-lying valley of the Struma which happened to be the most direct approach into Bulgaria but was a veritable mass breeding ground for the anopheline mosquito. Keogh had warned the General Staff that the malaria season would begin in June. This was reinforced by a note, prepared by the Royal Society of Medicine, sent to Keogh on 29 February 1916 by Sir Ronald Ross, discoverer of the mosquito cycle in malaria. This urged the necessity of dosing troops regularly with quinine and taking measures to reduce mosquitoes round encampments. Ross ended his letter *'You still have about two months grace before General Malaria comes in the field against you'.*[34]

But very little provision was made to protect the troops against mosquitoes and the administration of quinine was spasmodic and unmethodical. By the end of July 1916 over 3,560 cases had been admitted to hospital and the figures did not decrease until the end of October. Some 18,000 admissions to hospital were recorded for 1916. While the number of deaths did not amount to more than one per cent, whole units were often put out of action. A special War Office committee, set up to report on suitable prophylactic measures, concluded that *'we have had to do with a specially virulent type of malarial infection in a body of troops unseasoned to tropical conditions'.*[35] During the following winter, Ross himself carried out a survey of the malarial area and measures were drawn up to prevent a similar epidemic occurring in the summer of 1917. These included special dress, mosquito nets, masks, gloves, chemical repellants and the prophylactic issue of quinine. A special malaria laboratory was set up under C. M. Wenyon, a pathologist, with a biochemist and an entomologist to assist him. Schemes for drainage and clearance of brushwood round camps were carried out. Although hospital admissions continued to rise in 1917 and 1918, evidence emerged that primary infection was reduced, especially in 1918. Wenyon concluded that *'quinine failed to prevent infection in thousands of cases but at least protected a small number of individuals'.*[36]

In other theatres of war, such as Mesopotamia, Egypt and Palestine there was much less malaria, though the disease affected the latter stages of Allenby's advance in 1917–18.

The disease that worried Army doctors in Egypt was bilharziasis, or schistosomiasis as it is now called.[37] This disease is carried by a worm living on certain kinds of freshwater snails. Once the worm had established itself in a human body there seemed to be, at the time, no way of destroying it. Although strict orders were issued prohibiting bathing in fresh water, troops did not appreciate the danger involved and were unwilling to forgo the pleasure of a cool plunge. As the complete life history of the parasite was still uncertain, MRC supplied a team led by Robert Leiper, from the London School of Tropical Medicine, to investigate the problem on the spot. In a few months, Leiper and his colleagues discovered hosts of the worm and cheap and efficient means were introduced to render infected waters safe. These were brought into use at all military camps. Leiper's studies probably saved millions of pounds in treatment of existing cases for there were still a few men suffering from the disease incurred in the South African War and who were costing the Government about £6,000 a year. Companion studies to improve the early recognition of bilharziasis were made by Hamilton Fairley, already mentioned in connection with typhus.[38] He introduced a test which gave positive results in the early stages of the disease but was negative in all other conditions. It is worth noting in passing that Fairley would make important contributions to the suppression of malaria in World War Two. In 1941 he strongly advised General Wavell, when contemplating the landing of troops in Macedonia, that if unseasoned troops were sent there in the malarial season the experience of World War One would be repeated. At first Wavell reacted violently against this advice but subsequently admitted that he had been overhasty in his judgement and ordered the Army to go to Greece instead. At last the advice of scientists and medical authorities was being respected, though, as it happened, the campaign was over before the malarial season opened.

Oxygen Masks for Airmen

The rapid development of flying stimulated by the war generated its own special medical problems. It was the beginning of what is now called aviation medicine and specialist medical officers were appointed to approve tests for the selection of air crew, and study the effects on airmen of acceleration and fatigue.[39] One of the most important requirements was the provision of breathing apparatus for use at high altitudes. In both aerial combat and photographic reconnaissance the gaining of height was often a vital need. During the winter of 1916 pilots on the Western Front had to fly at heights of 20,000 feet and over and sometimes lost control of their machines through lack of oxygen.

The Germans were probably the first to develop compressed or gaseous oxygen equipment for their aeroplane and Zeppelin crews, but they found that it brought on sickness as a result of impurities in the oxygen. Taking advantage of their superiority in chemical research they developed, early in 1918, a small liquid oxygen apparatus (containing seventy to eighty per cent oxygen and the remainder nitrogen) manufactured by the firm Ahrendt & Heylandt. Liquid oxygen was an improvement over the compressed gas as it provided more oxygen for less weight. It was carried in a spherical double-walled metal flask (like a thermos) with charcoal suspended between the walls to maintain a better vacuum. It was based on the British design by the physicist James Dewar long before the war. The oxygen, after evaporating in an expansion chamber, was inhaled through the mouth by the pilot and his observer. Crews of *Gotha* bombers flying long distances at 15,000 feet and Rumpler photographic reconnaissance planes with a ceiling of nearly 24,000 feet used this equipment successfully.

The Allies, on the other hand, preferred to use compressed oxygen. Allied pilots were at first reluctant to use the equipment as it was uncomfortable to wear and unreliable at first, often freezing at great heights. According to an MRC report, it was only after discovering an oxygen apparatus attached to the pilot of a crashed *Gotha* bomber in the Thames that finally persuaded the British aviation authorities to make greater efforts to introduce breathing aids for high altitudes.[40] The only apparatus immediately available to the British was the Siebe Gorman outfit, specifically designed for diving and for rescue work in mines; but it was too heavy to be adapted for use in aircraft. However, it met the emergency as at least one reconnaissance squadron in France had become so handicapped by lack of oxygen apparatus that it was unable to carry out its assignments.

Meanwhile the pathologist Georges Dreyer turned his attention from the study of cultures for the control of enteric fevers to designing a more convenient breathing apparatus for aircrew.[41] It had an aneroid-controlled regulator which automatically increased the flow of compressed oxygen from 0.22 litres per minute at sea level to 2.32 litres per minute at 27,750 feet. The amount of residual oxygen in the cylinders was visible to the pilot, and there was a metal diaphragm which delivered a constant flow of oxygen irrespective of external conditions or continual use. The mask was small, light, comfortable, and could not cause frost bite. Dreyer's apparatus was approved for operational use just in time for the massive artillery bombardments at Messines in June 1917 when high level photographs of the results were essential. The Dreyer proved to be more popular among aircrew than either the French or American models; the Americans, in fact, modelled their equipment on Dreyer's and mass-produced it for the air service.

Manufacture of the British equipment took place at a small factory in Paris, each kit being sent immediately to the front by car as soon as it was ready. Even so, breathing apparatus was never used extensively; air combats were usually fought at heights of around 15,000 feet and high level reconnaissances were not so numerous; some pilots could not be persuaded to wear the masks. Moreover, production of the equipment was slow and complicated and the earlier models were unreliable. Nevertheless, by the end of the war sufficient aircrew had been educated to appreciate the advantages of breathing oxygen and were flying with their faculties unimpaired at heights of 20,000 feet and over for four hours at a time.

At the same time, there were other important aspects of flying that demanded the attention of medical men.[42] They included tests for the selection of aircrew; providing antidotes for the effect of G forces on pilots when diving or making sharp turns. This was an entirely novel field of study and was initiated to a large extent by the Department of Physiology at Bristol University. Its professor, Stanley Kent, carried out research on another extremely important but quite different field — industrial fatigue. He had begun these studies before the war, but after the extensive construction of munition factories and the large-scale employment of both men and women workers they assumed an even greater significance. The outcome of Kent's work was published in a White Paper and a Blue Book and led to the reduction of the long hours worked in munition factories in the early years of the war.

10

Aspects of Wartime Industrial Research

Britain's pre-war dependence on certain German manufactured goods and raw materials such as synthetic dyestuffs, synthetic drugs and optical glassware proved to be a serious handicap.[1]

In this chapter the measures that had to be taken to overcome two of these deficiencies essential for the war effort — optical glassware and nitric acid — will be described. Both products were based on the development of new knowledge about the processes of production and depended on recent discoveries in chemistry and physics.

British Deficiencies in Optical Glass

Just as the enormous growth of the artillery arm had created an unprecedented demand for high explosive, so too was there now a pressing need for greater quantities of rangefinders, telescopic sights, dial sights, clinometers, fire directors, field plotters and telemeters to improve the accuracy of fire. Special instruments too were needed for trench warfare, including compasses with luminous dials for night operations, periscopes (ranging from giant instruments twenty-four feet high for special observation purposes to trench periscopes designed to determine the bearing of a machine-gun nest) and telescopic sights for snipers' rifles. Anti-aircraft guns too needed very accurate sights whilst the Air Force was demanding not only sights for its machine guns but large quantities of photographic lenses to cater for extensive aerial photography, which had begun in earnest in 1915. High quality glass was also required for wireless set valves and for X-ray tubes.

The manufacture of optical glass demanded unusual skills. The glass had not only to be strong enough to resist the abrasive action of lens grinding and polishing, but at the same time had to be transparent and capable of transmitting light without diminution or distortion.[2] No one equalled the Germans in optical glass manufacture. They had achieved their pre-eminence through the efforts of the firm of Abbé and Schott in Jena, generously assisted by grants from the German Government. By 1886 these efforts had greatly increased the range of optical instruments available; advantage was taken of these developments by a competent school of opticians already in existence. Although the quality of French optical glass hardly rivalled Jena's products, it was good enough to export to the British in quite large quantities. The British glass industry, however, had become so dependent on German and French imports that it had declined into '*a comatose condition and was absolutely stagnant. There were probably not more than half a dozen men in the country that could be depended upon to design and compute the simple optical instruments required. The machinery that existed was antiquated and wholly inadequate. The workshops were mere shanties*'.[3] The Services were almost wholly dependent for their requirements upon one manufacturing firm — Messrs Chance Brothers of Birmingham.

Thus, at the outset of the war, all that was available to the Government was a small stock of Jena glass and the capacity to make about one thousand pounds a month, supplemented by imports from France. It did not take long for the General Staff to appreciate the implications of the loss of German supplies. A letter was sent to the Royal Society War Committee on 6 January 1915 asking it to suggest '*means for improving the processes of glass manufacture*'.[4] During that summer a special department was set up in the Board of Trade to deal with optical glass questions under the physicist and optical expert, Frederic Cheshire. It also had the benefit of advice from Sir Herbert Jackson, a well known chemist, and Professor Percy Boswell, a twenty-nine-year-old geologist from Liverpool University. The main tasks were to assist manufacturing firms with financial aid, provide technical advice, set up research centres and obtain supplies of privately-owned binoculars, compasses and telescopes and similar equipment for the armed forces. Cheshire was also allowed to form his own experimental section. As no military optical equipment, apart from rangefinders, and binoculars, had ever been made in Britain on a manufacturing scale, it can be imagined how important was the need for technical assistance. In June 1917, Cheshire left to become Director of the Technical Optics Department at Imperial College; his successor, S. W. Morrison, became responsible not only for providing advice on optical munitions but on ordinary glassware as well. Other scientists brought in included Professor J. W. Cobb of Leeds University to advise on furnaces and refractions and Professor Ernest Wilson of King's College, London to experiment on glass for wireless valves.[5]

Meanwhile, on account of the expansion of the artillery arm and the needs of new weapons for trench warfare, the demands for field glasses of various kinds had become so pressing that the War Office was compelled to open secret negotiations with the German Government for the supply of optical instruments through a Swiss intermediary. In return the Germans would be supplied with rubber, stocks of which had run low because of the Allied blockade. As a result some 20,000 German binoculars for infantry and artillery officers and up to 12,000 non-prismatic binoculars for NCOs were despatched to the British during August 1915. The Americans, before entering the war, provided the British Services with large numbers of binoculars, but so many faults were discovered that supplies were discontinued. The Crown Optical Company of Rochester *'later produced a better kind of instrument but was entirely dependent on British supplies of glass; the contract had to be abandoned'*.[6]

A New Process for Annealing

In Birmingham, Messrs Chance Brothers were trying both to solve the problem of limited amounts of raw materials and to increase their very limited output. They were handicapped by lack of knowledge about the properties of glass and found it difficult to estimate the correct temperatures for annealing the glass and the permissible rate of cooling during this process. Luckily for them, this problem had already been partially investigated by Frank Twyman, the managing director of Adam Hilger, a small London firm which since 1898 had made spectroscopes and other scientific instruments, and which was now engaged in making panoramic sights and other optical munitions for the armed forces.[7] In June 1915 Twyman was asked by Chance Brothers to discover (1) the proper annealing temperature of various kinds of glass and (2) the greatest permissible rate of cooling. It did not take Twyman more than a month to develop a process and suitable apparatus through which it was possible to ascertain the correct annealing temperatures of various samples of glass and the apparatus was immediately installed at the Chance works in Birmingham. It now took only about an hour to obtain the proper temperatures.

Twyman went on to develop a method by which from the annealing temperature a *'cooling curve'* could be obtained so that the best and most rapid cooling could be given to any sample of glass. This new method enabled the manufacturers to reduce the time taken in annealing so much that the whole process of filling and emptying of kilns was reduced from twenty-eight to seven days. They were thus able to increase their output threefold without having to build more kilns.

Although the production of optical glass was accelerated by the Twyman process, demands for specialised optical equipment continued to be received by the Ministry of Munitions as the techniques of warfare became more sophisticated, for example, periscopes were needed for tanks and sights for machine guns mounted in aircraft. In November 1916 the Advisory Council for Scientific and Industrial Research (formed just over a year earlier) was asked to establish a standing committee to cover research problems in connection with glass and optical instrument making. It was composed of scientists and representatives from the Royal Astronomical Society and other learned bodies, from the glass and instrument makers like Barr & Stroud, the Services and the Ministry of Munitions.[8]

It is worth noting that the committee system was already proliferating to such an extent that scientists found they were unable to spend as much time in their laboratories as they wished. The physicist, C. V. Boys, for example, when invited to join the above-mentioned committee accepted *'reluctantly and with some hesitation as I belong to so many committees already and I fear much of the time taken is wholly wasted'.*[9] Twyman, who was one of the original members, resigned after five months service on the grounds that his *'absence from the factory during hours is of too serious detriment to me to continue these pleasurable activities'.*[10] His opinion, which seems to have been shared by his fellow members, was that the numerous sub-committees of the Advisory Council had reached their limit and were hindering rather than promoting action. This particular problem was solved in 1918 by Sir Herbert Jackson, President of the Institute of Chemists, who proposed the foundation of a Research Association for Optical and Scientific Instruments. He himself became the first research director.

X-Ray Tubes

Despite these criticisms, a good deal of useful work was accomplished by the sub-committees of the Advisory Council. One of them was the Committee on X-Ray Glass Apparatus which is of interest because two of its members were to distinguish themselves in World War Two — F. A. Lindemann (later Lord Cherwell and scientific adviser to Churchill) and the spectroscopist, T. R. Merton.[11] Lindemann, who had written papers on aspects of X-ray equipment in Berlin, had applied himself to military problems since the war, one of which was a proposal for the detection of aircraft or ships by long range radiation. He was now employed on the scientific staff of the Royal Aircraft Factory. Here he had recently become celebrated for being the first pilot to obtain measurements while an aircraft was in a spin and thereby able to deduce the true nature of the motion. Less well known was his design for a regulator for obtaining a vacuum in X-ray tubes which he placed at the disposal of the committee. Merton was to make important contributions to the art of camouflage and smoke screens. The X-Ray Committee was especially concerned about the desperate shortage of valves for X-ray equipment for deep treatment in medicine being experienced by military hospitals which, by the end of 1917, were in *'a state of hand-to-mouth existence'.*[12] Earlier in the war reliance had been placed on supplies from America but when she became a belligerent, priority naturally had to go to the American forces. British Thomson-Houston was committed to manufacturing American pattern valves but, as already described, was swamped with urgent orders from the Navy and Air Force for wireless equipment.*

---

* X-rays were also used for detecting flaws in steel and for examining various articles such as unknown ammunition when it was necessary to know the internal structure before dismantling the parts.

A new factory for the production of valves by Cossor was completed in the spring of 1918 but by then the supply of American valves had been renewed *'subject to the requirements of the American Army'*[13] and even the small British glass industry had begun to show *'a vast improvement'*. As usual, British ability to improvise had saved the day but the serious deficiencies in British technology could not be overlooked. The extent and good, if somewhat cumbrous, design of German optical munitions were brought home to the British when Cheshire and a companion from the recently formed Admiralty Research Laboratory visited the great Zeiss factory at Jena several years after the war.

Allied Experiments in Nitrogen Fixation

Fortunately for the British the danger of running short of raw materials for the manufacture of high explosive never occurred as it did for the Central Powers. Ships carrying the precious cargoes of Chilean nitrate and similar imports from Scandinavia usually evaded the attentions of the U-boats. Furthermore the existence of a large urban gas industry, and numerous coke ovens with their by-products capable of producing ammonia, ensured that nitric acid, essential for the production of nitro-glycerine, dynamite and nitrotoluol, never ran short. Unlike Germany, the Allies did not have to face conflicting demands for nitrates from the farmers as well as the armaments industry as the great American wheat-belt did not need as much fertiliser as the impoverished soil of Central Germany.

Nevertheless, had the U-boat campaign been more successful, the British and the French would have been hard put to finding substitutes for nitric acid manufacture. The fact that some British scientists recognised that nitrogen fixation plants should be constructed, as in Germany, deserves a brief mention. Even before the war, one or two perceptive chemists had anticipated the possibility of the supply of nitrates from Chile being cut off in a war and had tried to interest the British chemical industry in the importance of being able to produce synthetic ammonia. But it needed the pressure of war for action to be taken. At a council meeting of the Faraday Society in March 1916, J. A. Harker, the forty-six-year-old Vice-President of the Society and chief assistant at the NPL, warned his colleagues that if the war were to continue for any length of time and if the supply of seaborne Chilean nitrates was threatened by U-boat attack, nitrogen fixation processes would have to be seriously considered. Harker was at once asked to investigate the matter.[14]

Although a certain amount of information had leaked into the scientific literature on the industrial preparation of synthetic ammonia, the process being so successfully applied by the Germans was naturally kept a closely-guarded secret. Even so, it took Harker little more than a month to collect enough data for a memorandum which he submitted to MID. The

Comptroller, Colonel Goold-Adams, quickly appreciated how necessary it was to have alternative sources of supply for raw materials for munitions. In June 1916 he formed a Nitrogen Products Committee which he chaired himself.[15] While the Department of Explosives Supply was well represented by Lord Moulton and his scientific advisers, the main responsibility for carrying out research lay with G. S. Albright, chairman of the chemical manufacturers, Albright & Wilson, who was put in charge of the processes sub-committee, and Harker who directed nitrogen research. The committee now had to discover which of the three principal processes was the most suitable for nitrogen fixation in the short time available and how expensive it would be in terms of materials, plant and electrical power.

A series of experiments on a semi-engineering scale was carried out that summer, mainly in the Ramsay laboratory of University College, London under the nitrogen expert, H. C. Greenwood with the assistance of H. A. Humphrey, an inventor and consulting engineer to the chemical firm, Brunner, Mond. Harker meanwhile visited Norway and Sweden to inspect plant operating the arc and cyanamide processes; (later on a journey to the United States he escaped with his life when his ship was torpedoed in mid-Atlantic). The results of the experiments at University College confirmed Harker's belief that, in the present emergency, the calcium cyanamide process was preferable to the Haber–Bosch process, described earlier, as so much more information was available on the former. The committee recommended to the MID that a nitrogen fixation plant should be built on these lines, but that before embarking upon the construction of a factory, a small scale commercial plant should be worked out in detail. This was approved and a small plant modelled upon the Haber–Bosch process was built at University College; it began to yield synthetic ammonia at the end of 1917.[16]

In the meantime, the U-boat campaign had intensified as a result of the German High Command's decision to allow unrestricted sinking of merchant ships in February 1917. Although there had been a critical period of losses in the spring and early summer of that year, disaster was averted by the introduction of the convoy system, improvements in the organisation of shipping, speeding-up turn-round times in ports and the selection of less vulnerable sea routes. Nevertheless, by the end of 1917, British stocks of nitrate of soda had fallen to 100,000 tons compared with 325,000 tons for the previous year and this was considered to be an uncomfortably low margin. The Ministry of Munitions, under Churchill, became convinced that a large-scale synthetic ammonia plant must be built as quickly as possible.[17]

Construction of a plant capable of producing some 60,000 tons of ammonium nitrate at that late stage of the war was an awesome prospect, especially as the cyanamide process required quantities of electric power. Harker and Humphrey warned the Ministry of Munitions that it would be impossible to start production before the end of 1918.[18] However, on

22 February 1918, the Munitions Council decided to go ahead, with the approval of the Cabinet, and built a national factory which would be now based on the Haber–Bosch process on the grounds that it could produce about five times more nitric acid than could be produced by the cyanamide process with the same amount of power.[19] A reluctant Treasury was persuaded to put up five million pounds. A site was chosen for the factory at Billingham-on-Tees, conveniently near a new electricity generating station. But it was soon realised that, as the scientists had predicted, there was no hope of completing the plant before the end of the war, and much of the engineering resources were therefore transferred to construction projects related to chemical warfare. By the Armistice, all that was visible at Billingham were a half-completed administrative building, a workshop and some contractors' huts.

After the war, occupied Germany was invaded by Allied technical missions, among them being one organised by Humphrey for the purpose of inspecting the *BASF* works at Oppau. Not surprisingly, the German staff proved to be far from cooperative, even to the extent of stealing an important part of the mission's luggage containing the written-up notes on technical processes. However, wrote Humphrey later, '*We arrived back in England with all our rough notes intact with complete flow charts*' which enabled the team to complete its report.[20] The British Government had now become well aware of the strategic importance of synthetic ammonia and had appreciated how necessary it was to avoid becoming dependent on overseas imports of nitrates. A new Nitrogen Products Committee was set up which, in due course, published a voluminous report urging that the Government should encourage the manufacture of synthetic ammonia both for military and civil purposes.[21] After a lengthy period of negotiation, the national factory at Billingham was taken over by Brunner, Mond (later Imperial Chemical Industries). A new company called Synthetic Ammonia & Nitrates was formed to run it and Humphrey was appointed the first managing director.

Both the French and the Americans were also dependent on Chilean nitrates for munition production during the war.[22] Like the British, the French decided to rely on the cyanamide process with the difference that ammonia rather than nitric acid was the end product. A number of large oxidising plants had therefore to be built for the manufacture of nitric acid, not all of which had been completed by the Armistice. Likewise, the Americans, on the advice of the British, decided to invest in cyanamide manufacture on a very large scale. Their first plant at Muscle Shoals on the Tennessee River in Alabama had a giant electric turbo-generator installed and hydro-electric development of the Tennessee River was begun so as to extend the production of ammonium nitrate for agricultural fertiliser.

During the next ten years, the Haber–Bosch process was almost universally adopted by industrial nations. By 1930, at least eighty per cent of the world's demand for nitrates was satisfied by nitrogen fixation plants. The threat of the cessation of imports of nitrates was no longer a matter of concern to governments when World War Two began. In Britain, three quarters of the supply of nitrates came from nitrogen fixation. Finally, it is worth noting that the Haber–Bosch process has never been superseded.

Conclusion

By 1918 there were few weapons or instruments of war including remedies for wounds and disease that had not been the concern of civilian scientists or technologists in or out of uniform. Contrary to what was anticipated early in the war, the value of civilian collaboration lay far less in '*inventions*' than in the extension of the boundaries of science for specific applications. '*The knowledge required*', wrote J. S. Ames of Johns Hopkins University and a member of the NRC, '*is not that of the amateur or even of the trained engineer, but definitely that of the scientific investigator, the man who by his own laboratory investigations has added to our store of knowledge*'.[1] And it is remarkable that most of the devices discussed in the previous chapters originated in the decade or so before the war — wireless, underwater acoustics, electrical transmissions for naval gunnery, poison gases, vaccination; even the tank was not original but evolved from an earth-moving tracked vehicle. In military aeronautics, however, the war stimulated great advances in power and armament of the aeroplane while, in a totally different area, notable progress was made in the possibilities offered by antiseptics and in the treatment of infectious diseases.

The Need for Practicality

It is not surprising that out of about 16,000 inventions offered to the NRC only five proved to be useful. In France out of the total of 44,976 proposals offered to the *Commission Supérieure des Inventions* possibly only 781 had any practical applications.[2] In Britain the pattern was similar. The BIR was swamped with 100,000 inventions of which perhaps thirty were likely to be of any use;[3] the MID received 47,949 of which 226 were useful;[4] the AIC received some 5,000[5] but the number adopted for use is not known: as we have seen, Horace Darwin was not optimistic at the outset. No comparable figures exist for Germany but it is unlikely that they would have told a different story. In war, time was of the essence and a premium was placed on fundamental research. The scientists who were most valuable to the war effort were those who were able to appreciate the nature of a problem rapidly and suggest a method for solving it. Such men were relatively few;

189

they included Fritz Haber who displayed a remarkable grasp of military matters and an ability to organise scientific research to meet operational schedules. In Britain the outstanding men were the Braggs, Beilby, Darwin, Hartley, Henderson, Hopkinson, Lowry. Pope, Rayleigh, Rutherford Threlfall and Thomson. In France Ferrié, Le Prieur, Langevin and Moureu should be singled out for special mention. In the States there were de Forest, Millikan and Mason. Hale, Moulton and Painlevé were the most competent scientific administrators. On another level, there were the practical technicians who were masters of some branch of engineering like Constantinesco, Dibowsky, Brock, Hazelton, Nash, Prince, Rotter, Round, Stokes, and Wimperis (they were less in evidence in Germany). Finally, there was the handful of professional service officers who appreciated how much technology could be applied to warfare like Du Cane, Hankey, Foulkes, Jackson, Thuillier and Swinton.

The Contribution made by Scientists

What was remarkable about the British scientific effort was the ability of academic scientists to adapt themselves to war research, especially the scientific departments of the 'red brick' universities such as Birmingham, Bristol, Leeds, Manchester and St Andrew's. Outstanding was Imperial College, which more than rivalled the Kaiser Wilhelm Institute in the variety of its contributions by chemists, physicists, metallurgists, mathematicians and engineers; while it might have been expected that Cambridge should offer a good quota of physicists and engineers, the new chemistry and pathological departments at Oxford fully justified their foundation. Characteristically, scientists were drawn in through the 'old boy network' of learned bodies like the Royal Society and the Institute of Chemistry; and the response came from the senior professors who were not eligible for military service and who usually received no payment for their work. The French academics were no less responsive but became part of the military machine. In America, the NRC drew on both the scientific departments of the universities and the industrial laboratories which were more highly developed than in Britain or France. In Germany, oddly enough, few scientists were recruited from the universities, in spite of the large number of eminent men who signed the patriotic manifesto at the beginning of the war. The main scientific effort seems to have revolved round the well-known figures of Fischer, Haber, Nernst and Willstaetter.

Although most scientists, apart from those serving at the Front, were not subjected to the hazards to which the fighting men were exposed, the lives of many of them were far from sheltered. In particular, chemists working with high explosives were often in danger and the bravery of at least one of them was publicly acknowledged. He was forty-year-old Andrea Angel, chief chemist at the TNT refinery at Silvertown in the East End of London and, until the war, lecturer in natural science at Brasenose College, Oxford. In January 1917, part of the plant was destroyed in an explosion. Angel, after ordering workers to disperse, helped firemen to quell the blaze until overwhelmed by the flames. He was one of the seventy killed and was posthumously awarded the Edward Medal for his efforts to save life.*

Not long before the end of the war, Bertram Hopkinson, the engineer who, as earlier described, had solved problems of underwater explosions and had then gone on to organise experimental work on aerial navigation and armament, was killed while flying a Bristol fighter from Martlesham Heath to London. Hopkinson had learned to fly at the age of forty-four in order to give himself greater authority over the officers committed to his charge and the Air Council later recognised '*the private self-abnegation with which he devoted his great abilities and scientific attainments to the public service*'.

The part played by women scientists should also not be neglected. Only one reference has been made to the part played by women — Ida Smedley Maclean, wife of Hugh Maclean the biochemist, who worked on acetone. There were several others who deserve mention such as Miss M. G. Micklethwaite of the Trench Warfare Department responsible for overseeing the filling of grenades. Abroad, Marie Curie, helped by her daughter Irène, made X-ray equipment available for the Front; similar duties were performed by the Austrian physicist, Lise Meitner, later to become celebrated for her discoveries relating to nuclear fission.

Their Relationship with the Fighting Forces

It was only to be expected that the fighting forces should resent the offering of scientific advice. For while scientists in France, Germany and the States were socially acceptable, in Britain they tended to inhabit the fringes of society; the term 'scientist' was a relatively new one. Difficulties even persisted through World War Two. What, then, were the points at issue? Firstly, status. With the exception of Haber, Fischer, some of the French scientists, and Hartley, Threlfall, and J. J. Thomson, most scientists found it difficult to speak on equal terms with senior officers and civil servants. Beilby went so far as to state that much of the work at BIR was '*rendered futile by the lack of interest of the naval authorities*'.[6] In England, especially, few civil servants had any scientific knowledge, let alone the military. Even at a late stage in the war William Pope complained that the '*process of appointing someone who knows nothing to supervise the work of someone who does seems to have been at the bottom of a great many of our misfortunes in the past*'.[7] He was referring to the Government's failure to support the

---

* As no decoration existed for heroism in this branch of war work, the decoration given to those involved in mine or quarry disasters (the Edward Medal) seemed the most appropriate.

chemical industry, but the same strictures could have equally applied to the scientists of BIR working on acoustics or the chemists working on chemical warfare, or to the Directorate of Artillery in regard to some of the weapons for trench warfare. As Thomas Merton was to remark at the end of World War Two, it was *'usually more difficult to ask the right questions than to get the right answers'.*[8]

Secondly, scientists and engineers frequently suffered from the disadvantage of rarely having enough information to enable them to judge the likely efficiency of their proposed device. Not only were scientists rarely encouraged to visit the Front, but they often could not obtain equipment with which they could carry out experiments. This applied less to German scientists who encountered a smaller amount of bureaucracy between the *'user'* and the industry making the equipment.

Thirdly, the degree of priority to be attached to a particular device was not often agreed by scientists developing it and the technical department responsible for supplying it to the *'user'*. The latter naturally demanded a product to be available as soon as possible, irrespective of future developments. But the scientists often needed to think out the problem starting from fundamental principles. Sir Oliver Lodge explained the dilemma concisely: *'Expectation of quick returns is an unfair handicap in an investigation. In making a real experiment no one can see the result . . . much of pioneer work must be groping more or less in the dark until a glimmer of steady light in some one direction . . . points the way to discovery. Official attempts to control details and to prevent overlapping are a mistake, for what one overlooks another may perceive; and it is by the combined efforts of many that the few can attain'.*[9]

Conflict Between Expediency and Long-term Research

As we have seen, military demands hardly permitted the luxury of prolonged research. Even so, a number of the scientific groups *had* to engage in fundamental research as post-war reports confirmed. For example, nearly half of the work done by Robertson's Research Department at Woolwich was pure research and included studies on the decomposition of explosives like nitrocellulose and nitroglycerine, the properties of mineral jelly, thermal analysis and so on.[10] Rotter, designer of the 106 fuse, wrote after the war that if the object of research was to provide more efficient explosives and armaments this could only be achieved *'by the elucidation and practical application of scientific principles'.*[11] The same applied to the work done at the NPL and the Royal Aircraft Factory. Other subjects touching on the frontiers of knowledge, like wireless valves and sonic equipment, also demanded the pioneer work to which Lodge referred. And there were, of course, dangers in premature employment of an equipment — the first use of the tank by the British being an outstanding example.

Achievements

Having pointed out some of the difficulties attending scientific research in the war, were there any outstanding or decisive applications? The introduction of toxic or lethal gases did not achieve the breakthrough that was intended. Likewise the tank, with the possible exception of the battle of Cambrai in November 1917, did not fulfil the expectations of its designers and promoters. But in both cases this was due less to technological failings than to failure on the part of the *'user'* to appreciate the capabilities and limitations of these new weapons. (In this respect the lack of liaison between technical officers and the scientists was a contributory factor.) In the war against the U-boat, acoustic equipment was greatly improved, but did not achieve any outstanding results. The new echo-ranging equipment required too much fundamental research to make it into a practical instrument in time, though had the war lasted a few months longer it would have been in operational use. (The first asdic was fitted into a British warship in 1922.)

The Allied success stories were to be found in the relatively simple pieces of engineering like the 106 fuse, direction finding aerials (which had such a notable impact on the gathering of naval intelligence), the Stokes mortar, the Mills bomb, the small box respirator, depth charges, the synchronised machine gun, gun and bomb sights for aircraft (several of these items were still in use in the Royal Air Force at the outset of World War Two). Outstanding initiative was shown by British chemists in the rapid development of TNT, RDB, Amatol, and improved armour-piercing explosives. Provision of substitute materials no longer available from Germany such as acetone for propellants and synthetic drugs for medical purposes were other examples of initiative. So was the research necessary for the manufacture of optical glass; and the experiments needed to keep abreast of the Germans in the processes of nitrogen fixation, while not required in the war, proved to be valuable for peacetime applications. Improvements in antiseptics and scientifically-controlled experiments to reduce disease in the field were further landmarks in the scientific waging of war.

Post-war Development

United Kingdom. All these innovations were sufficiently compelling for the Allied naval and general staffs to recognise the need to continue and even expand the number of scientists and research establishments working in peacetime. In Britain priority was given to strengthening naval scientific research. Two months before the Armistice, an interdepartmental committee was set up under Lord Curzon to consider a proposal by the Admiralty for a physical research institution for the Navy and was instrumental in founding the Admiralty Research Laboratory at Teddington referred to earlier. A more ambitious scheme was suggested by Admiral Bacon, recently Comptroller of MID, for an inter-service central research institute also situated near Teddington.[12] But interest in the proposal soon withered in the blight of post-war financial cuts. More enduring was an idea of Balfour's for a committee for the coordination of research in Government departments. It was intended to provide the coordination that had been so inadequate during the hasty expansion of scientific research during the war. Three coordinating boards were set up for chemistry, physics and engineering, similar in scope to the Radio Research Board, another recently-formed body which specialised in all aspects of radio communication. Beginning work in 1920 the new coordinating committee remained in being for nine years but then found itself unable to cope with the expanding requirements of defence research.[13]

Fundamental research in explosives was another field which had to be considered in the light of the importance it had assumed during the war. The Research Department at Woolwich had become used to investigating manufacturing processes and sources of raw materials — aspects which had never been considered before 1914. Although severely reduced in size, it now had time to tackle such pressing problems as the introduction of more stringent tests for armour-piercing shell and the necessity for a flashless propellant now that gun positions could be observed by aircraft.[14] The changing nature of war also affected the near-by Wireless Experimental Establishment which had to consider, among other things, inter-communication between tanks and the detection of hostile aircraft. In 1925, however, the acoustics branch was moved to Biggin Hill where aircraft were readily available.

But what exercised the mind of the post-war CIGS, Sir Henry Wilson, was the danger of neglecting chemical warfare which was entirely dependent on 'science and invention'.[15] He drew the attention of Churchill, then Secretary of State for War, to the fact that both the French and the Americans were investing large sums of money in chemical warfare research and in stockpiling materials. Actually, a committee of Service officers and scientists, known as the Holland Committee, had already concluded that it was a 'foregone conclusion'[16] that gas would be used in a future war and recommended that the War Office should be responsible for chemical warfare research and supply, for Porton, and for liaison with the chemical industry. At least this committee ended the separation of defensive and offensive preparations which had so bedevilled wartime gas policy and it ensured that scientific advice was at hand to deal with general policy and strategy at the highest level. The bogey of 'poison gas' especially when dropped in bombs was to haunt the minds of the general public in the inter-war years almost as much as nuclear weapons have done since 1945.

Oddly enough, the most technical arm, the Royal Air Force, though acquiring a Director of Scientific Research in the person of Wimperis five years after the appointment of a scientific adviser to the Admiralty, had to be content with the small wartime laboratory at Imperial College for research on weapons and equipment. But the NPL continued to be a centre for aerodynamic research while the testing of new aircraft, radio and navigational equipment and armament went on at Farnborough and Martlesham Heath. Perhaps inevitably, as the war receded, interest in defence declined and this was reflected in the lack of direction at Government establishments. But when the threat of war once more appeared to be imminent in the 1930s science again came to the fore. It was Wimperis, with his long experience of wartime research, who brought back science into the main stream of Air Staff thinking when he was authorised to form the Committee for the Scientific Survey of Air Defence choosing Tizard as chairman and A. V. Hill and P. M. S. Blackett, who had recently made his name as a physicist but who had served as a midshipman at the Falklands and Jutland, as members. These were the men who supervised the first British experiments in radar and persuaded the Air Staff to approve the building of a radar chain for the air defence of south-east England. Another member who later joined this committee was Lindemann; he played an important part in keeping the future wartime prime minister abreast of the latest scientific developments.[17]

An even more momentous committee which sprang from the side of the Tizard Committee was the famous 'Maud' Committee responsible for inaugurating British research on uranium in May 1940. Its chairman was G. P. Thomson, son of 'J. J.', who had been a member of the scientific team at Farnborough from 1915 onwards.[18]

Further acknowledgement of the scientific and industrial nature of war was provided by Sir Maurice Hankey, Secretary of the Cabinet and Committee of Imperial Defence, who, no doubt recalling the War Badges scheme taken advantage of by the Royal Society, suggested that steps be taken to conserve scientific manpower in the event of war. In 1938 his prodding led to the preparation of a central register containing the names of scientists and university administrators who were prepared to serve the country. Thus it was hoped to avoid the waste of talent which included men like H. G. J. Moseley, one of the most promising physicists of his generation who, ignoring the advice of friends that he should work in one of the scientific establishments, joined the Army as a signals officer and was killed at Gallipoli.[19]

France. Continuation of military scientific research in peacetime was the order of the day in France to begin with. Breton succeeded in keeping the *Sous-secretariat d'État des Inventions* alive under a new name the *Office National des Récherches Scientifiques et Industrielles et des Inventions* (similar to the British DSIR). New ideas of a strictly military nature continued to be examined by a *Comité d'Études et d'Expériences Physiques*.[20] Like the British, the French did not abandon chemical warfare research and when the Ministry of Armament was disbanded the chemical warfare department under General Ozil was transferred to the War Ministry; experimental work of an offensive and defensive nature did not cease and chemical warfare factories were kept in being so as to be capable of resuming production at short notice.[21] At the same time, the Army did not abandon its interest in keeping abreast of the latest developments in wireless. That remarkable pioneer of continuous wave sets, General Ferrié, remained in charge of the laboratory of the *Radio-télégraphie Militaire* stimulating developments in short wave radio and even encouraging the first French experiments in radio detection of aircraft until his retirement in 1928.[22]

But, like the British, French scientists soon lost interest in defence matters with no incentive to spur them on. Moreover, the political factions of the 1930s exposed the scientific community to the suspicions of the armed forces, for a number of the former were politically on the left, and even such a distinguished scientist as Paul Langevin was forbidden to continue work on submarine detection until the crisis of 1940 because of his sympathy with communism. Consequently, the gap between the scientists and their military counterparts was far wider in 1939 than it was in 1915 causing surprise to a senior British scientist who was accustomed to '*visit the service establishments and discuss fully the problems they are working on*'.[23]

The United States. Across the Atlantic, Hale's dream of an independent body which would coordinate the best scientific advice and '*utilise science to the full for military and industrial purposes*'[24] was never realised. As in Britain and France, once the war was over the scientists returned to their peacetime interests. Although the NRC was permanently established in May 1918 it did not succeed in providing the necessary link between civilian and military research. Among the reasons for its failure were the fact that the Council had to rely on funds from private sources; it had no official status and so won no support from Congress; and its committees were not sufficiently specialised to deal with specific military topics. In contrast, the National Advisory Committee for Aeronautics established by Congress in 1915 to undertake fundamental research on problems of flight was far more effective because it operated over a much more limited field. Results of its research were of direct benefit to the production of both civil and military aircraft.

It was left to the Service laboratories to initiate research. At the Naval Research Laboratory, opened in 1923, an attenuated team of civilian scientists managed to keep alive the flame of naval research lit in the energetic days of 1917 covering subjects such as radio, aircraft, torpedoes, gyroscopes, as well as defensive measures against submarines.[25] But lack of funds and of interest by the Navy and inadequate contact with the scientific world did not allow their work to prosper. One exception was the chance discovery by two members of the Laboratory in June 1930 that the radio detection of aircraft was a real possibility and this led to the beginning of

American research on radar. Eight months later independent radio experiments with a view to finding the position of aircraft were begun by the United States Signals Corps at Fort Monmouth, New Jersey. Since the latter months of 1918, the Signal Corps had taken a close interest in the development of direction finding equipment and airborne radio sets, and it now lost no time in introducing a programme of practical experiments in radar.[26]

Germany. So much for the outcome of scientific participation in the post-war years for the victors: what of the vanquished? A number of Allied technical missions visited the occupied region of the Rhineland in 1919 and confirmed the highly organised state of the German chemical industry. But very little was discovered about recent developments in either the chemical or the optical industries. Nothing prevented the factories, undamaged by war, from continuing production for peaceful purposes. Similar conditions appertained in the electrical and aeronautical industries. The German armed forces, though considerably reduced in size, could rely on the fruits of research from the industrial laboratories as they had done during the war. There was one important exception, however; it was not industry but the German Navy's signal research division that gave the German armed forces an entrée into radar in 1933, though this device was of greater value to those who had to defend themselves against German aggression. The *KWI* at Dahlem, which continued to be directed by Haber until his decision to leave Germany because of the Nazis in 1933, reverted to normal peacetime research. Haber himself took no further part in military research after 1918.[27] Though rumours of secret research and development of chemical weapons abounded in the 1920s and 30s they were never substantiated. In fact, not until Germany began to rearm in the 1930s was the future policy of chemical warfare considered.

Post-war reviews of the achievements of Allied scientists, of which there were a number, were usually studded with hubristic references to German scientific intervention in the war. But no one fully answered the question why, if German scientific education was so good and scientists so well organised, did not the latter have a greater influence on the war? This question has already been partly answered: the surprising fact that the experience of academic scientists was never fully tapped. Part of the answer also lay in the German temperament, '*the ease with which*', as Hartley wrote of the *KWI*, '*a scientist became a bureaucrat so that the worst he could say of an operation was that it was conducted in the "real professional manner"*'.[28] British war science, on the other hand, though at the start backward compared with France and the USA, at least allowed a good deal of individual initiative, both before and during the war which, as we have seen, accounted for the successful development under review.

Perhaps one of the fairest comparisons between Allied and German science was made by Sir Oliver Lodge, who as a pioneer of wireless and throughout the war Principal of Birmingham University which was heavily engaged in all kinds of military research, was as well qualified as anyone to give a judgement. In 1918 he wrote that although the Germans '*had trained and employed a host of comparatively mediocre workers', they had been preceded by a long period of disinterested research. In these higher directions our leaders in pure science have done equally well, though provided opportunities have been few'.*

Certainly the opportunities provided by the 'Great War' forced science out of the academic cloisters and private laboratories and its influence on society and the military world for better or worse was to become more and more apparent in the years ahead.

Sources

The following abbreviations are used for the location and designation of documentary sources:

Public Record Office (PRO)
ADM Admiralty
AIR Air Ministry
AVIA Ministry of Aviation
BT Board of Trade
CAB Cabinet
DEFE Ministry of Defence
DSIR Department of Scientific and Industrial Research
ED Ministry of Education
PRO Public Record Office Private Collections
T Treasury
WO War Office
Ministry of Defence (MoD)
NHL Naval Historical Library
OB Ordnance Board
Kriegsarchiv Vienna KA
Militärarchiv Freiburg-am-Breisgau MA
Churchill College Archive CC
Imperial College Archive IC
Medical Research Council Archive MRC
Royal Artillery Institution RAI
Royal Society Archive RS

Introduction
1. J. A. Fleming, Science in the war and after the war, *Nature*, *96*, pp. 150–54, 14 Oct. 1915.
2. One Hundred Years of Chemical Service: the Story of the Chemical Inspectorate, MoS, Chap 2, 1954.
3. WO 195/9187, External Ballistics Research in Great Britain; Dictionary of National Biography, Francis Bashforth, 1819–1912.
4. Maurice Crosland, Science and the Franco-Prussian War, *Social Studies of Science, 6*, 1976. Further details on Berthelot and French science will be found in Harry W. Paul, *From Knowledge to Power: The Rise of the Science Empire in France*, 1860–1939, CUP, 1985.
5. SUPP5/836, Report by Major J. H. Mansell on visit to some French experimental establishments, 1906.
6. Sir Frederick Abel, 'Smokeless Explosives', *Nature, 41*, 6 Feb. 1890.
7. W. J. Reader, *Imperial Chemical Industries. A History*, Vol. I, *The Forerunners, 1870–1920*, Oxford University Press, London, 1970, Chap 7.
8. SUPP6/645, Visit to Potsdam by R. B. and J. S. Haldane, 10 Apr. 1901.
9. Peter Alter, *Wissenschaft, Staat, Mäzene*, Publns of the German Historical Institute, London, Vol. 12, Klett-Cotta, 1982. A valuable account of British scientific policy from 1850–1920 with a comprehensive bibliography. The British Science Guild was founded by

Sir Norman Lockyer in 1905 to draw attention to the importance of science and to undertake the task of *applying scientific methods to public affairs*.
10. Paul, op cit, p. 308.
11. Ibid, p. 53.
12. Ibid, pp. 309–14.

Chapter 1. Prelude to Armageddon, 1900–14

1. O. F. G. Hogg, *The Royal Arsenal*, Vol. 2, Oxford University Press, London, 1963, Apps IV, XV and XVI.
2. DEFE15/22, R. C. Farmer, Lecture on Research Department, Woolwich to Staff College, 4 Sept. 1945.
3. SUPP5/807, Major F. L. Nathan's memo, 6 Apr. 1900.
4. Clive Trebilcock, 'War and the failure of industrial mobilisation', *War and Economic Development*, J. M. Winter (Ed.), Cambridge University Press, London, 1975.
5. SUPP5/807, op cit.
6. DEFE15/22, op cit.
7. DEFE15/22, op cit.
8. WO32/9063, Crookes's memo to Pres Ord Bd, 24 Jan. and 27 Feb. 1907.
9. WO32/9064, Trials of TNT; DEFE15/78, L. J. Redstone, History of Introduction of TNT, 31 Jul. 1918.
10. MUN5/191/1500/15, Interview with Tulloch, Chilworth Powder Co., 18 Dec. 1918.
11. WO32/9061, Introduction of new cordite MD, Report of Explosives Committee, 13 Oct. 1901.
12. ADM1/7758, Admiral Domville, Report on control of fire in action, 20 May 1904.
13. WO32/9040, Proposal to establish a Mechanical Research Department, Director of Artillery to Major General Ordnance, 9 Sept. 1905.
14. Ibid, Baker, Evolution of present type of gun, 2 June 1905.
15. R. C. Farmer, Sir Robert Robertson, *Obit Notices FRS, 6*, 1948–49, pp. 539–61.
16. T173/653, Pt 1 (Transcript) RCAI., J. B. Henderson, cross-levelling gear; description of fire director.
17. T173/88, Royal Comm on Awards to Inventors (RCAI), 1922. A collection of files relating to Pollen's claim in respect of a naval fire control system and which provides much detail on the Admiralty's attempts to develop a fire control system from 1905–12.
18. T173/204, RCAI, Rear Admiral F. C. Dreyer fire control tables; T173/205 and 613 (Transcript), Dumaresq instrument for rate of change; comparison of Admiralty system and Dreyer tables by W. E. Dalby.
19. Jon T. Sumida, 'British capital ship design and fire control in the Dreadnought era', *Jnl Mod. Hist, 51*, 1979, pp. 205–30; Jon T. Sumida (Ed.), *The Pollen Papers, 1901–16*, Navy Records Soc., Allen & Unwin, London, 1984.
20. Georg Siemens, *History of the House of Siemens*, Vols I–II, Karl Alber, Freiburg/Munich, 1957, Vol. I pp. 265 et seq.
21. F. E. Smith, Sir Henry Jackson, *RS Procs*, Vol. CXXVII, Al, 1930.
22. W. J. Baker, *A History of the Marconi Company*, Methuen, London, 1970, passim.
23. Gerald Tyne, *Saga of the Vacuum Tube*, Howard W. Sams, Indianapolis, 1970, passim.
24. WO32/8877, Appointment of Cttee to consider application of WT to the military service, 31 Jul. 1912.
25. WO32/8878-9, Final Rept of Cttee on WT, 1913.
26. Tyne, op cit, Chap. 10.
27. MoD NHL, *Technical History of the Navy*, Vol. IV, C. L. Fortescue, 'The development of continuous wave receivers during the War'; pp. 37–48.
28. AIR1/2100/207/28/1, CID, Sub-Cttee on Aerial Navigation, Dec. 1908.
29. AIR 1/725/102/1, Fmn of Advsy Cttee for Aeronautics, Apr.–May, 1909; AIR1/2100/207/208/12, Repts of Advsy Cttee for Aeronautics, 1909–18.
30. R. J. Strutt, *Life of J. W. Strutt, Third Baron Rayleigh*, Augmented Edn, Univ. of Wisconsin Press, Madison, Milwaukee and London, 1968.
31. J. L. Nayler, 'Early days of British aeronautical research', *Jnl Roy. Aero. Soc., 72*, Dec. 1968.
32. Ibid; Nayler, 'Aeronautical Research at the NPL', *A century of British aeronautics, Jnl Roy.*

Aero. Soc., 70, Jan. 1966. There is much valuable material in this number provided by pioneers of British aeronautics.

33. Nayler, 'Early days of British aeronautical research', op cit, p. 1049.
34. R. T. Glazebrook, 2nd Wilbur Wright Lecture, *Jnl Roy. Aero. Soc.*, 20 May 1914.
35. Trebilcock, op cit.

Chapter 2 Mobilising and Organising the Scientists

1. Lawrence Badash, 'British and American views of the German menace in World War I', *RS Notes and Records, 34*, 1979–80. A German 'Manifesto to the Civilised World' signed by leading scientists and physicians was issued in October 1914. Condemnation of the German so-called 'atrocities' in Belgium and the burning of the library at Louvain was expressed by British scientists in letters to *The Times*. In July 1917 a number of Oxford professors renounced their German honours.
2. Paul, op cit, pp. 320–3.
3. Morris W. Travers, *A Life of Sir William Ramsay*, Edward Arnold, London, 1956, p. 49 et seq.
4. RS 462CM B36 War Cttee, Mins of mtgs, Nov. 1914–Dec. 1916.
5. DSIR/10/127, RS War Cttee on WT, etc, Ramsay to Schuster (Secy) 22 Dec. 1914.
6. ED24/1572 and 1579. Proposals for Advsy Council for Ind. Res., June 1915 and ED24/1580, Appointment of Advsy Council for Sci. Res., May 1915.
7. G. D. Feldman, *Army, Industry and Labour in Germany, 1914–18*, Princeton, 1966, p. 45.
8. RS 463 CMB 37, War Cttee Mtd 17 June 1915.
9. Ibid, Schuster to W. G. Adams, War Badges Cttee, 26 Nov. 1915. War Service Badges were issued to men whom it was essential to retain in civilian employment for the purpose of carrying on work of national importance.
10. Letters to *The Times*, June to Jul. 1915.
11. CAB37/130/22; MUN43/263/8/26.
12. CAB/17/120A; ADM116/1430; Roy M. MacLeod and E. Kay Andrews, 'Scientific Advice in the War at Sea; 1915–17', *Jnl Contemp. Hist., 6*, 1971, pp. 3–40.
13. ADM116/1430, op cit, Sir J. J. Thomson memo, 30 Sept. 1917. Minutes of the meetings of the Central Committee and Panel of the BIR may be found in MoD NHL.
14. WO142/52, Mins Comm. Advsy and Sci. Advsy Cttee, 28 June 1915–7 June 1916, Addison to Roger, 25 June 1915.
15. MUN4/6870, Hist of the Trench Warfare Dept.
16. MUN5/43/263/8/7, Fmn of MID and transfer of functions from WO; MUN5/357/700/1 Fmn and org. of MID, June 1915–Oct. 1916.
17. MUN5/43/263/8/6, Fmn of MID; list of panel members MUN5/43/263/8/9.
18. MUN4/787, Sir Ernest Moir misc. corresp.; MUN5/43/263/8/16, Suggest fmn of inventions cttee in USA, Jan. 1916.
19. R. J. Q. Adams, *Arms and the Wizard*, Cassell, London, 1978, pp. 138–40.
20. AVIA2/2263, Burbidge Cttee Rept on Roy. Aircraft Factory, 17 Nov. 1916.
21. AIR1/731/176/6 Pts 1–3, Notes of Burbidge Cttee, Apr. 1916.
22. G. P. Bulman, 'Early Days', *Royal Aero. Soc. Centenary vol.*, op cit, p. 177.
23. Sir Roy Fedden, 'Reminiscences of Fifty Years in the Field of Aircraft Production', *Royal Aero Soc. Centenary vol.*, op cit, p. 170.
24. AIR1/824/204/5/84, Functions of Royal Aircraft Factory during War, 9 Aug. 1914.
25. CAB37/147, May 1916.
26. AVIA8/7, Fmn of Air Inventions Cttee, Jul. 1917.
27. ADM1/8493/167B, Org. of invention and research, Norman to J. T. Davis, 26 May 1917.
28. ADM116/1430; Willem Hackmann, *Seek and Strike*, Sonar, anti-submarine warfare and the Royal Navy, 1914–54, HMSO, London, 1984, Chap. II passim.
29. MUN5/43/263/8/18, Proposal for reorg of MID Admiral Sir Roger Bacon, Jan. 1918.
30. Paul Painlevé, *Les Raisons de la victoire des Alliés et ses consequences, Revue Scientifique*, 4 Jan. 1919.
31. Paul, op cit, pp. 320–25.
32. Ibid, p. 322.

33. Daniel J. Kevles, 'George Ellery Hale, the First World War, and the Advancement of Science in America', ISIS, 59, 1968, pp. 427–37; Helen Wright, Explorer of the Universe, E. P. Dutton, New York, 1960.
34. I. Bernard Cohen, 'American Physicists at War: from the First World War to 1942', Amer. Jnl Phys., 1945, pp. 333–41.
35. Kevles, The Physicists, Alfred Knopf, New York, 1978, Chap. VIII; Hackmann, op cit, Chaps II–IV.
36. L. F. Haber, The Poisonous Cloud, Clarendon Press, Oxford, 1986, pp. 128–9.
37. Kevles, The Physicists, op cit, Chap. IX.
38. ADM116/1430, Sir J. J. Thomson memo, 30 Sept. 1917, op cit.
39. V. I. Ipatieff, The Life of a Chemist, Stanford Univ. Press, OUP, 1946, Chap. XXXII.
40. MUN7/334, Italian Dept of Invention and Research, Rept by C. W. Rawes, 28 Aug. 1918.
41. Feldman, Army, Industry and Labour in Germany, op cit, p. 150.
42. Haber, The Poisonous Cloud, op cit, p. 2.
43. Feldman, 'A German Scientist between Illusion and Reality: Emil Fischer, 1909–19', Deutschland in der Weltpolitik des 19 und 20 Jahrhunderts, J. Geiss and B. J. Wendt (Eds), Dusseldorf, 1974.
44. W. Wien, Aus dem leben and Wirken eines Physikers, Ed. K. Wien, J. A. Barth, Leipzig 1930, pp. 36–7 and p. 63. For an imaginative insight into the mind of a German physicist during the war years based on original sources, see Russell McCormmach, Night Thoughts of a Classical Physicist, Penguin edn, London 1983.
45. Feldman, 'A German Scientist between Illusion and Reality', op cit, p. 355.
46. Ibid, T. Diehl to Carl Duisberg, 14 Feb. 1919.
47. J. H. Morrow (Jun), German Air Power in World War I, Univ. of Nebraska Press, Lincoln and London, 1982, p. 22.
48. D. H. Robinson, Giants in the Sky: A History of the Rigid Airship, Chap. IV.
49. A. Weinberg, 'Emil Fischers Tätigkeit während des Krieges', Die Naturwissenschaften, 46, 14 Nov. 1919, pp. 868–73.
50. K. Mendelssohn, The World of Walther Nernst. The Rise and Fall of German Science, Macmillan, London, 1973, p. 91.
51. KA, Technik im Weltkrieg, Nr 88, 16. Tätigkeitsbericht über die Erzeugung Chemische Produkte in den Jahren 1914–18. One of a series of monographs intended to form a complete history, but never finished.
52. T. von Karman, The Wind and Beyond, Little, Brown & Co., Boston, USA, 1967.

Chapter 3 'Science moves, but slowly slowly'
1. MUN7/320/1, Norman to MID; MUN5/236/8/14, Coordination with French Ministry of Inventions, 1915–16.
2. MUN7/327, Le Marquise de Chasseloup-Laubat to MID, 1917–18.
3. MUN5/386/1650/15, Major V. Lefebure, Liaison on chemical warfare with the French; Victor Lefebure, 1897–1947. Obit. Procs Chem. Soc.
4. MUN4/7038, Controller Gun Ammunition-Filling's Mission, Apr. 1918; MUN4/1752, Visit of French Mission to England, May 1918.
5. MUN4/735, British Armament Mission in Paris, 1918; misc. papers.
6. ADM1/8473/263, BIR cooperation with French Min. of Inventions.
7. ADM116/1430, BIR: Bridge to J. E. Masterman-Smith, Perm. Secy Admiralty, 14 Aug. 1916.
8. ADM1/8473/263, op cit.
9. MUN5/191/1500/13, Rept of Mission to Italy, Feb.–Mar. 1918.
10. MUN7/330, Italian Dept of Inventions and Research, op cit.
11. MUN4/1281, Supply of gas shells to Russia, Mar. 1916.
12. Tyne, op cit, Chap. 10.
13. AVIA8/3, Scientific liaison with America, 8 Jul. 1917.
14. R. A. Millikan, Autobiography, Macdonald, London 1951, Cohen, 'American Physicists at War', op cit.
15. MUN4/322, Rept on Arty Mission to USA by Major General Headlam, 16 Feb. 1919.

Chapter 4 'The Monstrous Thunder of the Guns'

1. B. H. Liddell Hart, *Thoughts on War*, Faber, London, 1944, p. 249; A. L. Tibawi, 'Chaim Weizmann's Scientific Work', *Arabic and Islamic Garland*, 1977, App. II, 'An assessment of the use made of acetone' — Note by Imp. War Mus. on expenditure of ammo.
2. DEFE15/78, L. J. Redstone Introduction of TNT, 31 Jul. 1918.
3. H. Fletcher Moulton, *The Life of Lord Moulton*, Nisbet, London, 1922, Chap. VII.
4. MUN5/144/1520/22, Memo by Moulton on production of HE, 27 Nov. 1914.
5. Frances Stephenson, *Lloyd George: A Diary*, Ed. A. J. P. Taylor, Hutchinson, London, 1971.
6. R. C. Farmer, RS Obit. Notices FRS, Sir Robert Robertson, op cit.
7. Sir Robert Robertson, 'The Research Department, Woolwich', *Nature, 105*, 5 Aug. 1920; DEFE15/92, Robertson memo on explosive research, 6 Nov. 1918.
8. MUN5/192/1500/14, R. C. Farmer, Chemical problems in the supply of explosives during the war, Feb. 1919.
9. MUN7/58, Research work on explosives at universities.
10. Sir William Pope, T. M. Lowry, *Obit. Notices FRS, 2*, 1936–38, pp. 287–93.
11. MUN4/1760, Major General Milman's evidence before Woolwich Cttee of Inquiry, Aug. 1918.
12. DEFE15/78, History of introduction of TNT, op cit.
13. T173/600, RCAI (Transcript), Craig, Robertson, Farmer, Development of TNT.
14. MUN7/26, K. B. Quinan: details of career.
15. MUN5/378/1500/1, Hist. of Explosives Supp. Dept, 14 Aug. 1914–Oct. 1917.
16. DEFE15/79, E. R. Deacon, Introduction of Amatol.
17. MUN4/1702, Reasons for Adoption of Amatol as an HE filling, 26 Sept. 1918; MUN5/194/1520/25, Moulton, Problem of providing HE for naval and military services, Apr.–May 1915.
18. W. J. Reader, *Imperial Chemical Industries*, op cit, pp. 266–347.
19. F. A. Freeth, 'Explosives in the First World War', *New Scientist* No. 402, 30 Jul. 1964. In World War Two Freeth worked on special devices for SOE.
20. DEFE15/79, op cit; MUN4/1669, Amatol 80/20-Repts on processes, 13 Aug. 1915.
21. T173/160 Pt I, RCAI, Visc Chetwynd, Improvements in filling of Amatol and HE shell; MUN5/379/1520/8, Supply of Amatol, Apr. 1915–Spring 1917, T. M. Lowry's statement, 4 Jul. 1918.
22. SUPP10/108, Lowry, Amatol papers; first Amatol conf., Guy's Hosp. 20–1 Apr. 1917.
23. Moulton, op cit.
24. T173/385, RCAI, P. J. Penney, AP lyddite shell burster.
25. ADM186/238, Progress in naval gunnery (CB902).
26. A. J. Marder, *From the Dreadnought to Scapa Flow*, Vol. III, Jutland and after, OUP, London 1966, pp. 169–75.
27. ADM186/167, Interim rept of Shell Cttee, 1917.
28. DEF15/92, op cit.
29. Marder, op cit, pp. 215–16.
30. ADM186/168, 2nd Interim Rept of Shell Cttee, 1918.
31. DEFE15/92, op cit.
32. Sir Robert Robertson, 'Some war developments of explosives', *Nature, 107*, 23 June 1921, p. 524.
33. Sir Frederick Nathan, 'The Manufacture of Acetone', *Soc. Chem. Inds., 38*, No. 14, 1919; L. F. Haber, The Chemical Industry, 1900–30, Clarendon Press, Oxford, 1971.
34. Tibawi, op cit.
35. Chaim Weizmann, *Life and Letters*, Series A Letters, Vol. V, 1907–13, OUP, London, 1974.
36. Weizmann, *Letters and Papers*, Vol. VII, Aug. 1914–Nov. 1917, Series A, OUP, London, 1975; Weizmann, *Trial and Error*, Harper Bros, London, 1949.
37. MUN7/235, Acetone: Dr Weizmann's experiments in Messrs J. W. Nicholson's distillery.
38. Ibid, MoM's representative's mtg with Graham Greene (Permanent Secretary Admiralty), 2 Aug. 1916.
39. MUN7/236, Weizmann's reports on acetone experiments.
40. MUN7/238, Acetone Reports relating to production plants. And Weizmann letters and papers VIII op cit, Weizmann to Nathan, 1 Mar. 1917.

41. MUN7/235, op cit, Weizmann to Nathan, 17 Aug. 1916.
42. ADM1/8451/65, Dr Weizmann's patents. Capt A. Desborough RN to G. B. Cobb, Contracts Dept, Admy, 9 Feb. 1916.
43. Paul, op cit, p. 167.
44. MUN5/186/1340/11/1, Rept on explosives and shell filling mission to France by Colonel Craigie, Directorate of Artillery; SUPP10/290, Rept on mission to French by Controller General, Ammo-Filling, Apr. 1918.
45. Haber, *The Chemical Industry*, op cit, pp. 84–168.
46. Mendelssohn, op cit, p. 80 et seq.
47. WO188/111, Rept on nitrogen fixing industry in Germany, 1919; MUN4/7056, Rept of British mission under Brigadier General H. Hartley appointed to visit enemy chemical factories in the occupied zone engaged in the production of munitions of war, 1–14 Feb. 1919.
48. Haber, *The Chemical Industry*, op cit, pp. 198–203.
49. SUPP10/109, Repts on synthetic ammonia. Interview with le Rossignol by Norman Wilsmore, Assistant Professor of Chemistry, Univ. Coll., London, 5–6 Jan. 1919.
50. Haber, *The Chemical Industry*, op cit, p. 355.
51. Robertson, 'Some war developments of explosives', op. cit.
52. T173/763, RCAI (Transcript), G. Rotter and Colonel L. C. Adams, 106 fuse.
53. MUN5/143/263/8/7, Fmn of MID and transfer of functions from WO. Note on prog. in adoption of French fuse.
54. T173/763, RCAI, Rotter and Adams, op cit; MUN4/2828, 106 fuse, 22 June–28 Mar. 1918.
55. MUN4/2834, German clockwork fuse. Secy Ord. Cttee to Dir. Gen. Mun. Design, 1 Sept. 1917.
56. MUN4/2834, op cit, Rept by Horace Darwin, 23 Aug. 1917.
57. MUN4/168, Relations of Gun ammo filling dept with Ord. Cttee and Chief Supt Ord. Firing. Trials with mechanical fuses, Shoeburyness.
58. MUN4/3517, op cit, WO to Dir. Muns Reqs and Stats, 21 Oct. 1918.

Chapter 5 Breaking the Deadlock
1. PRO30/57/49, Kitchener's Papers: Sir John French to Kitchener, 25 Dec. 1914.
2. MUN4/6870, History of Trench Warfare Supply Dept.
3. Ibid, Capt Leeming, History of Outside Engineers' Board.
4. MUN5/382/1600/8, Brigadier General Jackson, History of Trench Warfare Res. Dept, Aug. 1914–May 1915. 10 Dec. 1917.
5. T173/477 (Transcript), RCAI, Sir William Mills, Hand grenade.
6. T173/802 Pt II, RCAI, Vickery–Mills grenade; T173/791 Pts I–II (Transcript), Tunbridge, Vickery, Gibbons–Mills grenade.
7. T173/350, RCAI, Sir William Mills, Hand grenade.
8. *KA, Technik im Weltkrieg, Nr 7*, FZM Ceipek; M. Schwarte (Ed.) *Die Technik im Weltkriege*, Berlin 1920, Part A Land War, pp. 42–60; 'Austria's famous Skoda mortars', *Sci. Amer.*, 3 Jul. 1915.
9. Barbara W. Tuchman, *August 1914*, Constable, London, 1962, pp. 164–8.
10. Ibid, p. 190.
11. *KA. Kaiserlich and Königlich Technisches Militärkomitee*, TMK 1914/I/22-5/32, TMK 1915/I/1/22-4/3, TMK 1915/I/1/22-1/36, TMK 1915/I/1/36-1/64-12, TMK 1916/I/22-3/18.
12. MUN5/384/1611/1, Notes on Stokes gun, Jan. 1915–Mar. 1916.
13. T173/453, RCAI, Sir Wilfrid Stokes trench mortar. Enclosed is Sir W. Stokes, 'The Stokes gun and shell and their development', *Jnr Instn of Engineers, XXVIII*, Pt 10, 1918.
14. MUN5/384/1611/1, Notes on Stokes gun, op cit, D of Arty's min. 29 Apr. 1915; MUN5/196/1610/12, 'Early History of Stokes gun', Lieutenant F. A. Sutton's diary, 21 June 1915.
15. MUN5/196/1610/12, op cit.
16. T173/414, RCAI, Lieutenant R. H. G. Rimington, Stokes mortar safety catch; Major General C. H. Foulkes, *Gas! The Story of the Special Brigade*, Blackwood, Edinburgh and London, 1934, pp. 50–1; T173/701 Pt I, RCAI, W. H. Livens, Use of diphenylchloroarsine (DA) and smoke generator; Ibid Pt VII Defects of Stokes gun.
17. MUN5/384/1611/1, op cit, Entry 4 Sept. 1915.
18. OB. Procs Ord. Cttee, Min. 15,704, 3 in Trench How, 15 Sept. 1915.

19. MUN5/384/1611/1, op cit, Entry 28 Mar. 1916.
20. MUN7/455A, Proposal for Trench Mortar Cttee, 12 Dec. 1916; MUN4/6878, Trench Warfare Cttee papers.
21. Hauptmann Theune, *Flammenwerfer und Sturmtruppen*, Landes-Verlag, 1919.
22. Foulkes, op cit, pp. 49–50.
23. Ibid, pp. 111–12.
24. WO33/831, Sound Ranging, Mar. 1917.
25. John R. Innes, *Flash Spotters and Sound Rangers*, Allen & Unwin, London, 1935, Chap. 7.
26. RAI. Mil. Doc. 364, c. 1960s, Sir Lawrence Bragg, 'Sound Ranging in the 1914–18 War', pp. 1–7.
27. OB. Procs Ord Cttee, op cit, Min. 17069, Sound Ranging, 18 Nov. 1915. An apparatus was made by the Cambridge Instrument Co. and trials carried out under the direction of G. W. Walker FRS, but the apparatus was found to be too sensitive. See Min. 16,003, 30 Sept. 1915.
28. RAI, Bragg, op cit, pp. 4–5; T173/46, RCAI, W. S. Tucker, Hot Wire Microphone.
29. AVIA7/2768, Sound Ranging Notes.
30. RAI, Bragg, op cit, pp. 5–6.
31. WO195/196, Advsy Council on Sci. Res. and Tech. Dev: Gen. Phys. Cttee, June 1940, Note by A. J. Philpot, 'Sound Ranging based on experience in Palestine during the last war'.
32. Kevles, *The Physicists,* op cit, Chap. IX; Augustus Trowbridge, 'Flash Ranging', Bull. New York Pub. Lib., *43*, 1929.
33. AVIA7/2768, op cit, Bragg to Tucker, 12 Dec. 1918.
34. Lieutenant Colonel H. Hemming, 'Sir L. Bragg, Locating guns in war', *The Times*, 8 July 1971.
35. AVIA7/2768, op cit, Bragg to Tucker, 17 Jan. 1917.
36. Max Born, *Recollections of a Nobel Laureate*, Taylor & Francis, London, 1978, p. 172 et seq.
37. RAI, Bragg, op cit.
38. A. G. T. Cusins, 'Development of Army Wireless during the war', Jnl Inst. Elect. Engrs, *59*, 1920–1, pp. 763–70.
39. MUN7/320/1-4, Repts from France by Norman, Signalling from advanced front by means of earth currents, 25 Apr. 1916.
40. DSIR10/127, RS War Cttee, op cit, Lodge to Cttee, 30 Nov. 1914.
41. KA, *Technik im Weltkrieg Nr 90, Erdtelegraphie und die Verstärke lampe.*
42. Thomas Kuhn *et al.*, Sources for History of Quantum Physics, *Amer. Phil. Soc*, *68*, 1967. Interview with Richard Courant.
43. MUN7/32-/11-4, Norman reports, op cit, Norman to Secy MID, 19 Oct 1916.
44. Ibid, Norman to Goold Adams, 25 Apr. 1916.
45. Ibid, 9 June, 1916.
46. Ibid, Rept on *Parleur TM2* by Colonel Seaman, Asst Dir. Fortifications and Works, 6 Dec. 1916.
47. T173/224 and 627 (Transcript), RCAI, Major Fuller's Fullerphone.
48. KA, *Technik im Weltkrieg, Nr 90-1, Die Erdtelegraphie.*
49. RS 462 CMB 36, op cit, Rept of Physics Sub-Cttee, Apr. 1915, Experiments were made with equipment provided by the Cambridge Instrument Co.
50. WO158/132, Notes on listening to subterranean sounds. Methods and appliances instituted by French Military Telegraphy Service, June 1916.
51. Sir Robert Owen Lloyd, 'One Sapper's View of the First World War', *Roy. Engrs Jnl, 92*, June 1978, p. 81; WO106/387, Major General R. N. Harvey, Mining in France, 1914–17.
52. The literature on the development of the tank is large but from the technical point of view R. Ogorkiewicz, *Design and Development of Armoured Vehicles*, Macdonald, London, is comprehensive. For a short but accurate summary see *The Guinness Book of Tank Facts and Feats. A Record of Armoured Fighting Vehicle Achievement*, (Ed.) Kenneth Macksey, 3rd edn, Guinness Superlatives Ltd, 1980.
53. Walther Albrecht, *Gunther Burstyn, 1879–1945 und die Entwicklung der Panzerwaffe*, Biblio Verlag, Osnabrück, 1973.
54. MUN5/191/1500/15, Interview by MoM historian with Tulloch, 18 Dec. 1918; MUN5/210/1940/27, Trench Warfare Supp. Dept. Corresp. relating to historian MoM.

55. MUN4/6400, 'The evolution of the tank', Rept prepared for Tank (Awards) Cttee, 1919.
56. T173/16, RCAI, Winston Churchill's Notes on Tanks, including Hankey's paper, 28 Dec. 1914.
57. André Duvignac, *Histoire de L'Armee Motorisée*, Imprimat Nationale, Paris, 1947, pp. 283–91.
58. CAB17/120B, Development of the tank. Includes Swinton's historical memo on tanks, 19 Sept. 1916.
59. MUN5/210/1940/22, 'Admy papers on tanks. Murray Sueter's armoured cars.
60. ADM116/1339, Tanks (landships), inception and evolution, Feb. 1915–Sept. 1916.
61. CAB17/120B, op cit, Swinton to GHQ, 1 June 1915.
62. T173/475, RCAI, Sir William Tritton, Tanks; MUN7/112, Sir Albert Stern's corresp on tanks, 1917.
63. Kenneth Macksey, op cit, pp. 48–57.
64. CAB17/120B, op cit, passim.
65. B. H. Liddell Hart, *The Real War*, Faber London, 1930, p. 276.
66. Ibid, p. 265.
67. Sir Harry Ricardo, *Memories and Machines*, Constable, London, 1968, Chap. 11; Sir William Hawthorne, Sir Harry Ricardo RS Biog Memoirs, *22*, 1976.
68. MUN4/6400, Notes on tank economics by Lieutenant Colonel J. F. Fuller, 25 Jul. 1918.
69. WO158/818, Conference on tank policy, 28 Sept. 1917.
70. MUN5/210/1940/19, Tank conference, 8 Oct. 1917.
71. WO158/826, Positions and actions of Colonel Stern. Wilson's views on Moore and Stern will be found in A. Gordon Wilson, *Walter Wilson: Portrait of an Inventor*, Duckworth, London, 1986.
72. Duvignac, op cit; Macksey, op cit, French armoured development, pp. 58–9.
73. WO158/842, Sir Henry Wilson's memo on requirements for an armoured striking force for an offensive in 1918, 20 Jul, 1918.
74. A. J. Trythall, *Boney Fuller. The Intellectual General, 1878–1966*, Cassell, London, 1977, Chap. 3.
75. MUN4/5203, Tank engines, F. Shaw (Design Sect. Mob. Warfare Dept) to Comptroller MID, 8 Nov. 1918; MUN4/4979, Tanks: Stern, Rept on Liberty engine, 17 Oct. 1918.
76. MUN4/4979, op cit, Major Green's report on first Liberty engines, 2 April 1918; Mun4/5203, Tank engines, Lieutenant Colonel R. Johnson to Comptroller MID, Engines for Med. D tanks, 6 Jan. 1919.
77. MUN4/4979, op cit, Sir Percival Perry (Miss to USA) to MoM, memo on delays in Liberty engine prodn, Oct. 1918, MUN4/735, Brit. Arm. Miss., Paris, op cit, Notes on 'Tanks from the German point of view' by Stern. Contains interesting excerpts from German docs, for example, that the 'first realisation of the enormous possibilities of the new arm came after the French success in their counter-attack against the Soissons salient on 18 Oct. 1918'. For an informed newspaper comment, see 'Fabius' *Neue Freie Presse*, 15 Sept. 1918 (Trl in MUN4/4979, op cit). Compares the tank with the tremendous weight of shot of the Austro-Hungarian heavy howitzers (see p. 64) and their motor traction, thus fulfilling the need for a new weapon which would obtain a result with the minimum loss of life.
78. Macksey, op cit, German armoured development, pp. 59–60.
79. MUN5/198/166/13, Telpher Railway. Leeming's portable and collapsible aerial railway suggested by H. G. Wells and G. S. Coleman, extract from *Daily Chron.*, 19 Nov. 1917.
80. MUN5/383/1600/14, Development of Weapons used in Trench Warfare by Lieutenant Colonel O. F. Brothers, Chap. VII, 'The Newton Universal Military Tractor'; MUN4/3115, MT caterpillar tracks, Dir. of Supps and Tpt (WO) to Secy MID, 4 Jul. 1917.
81. MUN4/3467, Supply tractor, Seeley to Austen Chamberlain (War Cab.), 20 Aug. 1918; Ibid, WO to Secy MoM, 20 Sept. 1918.
82. MUN5/383/1660/14, op cit, Chap. V, Light aerial railways: MUN5/198/1660/13, Telpher rly, op cit. Aerial rlys would have been useful for transporting gas cylinders, cf Foulkes, op cit, p. 186.

Chapter 6 'The Ghastly Dew'

1. CAB45/289, Gas attacks, Western Front, corresp. with Brigadier General J. E. Edmonds (Official Historian).

2. Ulrich Trumpener, 'The road to Ypres. The beginnings of gas warfare in World War I', *Jnl Mod. Hist., 47*, 1975.

3. SUPP5/817, Sir William Ramsay and acrolein. General J. M. Grierson (Director Military Operations) quoting Decln 2 Hague Conv.; MUN5/385/1650/9, Offensive chemical warfare to formation of Chem. Advsy Cttee by J. D. Pratt.

4. Haber, *The Poisonous Cloud*, op cit, Chap. 2. This book is indispensable for the study of chemical warfare and was used extensively in the preparation of this chapter.

5. MUN5/385/1650/8, Organisation for chemical warfare research, 1914–18 by Capt J. D. Pratt, 30 Mar. 1919.

6. Haber, *The Poisonous Cloud*, op cit, pp. 23–4.

7. WO33/1072, Report on German CW organisation and Policy, 1914–18 by Harold Hartley; WO188/166, Questionnaire on German CW and anti-gas equipment by Mil. Inter-Allied Commn of Control, Armaments Sub. Sec., Question IVb deals with work of KWI from Aug. 1914 to Armistice.

8. Haber, *The Poisonous Cloud*, op cit, p. 27 et seq.

9. Otto Hahn, *My Life*, Trl by Ernst Kaiser and Eithne Wilkins, Macdonald, London, 1970, Chap. 7. A discussion of Hahn's views on the morality of using poison gas will be found in Chap. 8.

10. Charles Moureu, *La Chimie et La Guerre, Science et Avenir*, Masson et Cie, Paris, 1920, Chap. 3.

11. Haber, *The Poisonous Cloud*, op cit, p. 53.

12. MUN5/385/1650/8, Organisation for CW, op cit.

13. Foulkes, op cit, Chap. IV; WO32/5173, Employment of gas for offensive purposes: organisation of special unit.

14. M. J. Fox, *Corporals All. With the Independent Brigade RE*, 1915–19 (copy in Hartley papers CC Box Al).

15. Ernest Rudge, 'Chemists at War: In defence. The Central Laboratory in World War I', *Chemistry in Britain, 20*, Feb. 1984. Papers produced by the Cent. Lab. will be found in WO142/153.

16. Haber, *The Poisonous Cloud*, op cit, pp. 45–51.

17. CC. Hartley Papers, L. J. Barley to Hartley, 4 Jul. 1963.

18. Haber, *The Poisonous Cloud*, op cit, pp. 75–6, 101–2.

19. Ibid, pp. 67, 70, 74–5; WO33/1072, op cit, Development of protective devices.

20. Foulkes, op cit, p. 20.

21. Ibid, pp. 42–3.

22. Foulkes, op cit, Chap. V.

23. Ibid, pp. 87–8.

24. Ibid, pp. 165–73; T173/330 and 702 (Transcript), RCAI, W. H. Livens, Projector or mortar and bomb.

25. Haber, *The Poisonous Cloud*, op cit, pp. 180–2.

26. T173/702 Pt I, RCAI, Livens projector, op cit.

27. Foulkes, op cit, pp. 109–11.

28. Haber, *The Poisonous Cloud*, op cit, p. 38; CC Hartley Papers, Historical sketch of gas warfare, trench mortar gas bombs. Gas bombs ceased to play an important part in German trench warfare after the death in action at Verdun in 1916 of Major Lotus who had been an enthusiastic proponent of this weapon. Battalion commanders disliked using gas bombs.

29. Haber, *The Poisonous Cloud*, op cit, pp. 182–6.

30. Kenneth J. Franklin, *Joseph Barcroft, 1872–1947*, Blackwell Sci. Publns, Oxford, 1953, Chap. 5. Account by C. G. Douglas, physiological adviser to Foulkes; MUN4/2340, Arguments in favour of hydrocyanide.

31. T173/97, RCAI, S. J. M. Auld, Impregnating solution for phenate-hexamine gas helmets.

32. T173/314 and 683 (Transcript), RCAI, B. Lambert, Lime Permanganate granules.

33. F. H. Carr, Harrison Memorial Lecture, *Pharmaceutical Jnl and Pharmacist*, 26 Jul. 1919.

34. Sir William Pope, 'Chemistry in the National Service', *Trans Chem. Soc.*, 27 Mar. 1919.

35. Haber, *The Poisonous Cloud*, op cit, pp. 86–7, 95.

36. Ibid, p. 177.

37. WO142/58, Trench Warfare Res. Dept, Chem. Advsy Cttee, 1 May, 1916.

38. Ibid, Chem. Advsy Cttee to Thuillier, 12 June 1916.

39. Haber, *The Poisonous Cloud*, op cit, pp. 87, 164.
40. WO33/1072, Hartley Rept on German CW org., op cit, Develpt during 1914–16.
41. Ibid, Sub-sect. of the War Min. for prodn of gas.
42. MUN5/198/1650/26, Offensive and defensive measures of gas warfare, Apr. 1916; WO188/185, Levinstein claim for manufacture of mustard gas.
43. Haber, *The Poisonous Cloud*, op cit, pp. 131, 273.
44. CC. Hartley Papers, Hist. Sketch of devlpt of gas warfare by Germany, op cit, p. 8.
45. F. Guthrie, 'On some derivatives from the olefines', *Qtly Jnl Chem. Soc.,* *12*, 1860, pp. 109–20 and *13*, 1860–1, pp. 129–35; Victor Meyer, *Ueber Thiodiglykolverbindungen'*, *Berichte, 19*, 1886, pp. 3259–66; H. T. Clarke, 'On 4-Alkyl-1,4 Thiazans', *Jnl Chem. Soc, 101*, 1912, pp. 1583–90.
46. CC. Hartley Papers, Historical sketch, op cit.
47. Haber, *The Poisonous Cloud*, op cit, pp. 191–3.
48. Moureu, op cit.
49. Ibid; Haber, *The Poisonous Cloud*, op cit, p. 128.
50. Haber, *The Poisonous Cloud*, op cit, pp. 164–6.
51. WO106/332, Universities and the war, Cutting from *The Cambridge Magazine*, 'Professor Pope protests', 13 Oct. 1917.
52. MUN4/2735, Mustard gas, Lieutenant Colonel Starling to Master General Ordnance, 30 Aug. 1917.
53. WO142/71, Chem. Warfare Cttee mgts, 27 Oct, 1917–24 May 1917.
54. WO142/60, Chem. Advsy Cttee mtgs, June–Oct. 1917.
55. Ibid.
56. WO142/71, op cit, Pope's rept to Chem. Warfare Cttee, 17 Jan. 1918.
57. Sir William Pope, 'Mustard gas', *Procs Soc. Chem. Inds, 38*, No. 18, 30 Sept. 1919; A. R. Green, 'The history of mustard gas', *Procs Soc. Chem. Inds, 38*, No. 19, 15 Oct. 1919; T173/325 Pts I–V and 695 Pts I–III (Transcripts), RCAI, Herbert Levinstein, Manufacture of mustard gas.
58. MUN4/1673, Nat. Filling Factory No. 23, Chittening. General Milman's memo on visit to France, 10 Jul. 1918; Haber, *The Poisonous Cloud*, op cit, pp. 164–6.
59. Haber, *The Poisonous Cloud*, op cit, p. 189.
60. CC, Hartley Papers, Historical Sketch, op cit, Yellow Cross and Blue Cross shell.
61. WO33/1072, Rept on German CW org, op cit, Sect. K; Physical investigation of particulate clouds; Haber, *The Poisonous Cloud*, op cit, pp. 114–16, 189–90.
62. Foulkes, op cit, p. 99.
63. Haber, *The Poisonous Cloud*, op. cit, pp. 167–8.
64. Ibid, p. 191.
65. WO142/7, Chemical Warfare Service Laboratory, AEF.
66. Amos A. Fries, 'Chemical warfare', *Jnl Ind. and Engng Chem., XII*, 1920.
67. Haber, *The Poisonous Cloud*, op cit, pp. 36–9.
68. Ipatieff, op cit, Chap. XXXII.
69. Ibid. Ipatieff was being optimistic.
70. MUN4/1281, Supply of gas shell to Russia, op cit, Rept by Gardner, 24 Mar. 1916.
71. Ipatieff, Chap. XXXII, op cit.
72. Ibid; Haber, *The Poisonous Cloud*, op cit, pp. 76–7, 201.
73. Haber, *The Poisonous Cloud*, op cit, pp. 186–7.
74. MUN5/191/1500/13, Brit. Miss. to Italy, op cit.
75. WO142/193, Chemical Warfare, Italian offensive Repts.
76. Haber, *The Poisonous Cloud*, op cit, p. 243. An authoritative analysis of figures will be found in Chap. 10, 'Gas Casualties'.
77. Ibid, pp. 248–50.
78. WO/33/1072, German CW org., op cit, Conclusions.
79. H. Hartley, 'Chemical Warfare', *Brit. Assn, Repts on the State of Science*, 1919, p. 398.
80. WO188/143, Special weapon in chemical warfare, 1916–21: J. F. C. Fuller *Tank Notes, 20*, 21 Dec. 1918.
81. B. H. Liddell Hart, *Thoughts on War*, op cit, Instruments of War, No. 6 Chemical, p. 174.

Chapter 7 Failure and Success at Sea
1. T173/547 (Transcript), RCAI. A. H. Pollen, naval fire control system.
2. MoD NHL, Admy Tech. Hist. Vol. II, Fire Control in HM Ships, pp. 21–2.
3. Sumida, 'British capital ship design', op cit; Marder Vol. III, op cit, pp. 166–75.
4. Siemens, op cit.
5. T173/653 Pt II, RCAI, Henderson Fire control gear.
6. ADM1/8590/111, Prof. J. B. Henderson's inventions: note by Capt. F. C. Dreyer, 24 August 1917.
7. Ibid.
8. T173/201 and 612 (Transcript), RCAI, Lieutenant Commander J. S. Dove and H. Clausen, Gyro Director Training Gear.
9. ADM186/241, Repts on Dreyer Table, No. 1918–19.
10. R. W. Cheshire, 'The Admiralty Research Laboratory', *Jnl Roy. Nav. Sci. Serv.*, No. 19 , pp. 57–8.
11. T173/257, RCAI, Sydney Hardcastle, British Heater Torpedo.
12. Ibid.
13. T173/344 and 709 (Transcript), RCAI, H. J. Maskell, Rectifying device for torpedo gyroscope.
14. T173/6, RCAI, W. Duddell, R. T. Glazebrook and F. E. Smith, Direction finding.
15. T173/428, RCAI, H. J. Round, Direction finding.
16. T173/429, RCAI, Russell Clarke, WT inventions: statement by J. B. Henderson, 5 May 1919.
17. T173/428, RCAI, Round, op cit.
18. R. V. Jones, 'Alfred Ewing', RS *Notes and Records, 34*, No. 1, Jul. 1979.
19. Patrick Beesly, *Room 40, British Naval Intelligence, 1914–18* OUP, Oxford, paperback edn, 1984, p. 16.
20. Ibid.
21. T173/429, RCAI, Clarke, op cit.
22. H. J. Round, 'Direction and Position Finding', *Jnl Inst. Elect. Engrs, LVII*, 1920, pp. 224–57: remarks by Admiral Jackson.
23. Beesly, op cit, Chap. 10, Jutland; Marder, Vol. III, op cit, pp. 41–2.
24. T173/428, RCAI, Round, op cit.
25. Ibid.
26. Beesly, op cit, Chap. 15.
27. Tyne, op cit, Chap. 12.
28. MA/RM5/V 2 Bd, Nr 359, *Drahtlose Telephonie*, Mai 1913–Mai 1919: *Reichsmarine Amt* corresp. on wireless research and development, Alex Meissner, Development of tube transmitter by *Telefunken IRE Procs, 10*, 1922, pp. 3–22.
29. ADM1/8409/17, *Vernon*, Changes in the WT staff and equipment, Aug. 1914–Jan. 1916.
30. B. S. Gossling, 'The development of thermionic valves for naval uses', *Jnl Inst. Elect. Engrs, 58*, 1919–20, pp. 670–703.
31. ADM1/847/241, Long distance WT in submarines and destroyers, Fisher to Asst Dir. Trg, 20 Apr. 1915, passed to FSL.
32. Ibid, Churchill to Fisher, 23 Apr. 1915.
33. T173/398 and 742 (Transcript), RCAI, Poulsen WT Co, System of continuous wave telegraphy.
34. ADM1/8471/241, op cit, Capt L. Halsey RN, *Iron Duke*, to Secy Admy, 19 Oct. 1916.
35. Gossling, op cit, comments by C. L. Fortescue.
36. Hackmann, op cit, Chap. 1, 'Underwater acoustics before the first world war'.
37. Ibid, pp. 21–2.
38. Ibid, Chap. III, 'Acoustics at war: the development of the hydrophone'.
39. Ibid, Chap. III, pp. 50–6; A. B. Wood, 'From BIR to RNSS,' *Jnl Roy. Nav. Sci. Serv.*, Albert Wood Memorial, *20*, No. 4, Jul. 1965.
40. ADM212/157. Rutherford file, 1915–16, Bragg to Rutherford, 1 Nov. 1916.
41. Hackmann, op cit, pp. 55–6.
42. T173/829, RCAI, Hydrophones (General).
43. T173/357, RCAI, G. H. Nash *et al.*, 'Fish' hydrophone.
44. T173/357, RCAI, op cit, Captain Yeats Brown RN statement.

45. Hackmann, op cit, p. 62.
46. Ibid, pp. 62–3.
47. Ibid, pp. 56–60; Kevles, *The Physicists*, op. cit. Chaps VIII–X.
48. Hackmann, op cit, p. 59, Rept by Cdr H. R. Sawbridge, RN, Oct. 1918.
49. Ibid, pp. 64–71.
50. ADM189/99, Depth charge trials, 1907–19.
51. T173/786, RCAI, Thorneycroft depth charge thrower; MoD NHL, BIR Mins of Panel mtgs, 17 Apr. 1917.
52. Hackmann, op cit, p. 71.
53. Ibid, pp. 63–4.
54. MA/RM V 2Bd Nr 3250, *Unterwasser geräusempfangen 1918–19*. German underwater signalling apparatus for use in the North Sea and Adriatic for detection of Allied submarines was being developed in the latter part of the war, but the Navy was more interested in pro-submarine technology.
55. Hackmann, op cit, Chap. IV.
56. T173/161, RCAI, P. Langevin and C. Chilowsky, Underwater signalling apparatus.
57. Hackmann, op cit, pp. 77–83.
58. Ibid, pp. 83–9.
59. Ibid, p. 90; Kevles, *The Physicists*, op cit. Chap. IX.
60. ADM1/8547/340, Experiments on underwater protection of warships, 1913–17.
61. T173/607, RCAI, Commander Davies, RN Underwater bulge: statement by Sir E. Tennyson d'Eyncourt.
62. Ibid, Churchill to Rear Admiral Tudor (3rd Sea Lord), 23 Oct. 1914.
63. ADM1/8547/34, op cit, Cambridge and Portsmouth experiments.
64. MA/RM5/V 2 Bd Nr 3644, *Fernlenkboote*, Oct. 1918: details of operating wire and radio-controlled boats.
65. T173/803 PtI, RCAI, Rear Admiral E. E. Villiers Torpedo net defence, Ibid Pt II, Mine defence.
66. T173/147, RCAI, Lieutenant Commander C. D. Burney RN, Paravane.
67. ADM1/8566/240, Comments relating to a proposed book on the history of the paravane by Cope Cornford, 1919.
68. T173/251, RCAI, B. P. Haigh, Paravane.
69. ADM1/8659/273, Draft paper on Paravane and Otter to be delivered at Brit. Assn mtg, 1919 with comments by Dir. Merch. Shipping.

Chapter 8 'Tumult in the Clouds'

1. A. R. Weyl, *Fokker: the creative years*, Putnam, London, 1965. Chap. VI; AIR1/2430/305/30/1, Electric synchronising gear for German machine guns.
2. AVIA8/279, Claim for synchronising gear for firing Vickers machine gun through propellers.
3. AIR2/26/7899, Major F. Scarff, Invention relating to gun mountings and fire control gear; MUN5/212/1960/21, Synchronising gears.
4. T173/447, RCAI, Sopwith-Kauper, Synchronising gear.
5. MUN5/55, Constantinesco fire control gear, 1917; AIR2/1010, Constantinesco sonic transmission for propeller drive; T173/777 Pts I–II, RCAI, Synchronising gear group.
6. ADM1/8478/4, George Constantinesco, Jan 1917.
7. T173/610 Pts I–VII, RCAI, Captain V. Dibowsky and Major G. W. Hazelton, Speeding up rate of machine gun fire.
8. T173/261, RCAI, Major G. W. Hazelton, Speeded Vickers machine gun.
9. Ibid.
10. T173/405, RCAI, Captain Yves Le Prieur, Wind vane sight; Maurice Baring, Flying Corps Headquarters 1914–18, pp. 141–2.
11. T173/378 and 730 (Transcript), RCAI, Major G. H. Norman, Machine gun sights; *Roy. Aero. Soc. Centenary Jnl*, op cit, 'Gunsight trials at Orfordness, 1916–17, p. 247; T173/379, RCAI, Norman, Gun sight, American user; AIR2/AB275/1542, Norman, Gun sight.
12. Sir Geoffrey Taylor, 'When aeronautical science was young', *Roy. Aero Soc. Centenary Jnl*, op cit, p. 109.
13. Terence Heffernan, 'The Aeroplane and Armament Experimental Establishment', *Roy. Aero. Soc. Centenary Jnl*, op cit., p. 98.

14. T173/537 Pt II, RCAI, Wimperis Course-setting bombsight: US claim; T173/536 and 711 (Transcript), RCAI, Lieutenant Commander H. E. Wimperis Course-setting bombsight; T173/534, RCAI Wimperis Drift bombsight.
15. AIR2/38/03087/1917, Rept of trials of new CSBS fitted to large America 8665, Dec. 1917.
16. T173/537 Pt II, RCAI, Wimperis CSBS, Rept by Captain F. Short, US Ord. Dept, 28 Sept. 1919.
17. AIR1/733/178/1, WT in aircraft, Captain Fitzmaurice's rept, WT exptl stage up to Aug. 1914, Aeroplane, 1 Sept. 1920.
18. AIR1/733/183/1, Hist. of RFC wireless from outbreak of war, Major Orme and Major Prince; Sir Robert Telford, 'The growth of the avionics industry in the UK', (2nd Brabazon Memorial Lecture), Aerospace, Nov.–Dec., 1983.
19. AVIA8/510, C. E. Prince, Wireless Telegraphy, 1919–20, Prince to AIC, 22 Jul. 1920.
20. T. Vincent Smith, 'Wireless in the RAF during the war', Aeronautics, 9 Oct. 1919 (copy in AVIA8/510, Wireless in the RAF).
21. C. E. Prince, 'Wireless Telephony and Aeroplanes', Jnl Inst. Elect. Engrs, 58, 1920, pp. 377–90.
22. J. W. Stokes, Seventy years of radio tubes and valves, Vestal Press, 1982, p. 10.
23. T173/287 and 665 (Transcript), RCAI, F. Horton, Helium-filled thermionic valve.
24. Tyne, op cit, Chap. 11.
25. B. S. Gossling, 'The Development of Thermionic Valves for Naval Uses', op cit.
26. AVIA8/510, C. E. Prince, op cit.
27. AIR1/864/204/5/503, HQ, RFC, BEF Weekly reports on WT experimental work.
28. AIR1/725/97/1, WT 1917–18; AIR1/38/15/11/258, WT Cttee, 9 Mar. 1918–10 Jan. 1919.
29. AIR1/727/1543, Résumé of WT work in progress in RAF, BEF, 11 Nov. 1918.
30. AIR2/82/B4384, WT, request for trials to be carried out with tanks and aircraft: report by 8 Sqdn, RAF, 22 Jul. 1918.
31. AIR2/78/B1656, Repts on experiments in WT in the Independent Force.
32. T173/474, RCAI, J. S. E. Townsend, Portable electric wavemeter for use in WT.
33. WO106/333, Universities and the war: northern universities, Manchester School of Technology; AIR1/131/15/40/221, Periodical wireless repts from Brooklands (propeller-driven generator, 21 Jul. 1916).
34. AIR1/38/15/1/258, WT Cttee RAF, op cit.
35. AIR2/145/204452/20, Expts in development of wireless valves at Biggin Hill, Rept by Erskine Murray, 17 May 1920.
36. AIR1/727/1543, Résumé of WT work, op cit. CW ground intercommunication system.
37. AIR2/125/B11207, WT work in RAF BEF, Nov. 1918 and account of WT work by RNAS at sea.
38. T. Vincent Smith, op cit, p. 350.
39. J. G. G. Hempson, 'The aero engine up to 1914', The Newcomen Soc. Procs, 53, 1981–2; F. Nixon, 'Aircraft engine developments during the past half century', Roy. Aero. Soc. Centenary Jnl, op cit, pp. 150–3.
40. T173/560 Pts I–III (Transcript) and 113, RCAI, Captain W. O. Bentley, Rotary engine.
41. Hempson, op cit.
42. T173/282 and 699 (Transcripts), RCAI, W. R. Hodgkinson and Lieutenant Colonel H. A. Lewis, Incendiary shell; MoD OB. Procs OB for qtr ending 30 Sept. 1909, Dr Hodgkinson, New type of explosive against airships.
43. T173/252 and 645 (Transcript), RCAI, F. M. Hale, Aerial bomb.
44. T173/411, RCAI, Wing Commander F. Ranken, Dart.
45. CAB42/16, Discussions on explosive bullets by Curzon and Lloyd George, Jul. 1916; AIR2/48AB243/15, Conf. on anti-Zeppelin projectiles, 1 Sept. 1916.
46. Ibid; AIR1/2296/209/77/18, Use of RTS bullet, memo by Lord Derby, 13 Dec. 1917.
47. MUN4/429, Pomeroy bullet; AIR2/48/AB243/11, Repts on AA incendiary shells and bullets, 1916.
48. T173/135, RCAI, F. A. Brock, Incendiary bullet.
49. AIR2/719/35/8, The Buckingham incendiary bullet.
50. AIR2/48/AB243/18, Particulars and trials of Professor Threlfall's anti-aircraft shell.
51. Ibid, Brigadier General Groves to Sydenham, 9 Oct. 1916; MUN7/450, Shrapnel shell for aircraft attack (Threlfall), 13 Nov. 1916.

52. G. Hartcup, *The Achievement of the Airship*, David & Charles, Newton Abbot, 1974, p. 97.
53. MUN4/3259, Advsy Cttee AA Equipment; AVIA8/4, Procs AA Equipment Cttee, 15 Nov. 1917–27 Jan. 1918.
54. AVIA8/476, Rangefinding: Hill to Darwin re invitation to join AIC; MUN5/357/700/1, AA Exptl Sec.
55. A. V. Hill, *The Ethical Dilemma of Science*, Rockefeller Inst. Press, New York, OUP, 1966, p. 307.
56. MUN5/119/700/6/2, MID mthly repts, Nov. 1916–June 1917; MUN5/119/700/6/8, MID mthly repts, Dec. 1917–Apr. 1918.
57. T173/529, RCAI, J. E. Wilson and W. E. Dalby, AA gun director.
58. MUN5/119/700/6/8, MID mthly repts, op cit, 1 Apr. 1918.
59. Hill, op cit, pp. 266–7.
60. MUN7/309, Repts on sound locating trumpets and their cooperation with searchlights.
61. Ibid, Rept on sound locators by Major E. D. Henrici, 2 Jan. 1919.
62. MUN7/309, op cit, Rept by G. M. Moubray, 4 Apr. 1918.
63. MUN7/303, Tucker: location of aircraft by sound.
64. MUN7/308, Acoustical Research Sect. Repts.
65. MUN7/303, Tucker, op cit.
66. SUPP6/181, Ord. Bd papers, 1913: Min. 8070, Proposal by Mr Quaife for aerial torpedo, 13 Mar. 1913.
67. AIR2/36/28185/1916, Control of aircraft by wireless: comment by Samson, 14 May 1916.
68. D. W. Allen, 'A history of pilotless aircraft', *Aerospace*, Aug.–Sept. 1985, pp. 23–8.
69. R. Graham, 'Brennan — his helicopter and other inventions', *Jnl Roy. Aero. Soc.*, Feb. 1973, pp. 74–82.
70. MUN8/26, Brennan to Hutchins, Secy MID, 14 Oct. 1918.
71. MUN5/131/1000/88, Memo by Churchill to War Cab: 'Munitions Possibilities of 1918', 21 Oct. 1917.

Chapter 9 The Unseen Enemy

1. Stephen A. Pagaard, 'Disease and the British Army in S. Africa 1899–1900', *Military Affairs, 50*, No. 2, Apr. 1986, pp. 71–6. In the Crimean War about 75 per cent of the British deaths were caused by disease. In South Africa major epidemics of typhoid and dysentery occurred between Nov. 1899 and May 1900.
2. Sir Clifford Allbutt, 'Medicine in the Twentieth Century', *Greek Medicine in Rome with other Historical Essays*, Macmillan, London, 1921, pp. 541–50.
3. PRO30/57/80, Kitchener papers, op cit: Haldane to Kitchener, 2 Oct. 1914.
4. MRC/1472/I, Medical Research Cttee, History and Organisation, 1914–18.
5. RS 462 CMB 36, op cit, Chemistry Sub-Cttee mtgs, 26 Nov. and 16 Dec. 1914.
6. T173/309, RCAI, A. T. King, F. A. Mason and S. B. Schryver, B-eucaine. Includes 'Memorandum on Special Measures taken by National Health Insurance Commission (England) in relation to the Supply of Drugs and other Medical Stores during the War', May 1919.
7. WO106/341, Scottish universities and the war, St Andrews, 21 Sept. 1917; John Reach, J. C. Irvine, *Obit Notices FRS*, No. 22, Nov. 1953.
8. Reach, op cit.
9. T173/309, RCAI, A. T. King *et al.*, op cit.
10. F. W. Andrewes, 'The work of British pathology in relation to the War', *Brit. Med. Jnl*, 23 June 1917, pp. 830–1; H. D. Dakin, 'Biochemistry and War Problems', *Brit. Med. Jnl*, op cit, pp. 834–5.
11. Sir Percival Hartley, H. D. Dakin, *Obit Notices FRS, 8*, 1952–3, pp. 129–48.
12. MRC/PF2/1, General correspondence, 1914–16, Morant to Balfour, (1st Lord), 16 Sept. 1916.
13. MRC/152/Antiseptics, C. H. Browning, Bland Sutton, Inst. of Pathology, Middlesex Hosp., 1917; Andrewes, op cit, p. 831.
14. W. B. Leishman, *Roy. Soc. Obit. Notices* 1926; Leishman, 'Enteric fevers in the BEF', *Jnl RAMC, 36*, Jul. 1921.
15. Georges Dreyer, 1873–1934, *RS Obit. Notices*; Andrewes, op cit, p. 829.
16. WO158/797, Mobile bacteriological laboratories; Colonel Sir W. P. Herringham, 'Bacteriology at the Front', *Brit. Med. Jnl, 36*, Jul. 1921.

17. Major General Sir W. G. Macpherson, Hist. of the Great War, Medical Services, Gen. Hist., HMSO, London, 1921, Vol. I, Chap. IX, Enteric Fevers, Chap. XI Amoebic Dysentery, Chap. XII, Bacillary Dysentery.
18. Andrewes, op cit, pp. 829–30.
19. Dakin, op cit. p. 836.
20. Macpherson, op cit. Chap. XIII, Typhus.
21. WO32/9797, Prevention of Typhus Fever, 1941–48: historical note on epidemic typhus.
22. W. James Wilson, 'Typhus fever and the so-called Weil–Felix reaction', Brit. Med. Jnl, I, 1917.
23. J. Craigie, Arthur Felix, Biog. Memoirs FRS, 3, 1957, pp. 53–75.
24. John Boyd, Neil Hamilton Fairley, Biog. Memoirs FRS, 12, Nov. 1966, pp. 124–5.
25. KA, Technik im Weltkrieg Nr 183, Sanitäre Wacht aus der Pforte des Orients und Occidents. An account of medical work in the Austro-Hungarian Army on the Eastern Front.
26. Haber, The Poisonous Cloud, op cit, pp. 78–80, treatment of chlorine poisoning.
27. Ibid, p. 104, treatment of phosgene poisoning.
28. Ibid, pp. 253–7, treatment of mustard gas poisoning.
29. MRC/83, Trench nephritis and the WO; MRC notes on results of medical research in the war by W. M. Fletcher to C. Addison: trench nephritis; 'Nephritis', Brit. Med. Jnl, I, 4 Jan. 1919.
30. MRC/83A, Vol. I, Correspondence between Maclean and Fletcher.
31. MRC, Notes on results of medical research, op cit.
32. Andrewes, op cit, p. 829; 'Trench fever, Brit. Med. Jnl, I, 1918, p. 91 and Brit. Med. Jnl, I, 4 Jan. 1919.
33. Macpherson, op cit, Vol 1, Chap VIII, Prevention of Malaria.
34. WO32/5112, Question of prophylactic issue of quinine to troops during next malarial season (1917), Salonika, Ross to Keogh. 29 Feb. 1916.
35. WO32/5112, op cit, 12 Oct. 1916.
36. C. M. Wenyon, 'The incidence and aetiology of malaria in Macedonia', Jnl RAMC, 37, Jul.–Dec. 1921.
37. Andrewes, op cit. p. 832; MRC Note, op cit.
38. Boyd, Neil Hamilton Fairley, op cit, pp. 125, 133–4.
39. Douglas H. Robinson, The Dangerous Sky. A History of Aviation Medicine, G. T. Foulis, London, 1973, p. 75 et seq.
40. MRC Notes, op cit, Physiological problems of flying.
41. Macpherson, op cit, Diseases of War Vol. II, p. 231 et seq.
42. WO106/336, Universities and the war, Bristol, 1914–17.

Chapter 10 Aspects of Wartime Industrial Research

1. Ian Varcoe, 'Scientists, Government and Organised Research in Great Britain, 1914–16; the Early History of the DSIR,' Minerva. 8, 1970, pp. 192–216.
2. BT66/6/46, Record and history of the Optical Munitions, Glassware and Potash Prodn Dept; R. MacLeod and E. K. Andrews, 'Government and the Optical Industry in Britain, 1914–18' in War and Economic Development, (Ed.) J. M. Winter, CUP, 1975.
3. BT66/6/46, op cit, Pre-war conditions prevailing in optical trade.
4. RS 462CMB 36, op cit. The request was referred to Haldane's War Trades Cttee recently formed.
5. BT66/7/63, Record of work of Scientific, Technical and Research Branch, Optical Muns and Glassware Supp. Dept.
6. BT66/6/46, op cit, Negotiations with Germany and America for optical instruments, Aug. 1915.
7. A. C. Menzies, Frank Twyman, Biog. Memoirs FRS, 5, 1959, pp. 269–75.
8. DSIR3/315, Standing Cttees, Glass and Optical Instruments.
9. Ibid, Mins of Advsy Council, 3 Nov. 1916.
10. Ibid. Twyman's letter of resignation, 10 Mar. 1917.
11. DSIR3/387, Standing Cttee on Glassware and Optical Instruments Cttee on X-ray glass apparatus, 1917–18.
12. Ibid, 5th mtg, 18 Dec. 1917: statement by Colonel Reid.
13. Ibid, 20 Feb. 1918: statement by Colonel Darrell (USA).
14. MUN4/6352, Rept of Nitrogen Prods Cttee and corresp: Sir Robert Hadfield to Lord Inverforth, 17 Mar. 1921.

15. MUN4/6398. Fixation of atmospheric nitrogen, 1919–20; included account of original Nitrogen Prods Cttee.
16. MUN5/119/700/6/8, NPC Rept and Note, 27 Oct. 1917; MUN5/119/6/2, Exptl work at King's Coll. and Univ. Coll., London.
17. MUN5/131/1000/88, Memoranda submitted to War Cab. by Churchill Jan. 1918.
18. IC, H. A. Humphries papers F1, relating to MoM; MUN5/192/1510/15, Fixation of atmospheric nitrogen, Feb.–Mar. 1918.
19. MUN7/10, Negotiations with Mr Boor re Carlson Cyanamide Process; Muns Council Cttee No. 39, 22 Feb. 1918; Haber *The Chemical Industry*, op cit, p. 204 et seq.
20. IC, H. A. Humphries papers, op cit, Account of visit to Oppau works, May 1919.
21. SUPP10/299, Final Rept NPC, 1920.
22. MUN4/6352, op cit, 'The Nitrogen Problem at Home and Abroad in its Relation to National Defence' by J. A. Harker, pp. 5–6.

Conclusion

1. J. S. Ames, 'The trained men of science in the war', *Science, XLVIII*, 25 Oct. 1918.
2. Paul, op cit, p. 323.
3. Sir J. J. Thomson, *Recollections and Reflections*, Bell, London, 1936, p. 208.
4. Michael Pattison, 'Scientists, Inventors and the Military in Britain, 1915–19: The Munitions Inventions Department, *Social Studies of Science, 13*, No. 4, Nov. 1983, p. 538.
5. Ibid.
6. CAB27/64, War Cab. Res. Cttee, 6 Mar. 1919.
7. W. J. Pope, Speech at teachers' mtg, Regent St Polytechnic, *Manchester Guardian*, Oct. 1917.
8. Sir Thomas Merton, 'Science and Invention', *New Scientist*, 11 Feb. 1965.
9. WO106/336, Universities and the war, op cit, Sir Oliver Lodge, Principal Univ. of Birmingham to the Council, 17 Session, 1916–17, 4 Feb. 1918.
10. DEFE15/92, op cit, Sir Robert Robertson's memo on Explosives Research.
11. DEFE15/42, Duckham Cttee: Notes on org. of research for services; imperfections of present system by G. Rotter, 22 Mar. 1926.
12. MUN4/6404, Research for the Navy and Air Force, Proposal for National Research Inst. 1919.
13. CAB27/94, Rept, Procs and Memos of Cab. Cttee on Coord. of Sci. Res. in Govt Depts, 1919–21.
14. MUN7/244, Dr Silberrad's flashless propellant. (Silberrad had worked on this problem throughout the war and submitted results to Lord Moulton in Feb. 1918.)
15. WO32/5618, Gas Warfare, Memo by Field Marshal Sir H. Wilson for Churchill (Secy of State for War), 3 May 1920.
16. Haber, *The Poisonous Cloud*, op cit, p. 293.
17. Ronald W. Clark, *Tizard*, Methuen, London, Chap. 6.
18. Margaret Gowing, *Britain and Atomic Energy, 1939–45*, Macmillan, London, 1964, Chap. 2.
19. J. L. Heilbron, *H. G. J. Moseley: Life and Letters of an English Physicist*, Univ. of California Press, 1974. It is possible that Moseley's death, which was widely reported in the press, may have helped leading scientists to convince the public that '*scientific brains, being a national and even a military asset, should be conserved in time of war*'. It is worth noting that thirty-five Fellows of the Royal Society and fifty-five members of the Royal Institution were killed.
20. Paul, op cit, pp. 323–39.
21. MUN4/735, Brit. Armament Miss in Paris, op cit, Lefebure to Hartley, 3 Dec. 1918.
22. S. S. Swords, *Technical History of the Beginnings of Radar*, Peter Peregrinus, London, 1986, p. 122.
23. Spencer R. Weart, *Scientists in Power*, Harvard Univ. Press, 1979, J. D. Cockcroft to F. Joliot, 18 Feb. 1940.
24. Kevles, 'George Ellery Hale', op cit, Draft of order for NRC, 27 Mar. 1918.
25. Louis A. Gebhard, *Evolution of Naval Radio-Electronics and Contributions of the Naval Research Laboratory*, NRL Washington DC, 1979.
26. Swords, op cit, pp. 101–2, 112–13.

27. Haber, *The Poisonous Cloud*, op cit, p. 306. Haber did, however, continue to take an interest in anti-gas precautions.
28. WO33/1072, op cit, Hartley's conclusion to report on German CW organisation.
29. WO106/336, Universities and the War, op cit, Sir Oliver Lodge's statement to Council, op cit.

Select Bibliography

Addison, C: *Four and a Half Years. A Personal Diary from June 1914 to January 1919.* London, 1934.

Aitkin, H. G. J.: *The Continuous Wave: Technology of American Radio 1900–32,* Princeton University Press, New Jersey 1985.

Alter, P.: *Wissenschaft, Staat, Mäzene. Anfänge moderner Wissenschaftspolitik in Grossbritannien 1850–1920,* Klett-Cotta, Stuttgart, 1982.

Ashworth, T.: *Trench Warfare 1914–18. The Live and Let Live System,* Macmillan, London, 1980.

Baker, W. J.: *History of the Marconi Company,* Methuen, London, 1970.

Barnett, C.: *The Collapse of British Power,* Alan Sutton, Gloucester (paperback edn), 1984.

Beesly, P.: *Room 40. British Naval Intelligence 1914–18,* Oxford University Press, London (paperback edn), 1984.

Birkenhead, Earl of: *The Prof in Two Worlds. The Official Life of Prof F. A. Lindemann, Viscount Cherwell,* Collins, London, 1961.

Born, M: *My Life. Recollections of a Nobel Laureate,* Taylor & Francis, London, 1976.

Caroe, G. M.: *W. H. Bragg 1862–1942. Man and Scientist,* Cambridge University Press, London, 1978.

Clark, R.: *Tizard,* Methuen, London, 1965.

Crowther, J. G.: *Fifty Years with Science,* Barrie & Jenkins, London, 1970.

Dreyer, Sir F. C.: *The Sea Heritage. A Study of Maritime Warfare,* Museum Press, London, 1955.

Duvignac, A.: *Histoire de L'Armée Motorisée,* Imprimerie Nationale, Paris, 1947.

Feldman, G. D.: *Army, Industry and Labour in Germany 1914–18,* Princeton University Press, New Jersey, 1966.

Feldman, G. D.: 'A German Scientist between Illusion and Reality: Emil Fischer 1909–19', Geiss I. & Wendt, B. J. (Eds): *Deutschland in der Weltpolitik des 19 & 20 Jahrhunderts,* 2nd edn, Düsseldorf, 1974.

Foulkes, C. H.: *Gas! The Story of the Special Brigade,* Blackwood, Edinburgh, 1934.

Franklin, K. J.: *Joseph Barcroft 1872–1947,* Blackwell Scientific Publications, Oxford, 1953.

Fuller, J. F. C.: 'Science and War', *The Nineteenth Century, 103,* 1928.

Glazebrook, Sir R.: *Early Days at the National Physical Laboratory Teddington,* 1933.

Gusewelle, J. K.: *The Board of Invention and Research. A Case Study in the Relations between Academic Science and the Royal Navy in the First World War* (unpublished PhD thesis), University of California Press, Irvine, 1971.

Haber, F.: *Fünf Vorträger,* Springer, Berlin, 1924.

Haber, F.: *Aus Leben und Beruf,* Springer, Berlin, 1927.

Haber, L. F.: *The Chemical Industry 1900–30. International Growth and Technological Change,* Oxford University Press, London, 1971.

Haber, L. F.: *The Poisonous Cloud. Chemical Warfare in the First World War,* Clarendon Press, Oxford, 1986.

Hackmann, W.: *Seek and Strike: Sonar, anti-submarine warfare and the Royal Navy 1914–54,* HMSO, London, 1984.

Hahn, D.: *Begrunder des Atomzeitalters,* List Verlag München 1979.

Hahn, O.: *My Life*, (Trl) Ernst Kaiser and Eithne Wilkins, Macdonald, London, 1970.
Hanslian, R.: (Ed.) *Der Chemische Krieg*, (3rd edn.), Berlin, 1937.
Hartley, H.: 'A General Comparison of British and German Methods of Gas Warfare', *Journal of Royal Artillery*, 46, No. 11, 1920.
Heilbron, J. L.: *H. G. J. Moseley. Life and Letters of an English Physicist*, University of California Press, 1974.
Innes, J. R.: *Flash Spotters and Sound Rangers*, Allen & Unwin, London, 1935.
Ipatieff, V. N.: *The Life of a Chemist*, Stanford University Press, 1946.
Joll, J.: 'Walther Rathenau: Prophet without a Cause' *Three Intellectuals in Politics*, New York, 1960.
Kessler, I. H.: *Walther Rathenau: His Life and Work*, London, 1929.
Kevles, D. J.: 'George Ellery Hale, the First World War, and the Advancement of Science in America', *ISIS, 59*, 1968.
Kevles, D. J.: *The Physicists. The History of a Scientific Community in Modern America*, Knopf, New York, 1978.
Lanchester, F. W.: *Aircraft in Warfare*, London, 1916.
Liddell Hart, B. H.: *The Real War*, Faber, London, 1930.
Liddell Hart, B. H.: *Thoughts on War*, Faber, London, 1944.
Liddle, P. H.: (Ed.) *Home Fires and Foreign Fields. British Social and Military Experience in the First World War*, Brassey's, London, 1985. See Chap. 7, 'Scientists, Government and Invention: The Experience of the Invention Boards 1915–18' by Pattison, M.
MacLeod, R. M. and Andrews, E. K.: 'The Origins of the DSIR. Reflections on Ideas and Men, 1915–16, *Public Adminstration, 48*, 1970.
MacLeod, R. M. and Andrews, E. K.: 'Scientific Advice in the War at Sea', *Journal of Contemporary History, 6*, 1971.
Macpherson, Sir W. G. *et al.*: *The Medical Service: General History of The Great War 1914–18*, HMSO, London, 1921; *Diseases of War*, Vol. 2, HMSO, London, 1923.
Marder, A. J.: *From the Dreadnought to Scapa Flow*, Vol. III: *Jutland and After, May 1916–December 1916*, Oxford University Press, London, 1966.
Meadows, A. J.: *Science and Controversy. A Biography of Sir Norman Lockyer*, Cambridge, Mass. 1972.
Millikan, R. A.: *Autobiography*, Prentice Hall, New York, 1950.
Ministry of Munitions History (12 vols), limited edition, London, 1920–21.
Moseley, R.: 'The Origins and Early Years of the NPL. A Chapter in the pre-history of British Science Policy', *Minerva, 16*, 1978.
Moulton, Lord: *Science and War*, Rede Lecture, Cambridge University Press, 1919.
Moulton, H. F.: *The Life of Lord Moulton*, Nisbet, London, 1922.
Moureu, C.: *La Chimie et la Guerre: Science et L'Avenir*, Masson, Paris, 1924.
Ogorkiewicz, R. M.: *Design and Development of Fighting Vehicles*, Macdonald, London, 1968: Doubleday, New York, 1968.
Ogorkiewicz, R. M.: *Armoured Forces*, Arms & Armour Press, London, 1970.
Osler, Sir W.: *Science and War*, Oxford University Press, 1915.
Pattison, M.: *The Munition Inventions Department. A Case Study in the State Management of Military Science 1915–19* (Unpublished PhD thesis, Teesside Polytechnic), 1981.
Pattison, M.: 'Scientists, Inventors and the Military in Britain 1915–19: The Munitions Inventions Department', *Social Studies of Science, 13* No. 4, 1983.
Paul, H. W.: *From Knowledge to Power. The Rise of the Science Empire in France 1860–1939*, Cambridge University Press, 1985.
Ratsey, O. L.: Fifty Years of Admiralty Surface Weapons Establishment History, 1896–1946, Naval Historical Library, Ministry of Defence.
Reader, W. J.: *Imperial Chemical Industries. A History* (2 vols), Oxford University Press, London, 1970 and 1975.
Ricardo, Sir H.: *Memories and Machines*, Constable, London, 1968.
Robinson, D. H.: *Giants in the Sky. A History of the Rigid Airship*, G. T. Foulis, Henley-on-Thames. Oxon, 1973.
Robinson, D. H.: *The Dangerous Sky. A History of Aviation Medicine*, G. T. Foulis, Henley-on-Thames, Oxon, 1973.
Rose, H. and S.: *Science and Society*, Pergamon Press, London, 1970.

Schwarte, M. (Ed.): *Technik im Weltkriege. Unter Mitterwerkung von 45 technischen fachwissenschaftlichen Mitarbeiten*, E. S. Mittler, Berlin, 1920.

Scott, L. N.: *The Naval Consulting Board of the US Navy*, Government Printing Office, Washington, 1920.

Scott, Sir, P. M.: *Fifty Years in the Royal Navy*, Murray, London, 1919.

Sommer, D.: *Haldane of Cloane, Life and Times 1856–1928*, Allen & Unwin, 1960.

Strutt, R. J.: *The Life of John William Strutt, Third Baron Rayleigh*, London, 1924; augmented edn, University of Wisconsin Press, Madison, Milwaukee and London, 1966.

Sumida, J. T. (Ed.): *The Pollen Papers*. The privately circulated printed works of Arthur H. Pollen, Allen & Unwin for the Navy Records Society, 1984.

Thomson, Sir J. J.: *Recollections and Reflections*, Bell, London, 1936.

Terraine, J.: *The Smoke and the Fire*, Sidgwick & Jackson, London, 1981.

Terraine, J.: *White Heat. The New Warfare 1914–18*, Sidgwick & Jackson, London, 1982.

Travers, M. W.: *A Life of Sir William Ramsay*, Arnold, London, 1956.

Trebilcock, R. C.: 'A Special Relationship: Government, Rearmament and the Cordite Firms', *Economic History Review*, 2nd series *XIX* 1966.

Trythall, A. J.: *Boney Fuller. The Intellectual General 1878–1966*, Cassell, London, 1977.

Tyne, G. F. J.: *Saga of the Vacuum Tube*, Howard W. Sams, Indianopolis, 1977.

Whittemore, G. F.: 'World War I, Poison Gas Research and the Ideals of American Chemists', *Social Studies of Science, 5* No. 2, 1975.

Wiener, M. J.: *English Culture and the Decline of the Industrial Spirit 1850–1980*, Cambridge University Press, 1981.

Wilson, A. G.: *Walter Wilson: Portrait of an Inventor*, Duckworth, London, 1986.

Wilson, D.: *Rutherford: Simple Genius*, Hodder & Stoughton, London, 1984.

Winter, J. M. (Ed.): *War and Economic Development. Essays in Memory of David Joslin*, Cambridge University Press, London, 1975. See MacLeod, R. M. and Andrews, E. K. 'Government and the Optical Industry in Britain 1914–18' and Trebilcock, R. C. 'War and the Failure of Industrial Mobilisation, 1899 and 1914'.

Wright, H.: *Explorer of the Universe. A Biography of George E. Hale*, Dutton, New York, 1966.

Yerkes, R. M.: *The New World of Science: Its Development during the War*, Scribners, New York, 1920.

Index

The names of persons not directly related to scientific or engineering developments, as well as merely casual references, are not included in the Index.

Abbé and Schott, 181
Abel, Sir Frederick, 2, 3, 6, 8
Adair, J. F., 129
Adams, Lieut Col L. C., 57
Addison, Christopher, 25, 26, 66, 167
Admiralty, Board of Invention and
   Research, 24, 29, 118, 130, 136
   inventions submitted, 189
   Department of Experiment and Research,
      29
   Experimental Station, Hawkcraig, 129,
      130
   Experimental Station, Harwich, 131
   Landships Committee, 84
   Room 40, 7, 120, 125–7
Advisory Committee for Aeronautics, 16–18,
   19
Advisory Council for Scientific and Industrial
   Research, 22, 183
   Committee on X-Ray Glass, 183–4
Aerial ropeways, 92–3
Air Board (*later* Air Ministry), 28, 159–60
Air Ministry, Laboratory, 195
   Committee for the Scientific Survey of Air
      Defence, 195
Aircraft:
   aeroplanes: British, Martynside, 155;
      RE1, 19; SE5, 157; Sopwith Camel,
      156–7; Sopwith Snipe, 157; Sopwith 1½
      Strutter, 146; German, *Gotha*, 159, 160,
      178–9; French, Nieuport, 159
   engines: Bentley rotary, 156–7, 159, 165;
      German rotary, 157; Clerget rotary, 156;
      Green, 156; Hispano-Suiza rotary, 157;
      Le Rhone, rotary, 156
   weapons: bomb sights, 150–2; darts, 150–1;
      explosive bullets, 157–60; explosive
      darts, 158; machine gun sights, 148–50;
      synchronised machine guns, 145–8
   oxygen apparatus: British, 179; German,
      178–9
   pilotless aircraft, 164–5
   helicopter, 165
Airships:
   British, *Mayfly*, 19; German, Zeppelins,
      157–60

Photographic Reconnaissance, 178–9
Air Inventions Committee, 28
   submissions, 181, 189
American Civil War, 2
American Submarine Signal Co., 129
Ames, Prof J. S., 189
Andrade, E. N. da C., 73
Anaesthetics, 167–8
Anderson, John, 167
Angel, A., 190–1
Anti-aircraft weapons, 157–61
   predictors, 162
Arco, Count G. von, 15
Armstrong-Whitworth Co., 4
Arras, battle of, 58
Asdic, 139
   first used, 193
Auld, S. J. M., 103
Austria-Hungary:
   Academy of Sciences, Vienna, 36
   Aviation Arsenal, Fischamend, 37
   Technische Hochschule, Vienna, 36
Aviation medicine, 179

Bacon, Capt (*later* Adm Sir Reginald) RN,
   11–12, 17, 29, 83, 164, 165, 193–4
Baekland, L. H., 32
Baily, F. G., 77
Bairstow, L., 18, 19, 28
Balfour, Lord, 24, 40
   Declaration, 54
Baker, Sir B., 9
Baker, Prof H. B., 25, 95, 97
Balloon Factory *see* Royal Aircraft Factory
Barcroft, J., 102, 115
Barley, L. J., 98, 106
Bashforth, Rev F., 2
Battenberg, Adm Prince Louis of, RN, 141
Bauer, Maj M. (German Army), 34, 95, 96
Beatty, Adm Sir David, RN, 120, 126
Beilby, G. T. (*later* Sir George), 24, 97
   quoted, 191
Bentley, W., 156
Bingham, Maj Gen F. R. (*later* Sir Francis),
   65–6
Birmingham University, 104, 131, 190, 198

219

Blackett, P. M. S., 195
Blériot, L., 18
Borel, E., 30
Born, M., 75
Bosch, C., 55
Boswell, P. G. H., 182
Bourdillon, R., 151
Boyle, R. W., 138–9
Boys, C. V. (*later* Sir Vernon), 108, 118, 184
Brackenbury, Maj Gen Sir Henry, 6–7
Bragg, W. H. (*later* Sir William), 24, 71, 104, 130–1, 190
Bragg, W. L. (*later* Sir Lawrence), 71–5, 190
Braun, K., 127–8
Brennan, M., 165
Breton, J. L., 31, 195
Bridge, Cdr C. RN, 39, 40
Bristol University, 179, 190
British Expeditionary Force, GHQ, Experiments Committee, 26, 28, 71, 84; requests for grenades, 62; mortars, 66; travelling ballistic party, 162; report on *Parleur TM2*, 77
British Science Guild, 4
British Thomson Houston Co., 128, 155, 184
Brock, C. J. & Co., 62
Brock, F. A., 159, 190
Broglie, L. de, 40
Broglie, M. de, 15, 40, 138
Browning, C. H., 170
Bryan, G. H., 18
Bryant & May, 62
Buckingham, J. F., 159
Bull, L., 69, 71
Bumstead, H. A., 43
Burbidge, Sir Richard, 27
Burney, Cdr C. D., RNVR, 143–4
Burstyn, G., 81
Busk, E. T., 19

Callendar, Prof H., 164
Cambrai, battle of, 74, 89, 193
Cambridge Scientific Instrument Co., 17, 60
Cambridge University, 190
Cavendish Laboratory, 60, 128, 137
Caporetto, battle of, 36, 40, 113, 115
Centralstelle für Wissenschaftliche Technische Untersuchen, 3
Capper, Maj Gen Sir John, 87–8
Carpenter, Dr, 47
Carrell, A., 169
Chance Bros, Messrs, 182–3
Chasse-Laubat, Marquis de, 39
Chemical industry
British: Albright & Wilson, 186; Brunner, Mond, 48, 97, 186–7; Castner-Kellner Alkali, 24, 97, 99; Chance & Hunt, 109;

Imperial Chemical Industries, 187; Levinstein, Messrs, 109, 170; United Alkali Co, 97
French: dyeworks, 55, 97, 108; cyanamide, 187
German: 4; *Badische Anilin und Soda Fabrik*, 55–6, 105, 112, 187; *Farbenfabriken Bayer A.G.*, 34, 95, 96, 106; Haber-Bosch process, 55–6, 186–8; *Interessengemeinschaft Farbenindustrie*, 105
USA: Muscle Shoals, 187
Chemical warfare:
Austro-Hungarian, use of, 36, 113
British, use of, 95, 97–8, 99–101, 104, 108–9; Chemical Warfare Committee, 108–9; Central Laboratory, 98; Holland Committee, 194; Special Brigade, 106, 110; Special Companies, 97–9, 100, 106
French, use of, 96–7, 102, 108; *Secretariat Interallié*, 39; *Direction du Matériel Chimique de Guerre*, 96; *Compagnies Z*, 97
German, use of, 95–6, 102, 104–7, 110–11; 112; No. 35 Pioneer Regiment, 96
Italy, use of, 113–14
Russia, 33; War Chemical Committee, 112; Casualties, 114–15; treatment of, 174–5; Value of, 115–17
USA, Bureau of Mines, 33, 111; Chemical Warfare Service, 111
see also gases, war, masks, weapons
Cheshire, F., 182, 185
Chetwynd, Visc., 48–9
Chilowsky, C., 136–7
Churchill, Winston, 24, 29, 53, 66, 83, 86, 108, 124, 128, 139, 141, 165, 186
Clarke, R., 15, 124–6
Clausen, Lieut H., RN, 121
Clerk, D. (*later* Sir Dugald), 28
Cobb, Prof J. W., 182
Cocksedge, H. E., 48
Columbia University, 139
Compagnie Belge des Munitions Militaires, 62
Conant, J. B., 111
Constantinesco, C., 147, 190
Coronel, battle of, 50, 118
Cossors, 185
Cotton, A., 84
Courant, R., 77
Craig, Col R. A., 49
Crampton, Col R. E., 84
Creusot, Le, 4
Crimean war, 2, 6
Crookes, Sir William, 7, 8, 9
Crossley, A. W., 97, 106
Cummins, Col S. L., 106

Curie, Irène, 191; Marie, 191; Pierre, 137, 140
Curzon, Lord, 28, 40, 159, 193
Cushny, Prof A. R., 108

Dakin, H. D., 169–70
Dalby, W. E., 162
Dale, H., 172–3
Darwin, C. G., 73
Darwin, H. (later Sir Horace), 17, 26, 28, 42, 43, 60, 161, 165, 190
Davy, Sir Humphrey, 1
Deacon, E. R., 48
Department of Scientific and Industrial Research, 22, 195
d'Eyncourt, E. Tennyson, 83–4, 85, 87, 141
de Forest, Lee, 16, 42, 127, 190
Depth charges, 135
  Throwers, 135
Dewandre, A., 62
Dewar, Sir James, 3, 178
Dibowsky, V., 146–7, 148, 190
Diseases: bilharziasis, 177–8; dysentery, 172–3; enteric fever, 171–2; malaria, 176–7; trench fever, 176; trench nephritis, 175–6; typhoid, 170–1; typhus, 173–4
Dogger Bank action, 118, 120
Donaldson, Sir Frederick, 27
Donnan, F. G., 108
Dove, Lieut J. S., RN, 121
Dowding, Major H. C. T., 152
Dreyer, Cdr (later Captain) F. C., RN, 11–12, 50, 118–19, 121
Dreyer, Col J. T., 57, 67
Dreyer, Prof G., 171, 179
Drugs, 167–8
Du Cane, Maj Gen J. P., 26, 67, 190
Duddell, W., 123
Duisberg, C., 34, 95
Dumaresq, Lieut J. S., RN, 11
Durand, W. F., 43

Eastern front: gas attacks, 96, 112
Eccles, W. H., 138–9, 155
Echo ranging, 136–140
Edgewood Arsenal, 111
Edison, Thomas, 31
Ellis, Sir Charles, 39
Elles, Brig Gen H. J., 88
Esher, Lord, 16, 166
Estienne, Col J. E., 82–3, 89, 91
Ewing, Sir Alfred, 7, 22, 124

Fairley, N. H., 173, 178
Falkenhayn, Gen E. von, 96

Falkland Isles, battle of, 50, 118
Faraday, Michael, 2
Farman, H., 30
Farmer, R. C., 45, 47
Felix, A., 173–4
Fernbach, A., 52, 53
Ferranti, S. Z. de, 26
Ferrié, G. A., Col, 15–16, 30, 127, 190, 196
Fessenden, R. A., 136
Field, Prof A. B., 155
Fire control (naval):
  British instruments: Dreyer, 11–12, 118–19, 121; Pollen, 11–12; Clocks, Argo, 11, 12, 119; Vickers, 11; Dumaresq calculator, 11, 12
  German instruments: Siemens & Halske, 12–13
  French instruments: 14
Fire directors: British, 10, 118–19; Gyro Director Training Gear: British, 120–2, German, 118
Fischer, E., 22, 34–6, 110, 190, 191
Fisher, Adm Sir John (later Lord) RN, 11, 12, 24, 29, 128
Flamethrowers, 68; Livens, 68
Fleming, A., 169
Fleming, J. A., 28
Fortescue, Prof C. L., 128
Fokker, A., 146
Foulkes, Maj (later Maj Gen) C. H., 97, 99, 101, 106, 190
France: education and research, Academie des Sciences, 3, 21, École d'Écoute des Avions, 161; Collège de France, 5; École Municipale de Physique et Chimie Industrielles, 137; École Normale Supérieure, 5; Institut Aérotechnique de l'Université de Paris, 5; administration: Comité d'Études et d'Éxperiences Physiques, 195; Commission d'examen des Inventions les armées de Terre et de Mer, 3, 29; Commission supérieure chargé d'étudier et eventuellment d'experimenter des Inventions Intéressant la Défense Nationale, 29; inventions submitted, 189; Ministry of Armaments and Munitions: Sous Secretariat d'État et de la direction des Inventions, des Études et des Experiences Techniques, 31, 39, 195; renamed Office National des Recherches Scientifiques et Industrielles et des Inventions, 195; Section Technique de l'Aéronautique Militaire, 31, 40. See also Chemical warfare and Wireless
Fowler, Sir Henry, 27
Fowler, Gen Sir John, 78
Franck, J., 96
Franco-Prussian war, 2–3, 5

Frankland, Prof P., 28, 41, 106, 108, 113
Freeth, F. A., 48
French, Field Mshl Sir John, 26, 61
Fuller, Maj A. C., 78
Fuller, Col J. F. C., 90, *quoted*, 116
Furnival, J. M., 152, 155
Fuses: British No. 44, 57, No. 106, 58, 193; mechanical: (British), 60; (German) *Dopp Z 16*, 58; French: *Fusée instantée allongée*, 57

Gallipoli, 76, 169, 172
Gardner, D., 41, 112
Garros, R., 145–6
Gases, war: Acrolein, 94–5; Chlorine, 94, 96, 99–100; Chloropicrin, 102, 104, 111; Dianisidine chlorosulphate, 95; Diphenylcyarsine, 110; Diphenylchlorarsine (DA), 110–11; Diphosgene (Green Cross), 104; Mustard (Dichlordiethyl sulphide), 106–11; Hydrocyanide, 102; Phosgene, 95, 102–3, 104, 111; Ethyldichlorarsine, 110, 113; Xylyl bromide, 95; Yperite, 107–8
Gas masks: British, 98, 103, 193; French, 98, 103; German, 99; Italian, 113; Russian, 113; weapons: cylinders, 94, 96, 99–100, 110, 112; shell. *See* Shell; projectors: Livens, 101, 114; German, 102, 113
Gaza, third battle of, 74
Geddes, Sir Eric, 29
General Electric Co., 32, *quoted*, 139
Germany: education and research, *Deutsche Versuchsanstalt für Luftfahrt*, 35; *Kaiser-Wilhelm-Gesellschaft für Physikalische Chemie*, 4, 23, 34, 96; *Kaiser-Wilhelm Institut*, 4, 34, 105, 106, 110, 197; *Kaiser-Wilhelm-Stiftung für Kriegstechnische Wissenschaft*, 35; *Physikalisch-Technische Reichsanstalt*, 5, post-war research, 197; War Ministry: Chemical Section; Hindenburg Programme, 35, 105; *Kriegsrohstoffabteilung (KRA)*, 22, 34, 56
Army: Artillerie Prüfungs Kommission, 35. *See also* Chemical Warfare
Navy: U-boats, 128, 129, 133; quieter engines, 136; remote-controlled torpedoes, 142. *See also* Fire Control (Naval)
Gerrard, H., 130
Gibbons, F. J., 63
Gibson, C. S., 109
Gilbert,. Cdr A., RN, 161
Glazebrook, R. T. (*later* Sir Richard), 17–19, 28, 123, 161

Goettingen University, 16, 35
Goold-Adams, Col H. E. F., 26, 186
Gouldie, W. J., 161
Green, Prof A. G., 109
Greenhill, G. (*later* Sir George), 17
Greenwood, H. C., 186
Grenades: Hales, 158, Jam pot, 62, Mills, 62–3, 193, No. 23 Mk III, 63, No. 36, 63
Grignard, V., 97
Guthrie, F., 106, 108, 109
Gwynn, H. A., 65

Haber, Fritz, 34–5, 55–6, 95–6, 99, 105, 115–16, 190–1, 197
Hadden, Maj Gen. C. F. (*later* Sir Charles), 17
Hadfield, Messrs, 49
Hague Conventions, 1899, 94, 158; 1907, 158
Hahn, Otto, 96
Haig, B. P., 143–4
Haig, Field Mshl Sir Douglas, 58, 66, 67, 86, 158
Haldane, J. S., 98
Haldane, R. B. (*later* Lord), 5, 7, 9, 16, 44, 98, *quoted*, 166
Hale, F. M., 158
Hale, G. E., 32, 42, 140, 190, 196
Hamilton, Gen Sir Ian, 76
Hankey, Col M., 23, 82–3, 91, 190, 195
Hardcastle, Lieut S., RN, 122–3
Hardy, W. B., 25, 97
Harker, J. A., 185–6
Harrison, E. F., 103–4
Hartley, H. (*later* Sir Harold), 106, 115, 190, 191, *quoted*, 197
Harty, Lieut H., RNVR, 130
Haworth, W., 108
Hazelton, G. W., 148, 190
Henderson, J. B., 120–1, *quoted*, 126, 190
Hertz, G., 96
Hetherington, Maj T. G., 84
Hewitt, J. T., 45, 46
High explosives: main fillings, Amatol, 48–9, 193; Ammonium nitrate, 48; Ballistite, 3, 65; Lyddite, 8, 44, 47; Schneiderite, 48; Shellite, 50; Tetryl, 8; TNT, 6, 8, 10, 44, 45–8, 50, 193; synthetic ammonia, 55–6, 185–8; propellants: Acetone, 52–4; Cordite MD, 9, 51; Cordite RDB, 51, 193
Hilger, A., 183
Hill, A. V., 28, 161–2, 164
Hippisley, Col B., 124
Hodgkinson, W. R., 46, 157
Holland, Sir Sothern, 29
Hopkinson, B., 15, 24, 87, 142, 150, 165, 190, 191

Hopwood, Prof F. L., 130
Holt Manufacturing Co., 81
Hornsby-Ackroyd Co., 81
Horton, F., 128, 153
House, Col E. M., 32
Humphrey, H. A., 186–7
Hydrophones: Allied, 129–35; C/CS tube, 134; K tube, 134; Lancashire fish, 133; Morris-Sykes, 130–1; multiple velocity tube, 134; Nash fish, 133; Porpoise, 133; Walser gear, 132, 138; German, 135–6

Imperial College of Science and Technology, 5, 25, 95, 153, 155, 168, 190
Ipatieff, V., 33, 112
Irvine, J., 108, 167–8
Isherwood, H., 12, 121–2
Italy: Department of Invention and Research, 33–4; Navy's use of paravanes, 144. See also Chemical warfare

Jackson, Capt (later Adm Sir Henry) RN, 14–15, 22, 126
Jackson, Sir Herbert, 182
Jackson, Col (later Maj Gen Sir Louis), 23, 25, 26, 61–2, 97, 104, 190
Jakeman, C., 163
Jarny, Capt de, 38–9
Jellicoe, Capt (later Adm Sir John) RN, 11, 120, 126, 131
Joffre, Gen J. J. C., 82
Jones, B. M., 150
Jutland, battle of, 50, 119

Karman, T. von, 37
Kauper, H., 147
Kennedy, Sir Alexander, 26, 28, 161
Kent, Prof A. F. S., 179–80
Kent, Messrs, 60
Keogh, Sir Alfred, 97, 166, 177
Keyes, Maj, 111
King, A. T., 168
Kitchener, Field Mshl Lord, quoted, 25, 26, 48, 61, 86, 154, 166
Kling, A., 97, 105
Krupp, 4, 58, 64

Lamb, Prof H., 129, 130, 131
Lambert, B., 103
Lambert, L., 124
Lancashire Anti-Submarine Committee, 133
Lanchester, F. W., 17, 26

Langevin, P., 40, 137–8, 140, 190, 196
Lawrence, T. E., 67
Leeds University, 190
Leeming, Capt J. A., 61, 92
Lefebure, Capt V., 39
Leiper, R., 177
Leishman, Sir William, 167, 171
Le Prieur, Y., 148, 150, 159, 190
Lewis, G. N., 111
Liddell Hart, B. H., quoted, 116
Lieben, R. von, 127
Liège, siege of, 64
Lindemann, F. A., vii, 184, 195
Livens, Capt W. H., 68, 100–1, 116
Lloyd George, David, 26, 38, 45, 66, 86
Lodge, Sir Oliver, 22, 24, 76, quoted, 192, quoted, 198
London University: King's College, 128; Royal Holloway College, 128; University College, 186. See also Imperial College of Science and Technology
Loos, battle of, 100, 114, 153
Lowry, M., 46, 50, 190
Luebbe, H., 146
Lyman, T., 75

Maclean, H., 175–6
Maclean, I. S., 53, 191
Madden, Adm C. (later Sir Charles) RN, 121
Madelung, E., 96
Madge, H. A., 15, 128
Mallock, H. R. A., 17
Manchester University, 52, 130–1, 190
Marconi Co., 41, 152
Marconi, G., 14, 128
Marriott, H., 123
Maskell, H. J., 123
Mason, C. C., 60
Mason, F. A., 168
Mason, M., 134, 190
'Maud' Committee, 195
Medical Research Committee, 25, 44, 167, 170, 171, 172, 175, 177, 179
Meissner, A., 127
Meitner, L., 191
Merton, T. R., 184, quoted, 192
Merz, C. H., 29
Messines Ridge, 80, 179
Meteorological Office, 162
Meurthe, H. D. de la, 18
Meyer, V., 106, 108, 109
Micklethwaite, M. G., 191
Millikan, R. A., 32, 190
Milman, Brig Gen L. C. (later Sir Louis), 46, 49
Mills, W. (later Sir William), 62–3

Milne, E. A., 162, 163
Mines
  land, 74–80
  sea, 135
Mittasch, A., 55–6
Moir, E. W. (*later* Sir Ernest), 26
Mole, L. A. de, 81
Montagu, E. S., 86
Moore, Adm A. G. H. W., RN, 88
Morecroft, J. H., 139
Morgan, W., 62
Morrison, S. W., 182
Mortars: British, Stokes, 25, 65–8; used for
  gas bombs, 101; 4 inch, 64; 3.7 inch, 65;
  Austrian–German, 64
Moseley, H. G. J., 195
Mouat Jones, B., 98
Moubray, Lieut G. M., 163
Moulton, Lord, 44–5, 48, 49, 53, 66, 190
Moureu, C., 97, 107, 190
Mullard, S. R., 153, 155
Munitions, Ministry of: Anti-Aircraft
  Experimental Section, 161; Department
  of Explosives Supply, 45, 186;
  Explosives Research Laboratory, 45;
  Gun Ammunition Filling Department,
  46; Mechanical Warfare Supply
  Department, 88; Munitions Invention
  Department, 26, 42; Aeronautical
  Committee, 151; inventions submitted,
  189; Nitrogen Products Committee, 186;
  Outside Engineers Board, 61; Trench
  Mortar Committee, 67; Trench Warfare
  Department, 25, 61; Trench Warfare
  Research Department, 25; Travelling
  Ballistic Party, 162
McEvoy, Capt C. A., RN, 129
Mcgregor Morris, J. T., 130

Nash, G. H., 133, 190
Nathan, Col F. L. (*later* Sir Frederick), 6,
  52–3
Namur, siege of, 64
HQ German Army Listening Service, 77
National Health Insurance Commission, 167
National Physical Laboratory, 4–5, 17, 18,
  22, 23, 77, 123, 157, 161, 163, 192, 195
Nayler, J. L., 18
Nernst, H. W., 34, 36, 55, 95, 102, 190
Neuve Chapelle, battle of, 44, 95
Newton, Lieut Col H., 92
Nicholson, Gen Sir William, 16–17
Nobel, A., 3, 65
Nobel Explosives Co., 52
Noble, Sir Andrew, 7, 9
Nordmann, C., 69
Norman, G., 150

Norman, Sir Henry, 15, 28, 38–9, 77
Noyes, A., 32
Nuttall, J. M., 73

O'Gorman, M., 17, 19, 27, 165
Optical glass, 181–4
Orme, R., 152, 155
Osram Robertson, 128
Oxford University, 140
Ozil, Gen, 96, 105, 196

Paget, Sir Richard, 130–1, 139–40
Painlevé, P., 30–1, 38, 137, 190
Paravanes, 142–4
Parsons, Sir Charles, 24
Pearson, Prof K., vi, 161–2
Pedrail Co., 81
Peirse, Vice Adm Sir Richard, RN, 118
Perkin, Sir W. H., 4, 51
Perkin, Prof W. H., 51, 52
Perrin, J., 161, 163
Petavel, Sir Joseph, 17, 28
Pichon, P., 41
Pollen, A. H., 11–12, 118–19
Pomeroy, J., 159
Pope, W. J. (*later* Sir William), 28, 39,
  quoted, 103, 106, 108–9, 138, 190,
  quoted, 191
Porton (Chemical Warfare Experimental
  Establishment), 106
Prandtl, L., 35
Prince, C. E., 152–3, 154–5, 165, 190

Quinan, K. B., 47, 51, 108, 109

Radar, 164, 195, 196–7
Radio Research Board, 194
Ramsay, Sir William, 4, 21–2, 94–5
Ranken, Cdr F., RN, 158
Raps, A., 14
Rathenau, W., 34, 45
Rawes, Capt C. W., 41
Rayleigh, Lord, 4, 7, 9, 16–18, 22, 129, 130,
  131, 163, 190
Rayner, E. H., 161
Redwood, Sir Boverton, 25
Regener, Prof E., 110
Renault Co., 89
Ricardo, H., 87–8
Richardson, O. W., 153
Rimington, Lieut Gen M. F., 66
Rimington, Lieut R. H. G., 66
Rintoul, W., 52
Roberts-Austen, Sir William, 7

Robertson, R. (*later* Sir Robert), 9–10, 45, 47, 50, 192
Robinson, H., 71
Roger, A. F. P. (*later* Sir Alexander), 25, 61
Roland, Capt L., 62
Rossignol, R. le, 55, 56
Ross, Sir Ronald, 177
Rotter, G., 57–8, 190, *quoted*, 192
Rotherham, Messrs, 60
Round, H. J., 123–6, 127, 190
Royal Aircraft Establishment, 27, 195
Royal Aircraft Factory (formerly Balloon Factory), 17, 19, 27, 31, 157, 184, 192
Royal Army Medical College, 97, 106, 166, 171
Royal Commission on Awards to Inventors, 63, 119–20, 123
Royal Flying Corps (*later* Royal Air Force), 28; Aircraft Armament and Gunnery Establishment, 150; Central Flying School, 150; No. 9 Squadron, 152
Royal Naval Air Service, 27, 28, 146, 148, 151, 156, 158; armoured cars, 83; Armament Works, 148
Royal Naval College, 120, 128
Royal Navy: shore establishments, *Excellent*, 10, 161; Royal Naval Cordite Factory, 53; Signal School, 129; *Vernon*, 8, 14–15, 128–9, 143
Royal Society: 4, 22, Advisory Committee on Raw Materials, 22; exemption of scientists from national service, 23; War Committee, 22, 23, 25, 65, 97, 123, 167, 182
Russia: Council of Defence, 33; Navy, 143
Russo-Japanese war, 62, 76, 79, 95, 140, 166; Tsu Shima, battle of, 16
Rutherford, Sir Ernest, 24, 33, 130, 133, 137, 190
Ryan, Cdr C. P., RN, 129–31, 133

Salonika, 176–7
St Andrew's University, 108, 167–8
Samson, Cdr E. R., RN, 164–5
Scarff, F. W., 146
Schneider, F., 146
Schneider Co., 4, 83, 89
Schryver, S. B., 168
Schütte-Lanz Co., 36
Scott, Capt (*later* Vice Adm Sir Percy), RN, 10, 118
Scott-Moncrieff, Maj Gen Sir George, 84
Seely, Gen J., 92
Selby, F. J., 17
Shaw, Rendle, 170
Shaw, W. N., 17
Sheffield University, 168

Shell: British, armour-piercing, 49–50; high explosive, 7–8; star, 50; gas-filled, 104, 115; mustard gas-filled, 109, 115; German: gas-filled, 104, 115; mustard gas-filled, 107, 110
Sibert, Gen W. L. (US Army), 111
Sidgwick, Prof N. V., 51
Siemens & Halske, 12–13, 127
Silberrad, O., 7, 8, 9
Skoda, 64
Slaby, A., 15
Smith, F. E. (*later* Sir Frank), 123
Smith, Prof L., 169
Soddy, Prof F., 108
Somme, battle of, 44, 48, 68, 75, 104
Sommerfeld, A., 77
Sound locators: British, 163–4; Baillaud mirror, 163; Tucker microphone, 163–4
Sound ranging: British, 71–5; French, 68–71; German, 75–6; US Army, 74–5
South African war, 6, 8, 19, 166, 168–9
Sperry, E. A., 32
Squier, Col (*later* Gen) G. (US Army), 15, 33, 42
Stanton, T. E., 17–18
Starling, E. H., 108
Stead, G., 128, 153
Stern, A. (*later* Sir Albert), 86, 88–9
Stokes, W. (*later* Sir Wilfrid), 26, 65–7, 165, 190
Submarine Signal Co., 136
Sueter, Capt Murray, RN, 17, 83–4, 86
Sutton, Capt F. A., 66
Swinton, Lieut Col (*later* Maj Gen), 82, 84, 86, 91, 190
Sykes, A. F., 130

Tanks: 80–2, 91; British, 83–90, 193; Heavy Branch, Machine Gun Corps, 86; French, 82–3, 89; German, 91; USA, Liberty engine, 90
Tappen, H., 95
Taylor, E. P., 155
Taylor, G. I. (*later* Sir Geoffrey), 150, *quoted*, 151
Telephones, field: British Fullerphone, 78; earth telegraphy, 76–8; French *Parleur TM2*, 77–8; German *Utel*, 78
Telefunken, Co., 15, 16, 35, 41, 127
Thomson, G. P., 195
Thomson, Sir J. J., 23, 24–5, 26, *quoted*, 33, 43, 122, 128, 190, 191
Thorneycroft, Sir John, 135
Thorpe, Prof J. F., 25, 95
Threlfall, R. (*later* Sir Richard), 102, 129, 131, 160, 190
Threlfall, W. B., Lieut, RNAS, 160

Thuillier, Brig Gen H. F., 106, 108, 190
Tiverton, Visc., 40
Tizard, H. T., vii, 151, 164, 195
Torpedoes, 122–3
Townsend, Prof J. S. E., 155
Tracked vehicles, 91–2
Tritton, W. (later Sir William), 85
Tucker, W. S., 72–3, 163–4
Tulloch, Maj T. G., 8, 29, 82
Twyman, F., 183
Tyrwhitt, Adm Sir Reginald, RN, 131

United States of America: National Academy of Sciences, 2, 32; National Advisory Committee for Aeronautics, 196; National Research Council, 32–3, 42–3; inventions submitted, 189; hydrophones, 133–4. See also Chemical Warfare
United States Army: Inventions Board, 32; Ordnance Department, 58; Signals Corps, 33, 197
United States Navy: Naval Consulting Board, 31–3; Naval Experimental Station, 139; Naval Research Laboratory, 196; Secretary of, 31
Urbain, Prof G., 102

Villavecchia, V., 113–14
Villiers, Rear Adm E. E., RN, 142–3
Vincent, Capt F. C., 68
Vincent, Prof J. H., 97, 171
Verdun, battle of, 56, 104, 114
Volterra, V., 33–4

Walser, Lieut G. (French Navy), 132
Warneford, Flight Lieut R. A., 158
War Office: 2, 9, 167; negotiations with German Government, 182; Army Council, 60, 166; Artillery Mission to USA, 43; Commercial Advisory and Scientific Advisory Committee (later Chemical Advisory Committee), 25, 97, 104, 108; Directorate of Artillery (A4), 26–7; Explosives Committee, 7–9; Master General of Ordnance, 67, 157; Ordnance Board, 8, 9, 26, 27, 67, 72, 160; Ordnance Committee, 45, 57, 60, 66–7; Ordnance Research Committee, 9; Wireless Committee, 15
Warships, anti-torpedo nets, 143; defence against underwater attack, 140–2
Watson, Prof W., 98
Wavell, Gen Sir Archibald, 178

Weil, E., 173–4
Weiss, P., 71
Weizmann, C., 52–4
Wells, H. G., 24, 81, 92, 157
Wenyon, C. M., 177
Western Electric Co., 32
Whitehead, A. N., 72
Westphall, W., 96
Whiddington, R., 152, 153
Wien, W., 35, 127
Willstaetter, R., 99, 190
Wilson, Adm Sir Arthur, RN, 12
Wilson, D. M., 110
Wilson, Field Mshl Sir Henry, 89–90, 194
Wilson, J. E., 162
Wilson, W., 85, 87
Wilson, Pres W., 32
Wilson, W. J., 173
Wimperis, H. E., 151–2, 164, 165, 190, 194–5
Winterbotham, Col H. St J. L., 71
Wireless Telegraphy: British Army, 15, 76; French Army, Radio-télégraphie Militaire, 15–16, 41, 132, 137, 196; Royal Navy, 14–15, 128; Poulsen arc system, 16, 128; French Navy, 15; German Navy, 15, 127–8; Japanese Navy, 16; Russian Navy, 16; valves: Audion, 16, 41, 127; Round/Marconi, 76, 127–8, 153; R5, 153; H.F. alternator, 155; wavemeter, 155; direction finding, 123–7; listening for subterraneous noises, 80; airborne wireless: British, 16, 23, 152–4; German, 156; wireless telephony: 154–6
Wood, A. B., 130
Woolwich: Chemical Research Department (later Research Department), 2, 7–10, 26, 27, 45–7, 48–9, 50, 51, 192, 194; Metallurgical Section, 9; explosion, 9; Proof and Experimental Establishment, 7, 9, 27; Royal Laboratory, 7, 57, 62; Wireless/Signals Experimental Establishment, 15, 194
Wright, Sir Almroth, 169, 170–1
Wright Bros, 16
Wright, W., 30

X-rays, 184–5

Ypres, 3rd battle of, 107

Zeiss Co., 185
Zeppelin Airship Works, 36